Learning from a Disaster

Learning from a Disaster

IMPROVING NUCLEAR SAFETY AND SECURITY AFTER FUKUSHIMA

Edited by

Edward D. Blandford and Scott D. Sagan

Stanford Security Studies

An Imprint of Stanford University Press

Stanford, California

Stanford University Press
Stanford, California

Printed in the United States of America on acid-free, archival-quality paper

Library of Congress Cataloging-in-Publication Data

Learning from a disaster : Improving nuclear safety and security after Fukushima / edited
by Edward D. Blandford and Scott D. Sagan.
    pages cm.
  Includes bibliographical references and index.
  ISBN 978-0-8047-9561-6 (cloth : alk. paper) —
  ISBN 978-0-8047-9735-1 (pbk. : alk. paper)
    1. Nuclear power plants—Japan—Safety measures.   2. Nuclear power plants—Security
measures—Japan.   3. Nuclear power plants—Safety measures.   4. Nuclear power
plants—Security measures.   5. Fukushima Nuclear Disaster, Japan, 2011.   I. Blandford,
Edward D. (Edward David), editor.   II. Sagan, Scott Douglas, editor.

TK1365.J3L43 2016
621.48'35—dc23   2015034996

Typeset at Stanford University Press in 10/14 Minion

ISBN 978-0-8047-9736-8 (electronic)

CONTENTS

Acknowledgments

This volume would not have been possible without the generous support of the Japan Foundation Center for Global Partnership, which provided a grant that enabled us to conduct two authors' workshops, one in Palo Alto and one in Tokyo. We also thank the Center for International Security and Cooperation (CISAC) at Stanford University and Hitotsubashi University for hosting those workshops. The feedback provided on draft chapters from both the other authors and independent scholars and practitioners at these workshops greatly improved the final product.

We thank Geoffrey Burn at Stanford University Press for his interest in this subject and support for this project. In addition, we thank the two anonymous reviewers of the manuscript who gave us most detailed and demanding feedback. Addressing the substantive issues they raised required both additional research and considerable revision, but we feel the book is much better because they took their reviewers' responsibilities so seriously.

We thank all of our coauthors for their dedication to this project. Nobumasa Akiyama from Hitotsubashi University deserves special recognition for both helping us identify the best Japanese authors for various chapters in the book and for hosting, with efficiency and grace, the authors' workshop at his university. This book would not have been possible without his assistance.

Finally, we want to thank Reid B.C. Pauly and Anna C. Coll for their superb work at CISAC from the start to the finish of this project. Reid was present at the creation, helping write the grant proposal, organizing the Stanford and Tokyo workshops, and writing reviews for each author. Anna was essential to bringing the book across the finish line: her keen analytic acumen and her stellar editing skills improved every chapter in the book. We deeply appreciate the patience and persistence she displayed in helping us turn a manuscript into a book. We also thank Maral Mirshahi for coordinating the final editing changes and bringing the volume across the finish line.

Edward D. Blandford

Scott D. Sagan

Contributors

Nobumasa Akiyama is a Professor in the Graduate School of Law at Hitotsubashi University and an Adjunct Research Fellow for the Japan Institute of International Affairs (JIIA). Previously, he served as a Senior Research Fellow at the Center for the Promotion of Disarmament and Non-Proliferation, JIIA (2004–7), and a Lecturer at Hiroshima Peace Institute, Hiroshima City University (2001–4). His research focuses on the international non-proliferation regime and the nuclear order in northeast Asia. He received his Ph.D in law from Hitotsubashi University.

Edward D. Blandford is an Assistant Professor in the Nuclear Engineering Department at the University of New Mexico. His research focuses on reactor thermal-hydraulics in support of the safety of nuclear installations, probabilistic risk assessment and risk-informed design guidance, and physical protection strategies for future nuclear infrastructure. He received his Ph.D. in nuclear engineering from the University of California, Berkeley.

Toshihiro Higuchi is an Assistant Professor in the Department of History and the School of Foreign Service at Georgetown University. Trained as an international environmental historian, Higuchi studies the problem of radioactive fallout to trace the changing interfaces among science, ethics, and politics in the globalizing twentieth-century world. He received his Ph.D. from Georgetown University in 2011.

Trevor Incerti is an Analyst at Compass Lexecon, an economic consulting firm. He previously served as a Researcher at the Walter H. Shorenstein Asia-Pacific Research Center at Stanford University.

Kenji E. Kushida is the Japan Program Research Associate at the Walter H. Shorenstein Asia-Pacific Research Center at Stanford University. Kushida's research focuses on institutional and governance structures of Japan's Fukushima nuclear disaster; political economy issues surrounding information technology; political strategies of foreign multinational corporations in Japan; and Japan's political economic transformation since the 1990s. He holds a Ph.D. in political science from the University of California, Berkeley.

Phillip Y. Lipscy is Assistant Professor of political science at Stanford University. He is also the Thomas Rohlen Center Fellow at the Shorenstein Asia-Pacific Research Center at the Freeman Spogli Institute for International Studies. His fields of research include international and comparative political economy, international security, and the politics of East Asia, particularly Japan. Lipscy obtained his Ph.D. in political science at Harvard University.

Michael May is Professor Emeritus (Research) in the Stanford University School of Engineering and Senior Fellow Emeritus with the Freeman Spogli Institute for International Studies at Stanford University. May is a director emeritus of the Lawrence Livermore National Laboratory, where he worked from 1952 to 1988. May was a technical adviser to the Threshold Test Ban Treaty negotiating team; a member of the US delegation to the Strategic Arms Limitation Talks; and at various times has been a member of the Defense Science Board, the General Advisory Committee to the AEC, the Secretary of Energy Advisory Board, the RAND Corporation Board of Trustees, and the Committee on International Security and Arms Control of the National Academy of Sciences.

Kaoru Naito is former President of the Nuclear Material Control Center. He received a master's degree in nuclear engineering from the University of Tokyo and a master of public systems engineering from the University of Michigan. He joined the Japanese government Science and Technology Agency in 1971, working mostly in the area of nuclear safety, security, and safeguards regulations. He was a Deputy-Director General when he left the government in 2001, after almost thirty years of service. Naito has also served with the IAEA two times, for a total of seven years. He served as a member of the Standing Advisory Group for Safeguards Implementation until 2006 and a member of the Advisory Group on Nuclear Security until 2014, both advisory bodies to the IAEA Director General. He is a fellow of the Institute of Nuclear Material Management.

Scott D. Sagan is the Caroline S. G. Munro Professor of Political Science, the Mimi and Peter Haas University Fellow in Undergraduate Education, and Senior Fellow at the Center for International Security and Cooperation and the Freeman Spogli Institute at Stanford University. He also serves as Project Chair for the American Academy of Arts and Sciences' Initiative on New Dilemmas in Ethics, Technology, and War. He is the author of *Moving Targets: Nuclear Strategy and National Security* (Princeton University Press, 1989); *The Limits of Safety: Organizations, Accidents, and Nuclear Weapons* (Princeton University Press, 1993); and, with co-author Kenneth N. Waltz, *The Spread of Nuclear Weapons: An Enduring Debate* (W.W. Norton, 2012). Sagan was the recipient of the National Academy of Sciences William and Katherine Estes Award in 2015 and the International Studies Association's International Security Studies Section Distinguished Scholar Award in 2013.

Kazuto Suzuki is Professor of international political economy at the Public Policy School of Hokkaido University in Japan. He served as a member on the Panel of Experts established pursuant to Resolution 1929 (2010) on Iran at the United Nations from 2013 to 2015. Suzuki graduated from the Department of International Relations, Ritsumeikan University, and received his Ph.D. from Sussex European Institute, University of Sussex, England. His research is focused on the transformation of national policies with a perspective on security, technology, and economy.

Gregory D. Wyss is a Distinguished Member of Technical Staff in the Security Systems Analysis Department at Sandia National Laboratories, Albuquerque, NM. Dr. Wyss has worked in the areas of risk, reliability, and vulnerability assessment at Sandia National Laboratories for more than twenty-five years. He has performed risk assessment studies for nuclear reactors, space vehicle launches, nuclear test facilities, telecommunications facilities, and various other high-integrity and potentially high-consequence systems. His research interests include assessment of preattack planning, insider threats, decision support, and synergistic effects between cyber and physical security systems. Wyss holds a Ph.D. in nuclear engineering from the University of Illinois at Urbana-Champaign.

PART I: The Fukushima Accident

Introduction: Learning from a Man-made Disaster

Scott D. Sagan

Numerous official governmental and independent commissions have published inquiries into the causes and consequences of the March 11, 2011, accident at the Fukushima Daiichi nuclear reactor, and many serious independent scholarly analyses have also appeared.[1] This collection of essays, however, is highly unusual and therefore especially valuable in four different ways. First, unlike most reports on Fukushima, which offer single perspectives on the causes of the accident and then provide consensus opinions about what lessons should be learned, the authors of these chapters present diverse perspectives on both the technical and the organizational failures that led to the accident and its tragic consequences and then provide insights into what lessons the Japanese government and nuclear industry and foreign governments and industries have actually learned and not learned. Their explicit focus on governmental and organizational learning successes and failures opens up a new window for studying the long-term consequences of a serious nuclear accident.

Second, virtually all studies of the Fukushima disaster have focused on the lessons to be learned regarding nuclear safety, which is defined as the prevention of nuclear accidents. That focus is perfectly understandable, of course, because of the nature of the Fukushima disaster. The authors of this book, however, recognize that although the Fukushima accident was the result of the combined effects of the 9.0 magnitude earthquake and the subsequent massive tsunami that hit Japan on March 11, 2011, it could just as well have been caused, in theory, by an external terrorist attack or an insider act of malicious sabotage, which are security problems, not safety problems.[2] This volume therefore includes analyses of both the nuclear safety and nuclear security lessons that have been learned, or in many cases have not been learned, since the accident.

Third, the authors of this collection represent an unusually diverse and interdisciplinary group of scholars and practitioners. The authors are diverse both in terms of nationality (Japanese and American) and in terms of past and current affiliations (universities, national laboratories, and government agencies). The volume has also benefited from the highly interdisciplinary nature of the collaborating authors, with political scientists, nuclear engineers, historians, and physicists working together and commenting on each other's draft book chapters.

Fourth, many previous studies of the Fukushima accident were written either by traditional critics of nuclear energy or advocates of nuclear power. Not surprisingly, the books and articles by the first group generally stress that the Fukushima accident could have been much worse than it was in terms of lives lost and costs to the Japanese and international economy had specific close-call decisions not been made by nuclear operators and government bureaucrats. These critical studies also generally emphasize the role of good fortune over good planning, and thus pessimists see the fact that the Fukushima accident did not produce massive fatalities in Japan as a "homage to plain dumb luck."[3] Also not surprisingly, the studies written by traditional advocates of nuclear energy have tended to emphasize the resilience of Japanese society during the emergency and the fact that no individuals were killed immediately by the nuclear accident (estimated long-term health effects are still disputed), compared with the many who died immediately by the earthquake and the tsunami in northern Japan. If a nuclear reactor complex can survive this magnitude of natural disaster, optimists argue, then we should be reassured about the future.

Such mixed opinions about the appropriate lessons to be drawn from "near misses" or "close calls" are common, indeed perhaps inevitable, after such events. As James March, Lee Sproull, and Michal Tamuz have noted in a similar context:

> Every time a pilot avoids a collision, the event provides evidence both for the threat and for its irrelevance. It is not clear whether the learning should emphasize how close the organization came to disaster, thus the reality of danger in the guise of safety, or the fact that disaster was avoided, thus the reality of safety in the guise of danger.[4]

The appropriate perspective on Fukushima must, however, include a basic awareness that the disaster could have easily, very easily, been much worse in terms of loss of life and economic damage to Japan and even surrounding countries. And yet we must also acknowledge the presence of some robustness in the accident mitigation system and astute decisions made by both leaders in Tokyo and especially by plant officials and workers in Fukushima. The authors of this volume recognize both sides of the accident's history and offer a balanced perspective reinforced by the diversity of opinion within the group. In contrast to contributors to most reports, the authors of this volume range from strong advocates, to agnostics, to skeptics about the role nuclear power should play in producing energy today and into the future. We hope the range of opinion on this central issue among the various authors adds to the interest and objectivity of the volume as a whole.

A NATURAL OR MAN-MADE DISASTER?

Although the proximate cause of the Fukushima accident was clearly a mixture of natural phenomena—the massive earthquake and tsunami that struck Japan—the authors in this volume see the accident not as a natural disaster but rather as a man-made disaster, in five different but related ways. First, as the report of the Independent Investigation Commission has recognized, the potential for a tsunami as large as the one on March 11 that breached the 10-meter-high seawall outside Fukushima was understood by many officials and regulators in Japan prior to the accident, but their recommendations to build stronger protection against such a possibility were ignored by Tokyo Electric Power Company (TEPCO), which owned and operated the plant.[5] Second, again as recognized by some official reports, common traits in Japanese culture played a significant role in permitting unsafe conditions to be overlooked in the name of social unity and group cooperation. As Kiyoshi Kurokawa, chairman of the Japanese Diet's Independent Investigation Commission, wrote in the commission's report on the accident:

> What must be admitted—very painfully—is that this was a disaster "Made in Japan." . . . Its fundamental causes are to be found in the ingrained conventions of Japanese culture: our reflexive obedience; our reluctance to question authority; our devotion to "sticking with the program"; our groupism, and our insularity.[6]

Third, a number of our authors analyze the causes and consequences of what the Independent Investigation Commission called "the myth of absolute safety":

the widespread public belief that Japanese nuclear plants were so well designed and operated that a serious accident was impossible, a belief that was strongly promoted by the nuclear industry and government in an effort to encourage public willingness to permit the construction and continued operation of nuclear power reactors in their local communities. Such a myth discouraged national and local officials from conducting realistic planning and emergency exercises, leading to multiple failures when the real emergency occurred in March 2011. Fourth, Toshihiro Higuchi compellingly identifies another way in which Fukushima was a man-made disaster in his chapter in this volume: Japanese officials dangerously adjusted the estimates of acceptable radiological exposure dosages before the accident to restore public trust. This policy, Higuchi argues, was not intended to create undue risk for Japanese citizens, but nonetheless produced emergency evacuation rules that unnecessarily exposed local men, women, and children to dangerous levels of radioactivity after the accident. Fifth, and finally, Kaoru Naito and Kazuto Suzuki discuss Japan's failure to learn lessons that were relevant for improving safety and security from the September 11, 2001, terrorist attacks in New York City and Washington, DC. After the 9/11 attacks, the US Nuclear Regulatory Commission (NRC) reviewed the relevant design, defense, and mitigation strategies in case terrorists attacked or sabotaged a nuclear reactor and developed new rules that all US nuclear operators were forced to adopt to reduce such risks. Although senior officials within Japan's nuclear regulatory agency were informed of the implementation of improved nuclear safety and security measures in the United States, they chose not to adopt similar rules for the Japanese nuclear operators and power plants.

VICARIOUS LEARNING

Otto von Bismarck, the German chancellor, is said to have remarked that "only a fool learns from his mistakes; wise men learn from other people's mistakes." This observation holds in the context of promoting nuclear safety and security. It will be important, going forward, that the appropriate lessons from the Fukushima accident be internationally understood and that organizational learning not be confined to Japan. This process is difficult, however, not only because government structures, regulatory systems, safety cultures, and reactor designs may vary across countries, but also because of a common tendency, which was seen in Japan after the Three Mile Island accident and the 9/11 attacks in the United States, to assume that failures occurring in other countries are unlikely to be repeated in one's own.

This volume is therefore designed to encourage improved *vicarious learning*, learning from the mistakes of others, not just one's own. After an initial chapter by Kenji Kushida outlines the progression of events before, during, and following the March 11, 2011, earthquake and tsunami, the volume presents a series of chapters about what went right and what went wrong in designing the safety and security systems for Japanese nuclear plants and in implementing appropriate measures during crises and after accidents. Gregory Wyss starts with a chapter analyzing how stakeholders set standards for risk acceptance, so-called design-basis criteria, by which nuclear facilities are designed, constructed, and operated. These criteria address possible procedural accidents, failed parts, natural disasters, or threats such as insider or terrorist attacks. Wyss is highly critical of the procedures used to produce the design-basis criteria for the Fukushima nuclear plant and outlines a set of improvements in the design and testing process that could improve nuclear safety and security in the future. Kaoru Naito then reviews the record of Japanese domestic institutions and international organizations that are responsible for promoting nuclear security and ensuring the safe transport of nuclear material. He finds that there were rapid improvements in security procedures after Fukushima in areas like access control, but that progress in other areas—notably the creation of a system for trustworthiness checks for workers in nuclear facilities—was not approved until October 2015 and, as of this writing, has not yet been implemented. In addition, steps remain to better integrate approaches to enhance nuclear safety and security. Nobumasa Akiyama follows with a chapter reviewing the many failures in nuclear emergency planning and response that were exposed during the Fukushima accident and its aftermath. Akiyama usefully focuses attention on both the failures of advance planning, caused by the "myth of absolute safety," and the mismatch during the crisis between the micromanagement leadership style of Prime Minister Naoto Kan and the weaknesses of information gathering and communication between the government, TEPCO, and the Fukushima plant.

The next chapters examine the complexity of creating and maintaining strong domestic and international learning processes around nuclear issues. Toshihiro Higuchi analyzes the failures in Japan to learn from international best practices regarding how to measure safety in radioactivity levels. His detailed chapter demonstrates how easily the Japanese government fell into the trap of what organization theorists call "goal displacement," whereby the measure chosen to represent "safe" levels of exposure became a goal for operators to achieve in its own right, encouraging them to ignore local conditions that might impact the actual level of safety of exposure during and after an accident like the one that occurred at Fukushima. Kazuto Suzuki's chapter on transnational organizational learning rounds out this part of the book. Suzuki focuses on why the Japanese government and nuclear industry too often ignored the best practices and lessons learned by the United States, the International Atomic Energy Agency, and industrial peer review organizations, before the Fukushima accident. His review of reforms proposed and implemented in Japan after the accident is decidedly pessimistic. He argues that the myth of absolute safety has not gone away and that there is a continuing misguided tendency for non-TEPCO operators to resist substantial investments in improved safety and security systems, since their plants did not suffer as much damage as the Fukushima plant after the March 11 earthquake and tsunami.

Finally, *Learning from a Disaster* concludes with two chapters examining international nuclear safety and security in a broader comparative manner. The chapter by Phillip Lipscy, Kenji Kushida, and Trevor Incerti studies whether Japan's nuclear industry was uniquely ill prepared for serious natural or man-made disasters. Their detailed data show that Japan was relatively unprepared for the kind of natural disaster that occurred on March 11, but that it was not the only country that would have faced severe nuclear safety challenges in the event of such a severe "double-whammy" of an earthquake and tsunami. Finally, Edward Blandford and Michael May provide both a summary of the lessons learned and debated by the authors in this volume and their own assessment of the difficulty of organizational learning through an examination of ways that nuclear operators and regulators have learned (or not learned) from accidents and failures in other countries since the introduction of civilian nuclear power. Their chapter ends with a set of concrete recommendations on how to improve and incentivize vicarious learning after nuclear incidents and accidents and thus provides an optimistic final word about our nuclear future. This chapter should be seen as a final plea for better "vicarious learning." The appropriate lessons for improved safety and security gleaned from the Fukushima tragedy must be carefully implemented, not only in Japan but also by the global nuclear community.

NOTES

1. Important studies and analyses of the Fukushima accident include "Official Report of the Fukushima Nuclear Accident Independent Investigative Commission," National

Diet of Japan, Tokyo, 2012, available at http://warp.da.ndl.go.jp/info:ndljp/pid/3856371/ naiic.go.jp/en/; Independent Investigation Commission on the Fukushima Nuclear Accident, *The Fukushima Daiichi Nuclear Power Station Disaster: Investigating the Myth and Reality*, ed. Mindy Kay Bricker (New York: Routledge, 2014); Richard J. Samuels, *3.11 Disaster and Change in Japan* (Ithaca, NY: Cornell University Press, 2013); Tokyo Electric Power Company (TEPCO), *Fukushima Genshiryoku Jiko Chousa Houkoku sho* [*Fukushima Nuclear Accident Investigation Report*] (Tokyo: Tokyo Electric Power Company, 2012); Institute of Nuclear Power Operators (INPO), *Lessons Learned from the Nuclear Accident at the Fukushima Daiichi Nuclear Power Station*, INPO Special Report, INPO 11-005 (Atlanta, GA: Institute of Nuclear Power Operators, 2011); INPO, *Lessons Learned from the Nuclear Accident at the Fukushima Daiichi Nuclear Power Station*, INPO Special Report, INPO 11-005 Addendum (Atlanta, GA: Institute of Nuclear Power Operators, 2012); Charles Perrow, "Nuclear Denial: From Hiroshima to Fukushima," *Bulletin of Atomic Scientists* 69, no. 5 (September/October 2013); *Lessons Learned from the Fukushima Nuclear Accident for Improving Safety of U.S. Nuclear Plants,* (Washington, DC: National Academies Press, 2014); and James Acton and Mark Hibbs, "Why Fukushima Was Preventable," Carnegie Endowment for International Peace, March 6, 2012, available at http://carnegieendowment.org/2012/03/06/why-fukushima-was-preventable/a0i7.

2. For an analysis of insider threats to nuclear facilities, see Matthew Bunn and Scott D. Sagan, "A Worst Practices Guide to Insider Threats: Learning from Past Mistakes," occasional paper, Cambridge, MA, American Academy of Arts and Sciences, 2014.

3. The phrase was famously used by former secretary of state Dean Acheson to describe the Kennedy administration's successful diplomacy during the Cuban Missile Crisis; Dean Acheson, "Dean Acheson's Version of Robert Kennedy's Version of the Cuban Missile Crisis: Plain Dumb Luck," *Esquire*, February 1969, 76.

4. James G. March, Lee S. Sproull, and Michal Tamuz, "Learning from Samples of One or Fewer," *Organization Science* 2, no. 1 (February 1991): 10. For more on learning from close calls and near misses, see Scott D. Sagan, *The Limits of Safety* (Princeton: Princeton University Press, 1995).

5. See Independent Investigation Commission on the Fukushima Nuclear Accident, *The Fukushima Daiichi Nuclear Power Station Disaster,* 100–106.

6. Kiyoshi Kurokawa, "Message from the Chairman," in *Official Report of the Fukushima Nuclear Accident Independent Investigation Commission*, 9.

1 Japan's Fukushima Nuclear Disaster: An Overview

Kenji E. Kushida

The Tohoku earthquake that struck off the northeastern coast of Japan on March 11, 2011, had a magnitude of 9.0, the world's fourth largest in modern recorded history. The island of Honshu moved 2.4 meters to the east. A massive tsunami followed shortly thereafter, reaching an estimated height of over 30 meters in some places. A 500-kilometer section of Japan's northeastern coast was devastated, with a death toll of more than 15,000 people. Damage from the earthquake and tsunami led to one of the world's most serious nuclear disasters, at the Fukushima Daiichi (number one) Nuclear Power Station on Japan's eastern coast, owned and operated by the Tokyo Electric Power Company (TEPCO).

The Fukushima Daiichi plant had six nuclear reactors, three of which were in operation at the time of the earthquake and tsunami, with the rest undergoing routine maintenance. As the earthquake hit, the active reactors were successfully scrammed (that is, placed under emergency shutdown). All off-site power from the external power grid was lost as a result of severed power lines and earthquake damage to transformer stations, but the on-site emergency backup power sources, consisting of diesel generators and batteries, immediately came online to operate the cooling pumps and other functions.

The tsunami hit the plant approximately forty minutes later, reaching a height of over 12 meters. It well exceeded the maximum safety design of 5.7 meters and obliterated the 10-meter-high seawall. The tsunami destroyed almost all on-site backup power sources, as well as most of the pumps necessary to cool the reactors. Over the next three days, despite desperate attempts on the ground to restore cooling, the three reactors that had been active before the earthquake experienced fuel core meltdowns, and hydrogen explosions blew away the roofs, walls, and upper floors of three reactor buildings.

Although the catastrophe at Fukushima Daiichi emitted at least 168 times the amount of radioactive cesium 137 as the Hiroshima atomic bomb, there were no direct deaths from radiation exposure. A mandatory evacuation zone with a radius of 10 kilometers was imposed in the early hours of March 12, expanded to 20 kilometers later that day, displacing more than eighty thousand residents. The disaster was eventually declared level 7 on the International Nuclear Event Scale (INES)—the maximum level on that scale. Chernobyl was the only other level 7 nuclear accident to date, although it released approximately six times the amount of radioactive material as Fukushima, since it was an explosion of the core reactor during active operation. At Fukushima, sea water pumped into the reactors and used fuel storage pools created more than 100,000 tons of contaminated water, about a tenth of which had been released into the ocean, by the end of 2011.

The following account of Japan's nuclear disaster is based on a variety of sources and studies published after the disaster. It is designed as an overview, presenting the basic facts about the disaster to set up subsequent chapters. Readers interested in further technical details and analyses about the causes of the accident, such as failures at the level of plant design, emergency preparedness, Japan's nuclear energy and electricity industry governance structures, and broader social, cultural, and political factors can refer to the reports themselves. The most reliable and extensive reports include the following: an accident report compiled by a government committee;[1] an independent commission convened by the National Diet;[2] private sector independent accident investigation commissions and projects;[3] TEPCO's own report;[4] reports from international organizations such as the International Atomic Energy Agency (IAEA) and other regulatory and industry bodies including the Institute of Nuclear Power Operators (INPO);[5] numerous credible accounts by investigative journalists;[6] works by academics and independent nuclear experts;[7] and accounts by some political leaders.[8] Most reports and accounts draw from extensive interviews, many of which are publicly available. The author also interviewed several experts involved in writing the independent reports.

Unless otherwise noted, factual information in this chapter relies on investigation commission reports where they are duplicated and are therefore considered common knowledge.[9]

THE DISASTER AS IT UNFOLDED

The nuclear accident ensued from the combination of two natural disasters: the earthquake and the tsunami it caused. Each brought a different type of destruction, and although four nuclear power plants along Japan's northeastern coast were struck by the March 11 earthquake and tsunami, the combination of damage at Fukushima Daiichi was catastrophic.

The Earthquake

The magnitude 9.0 earthquake occurred at 2:46 p.m. on March 11, 2011. The quake itself caused major damage at the Fukushima Daiichi nuclear plant, much of which was more than forty years old. In particular, most of the operations center buildings were catastrophically damaged, to the point of becoming unusable. The earthquake severed all external power lines to Fukushima Daiichi, making it completely dependent on its on-site backup power sources.

After the earthquake hit, staff at the Fukushima Daiichi operations headquarters quickly evacuated to a newly constructed emergency operations center, built on slightly higher ground and designed to withstand strong earthquakes. Had this structure not existed, the lack of a viable on-site staging ground for the rescue operation would have likely led to a significantly worse outcome. This seismically reinforced operations center had been completed just eight months prior to the earthquake.

The Tsunami: Devastating Excess and Critical Deficiency of Water

The tsunami hit in multiple waves, starting at 3:27 p.m., forty minutes after the earthquake. The second wave, which hit at 3:35 p.m., was higher, exceeding 12 meters at the site of the Fukushima Daiichi plant. It obliterated the 10-meter-high concrete seawall designed to stop a tsunami of only up to 5.7 meters. The tsunami destroyed much of the cooling system, largely consisting of pumps responsible for pumping seawater into the reactor building to cool the fuel rods. Critically, it also irreparably damaged almost all of the on-site backup power sources and infrastructure—the diesel generators, batteries, and circuit boards for the plant. The plant had lost the capability to cool the reactors.

The need for massive quantities of water for nuclear reactors cannot be exaggerated. The Fukushima Daiichi Reactors 1, 2, and 3, which were operating at the time of the disaster, were boiling water reactors (BWR). In a BWR, heat from the nuclear reactions of fuel rods within a sealed chamber boils water under high pressure, creating steam that rotates turbines to generate electricity.

The primary, or first-stage, cooling system for the Fukushima reactors required 5,600 tons, 7,570 tons, and 7,760 tons of seawater, respectively, per hour during normal operations. An additional 20 tons of seawater per second, or 1.7 million tons per day, were required to cool the steam and convert it back to water.[10] Therefore, the total seawater requirement was almost 1.9 million tons daily for this one plant.

In the Fukushima Daiichi plant, the initial scrams—emergency shutdowns of the fuel core reactions—as the earthquake hit were successful. However, even after shutting down, the fuel rods retained considerable heat, requiring large amounts of water for cooling. The three reactors combined required approximately 70 tons of water per hour for ten days, even after shutting down, to avoid a catastrophe.[11] Restoring cooling capabilities was of paramount importance. Yet, with the complete loss of off-site power as well as on-site backup power, along with damage to most of the cooling systems, the plant faced an acute crisis.

At 4:30 p.m. on March 11, when it had become clear that emergency teams had not been able to cool the reactors and could not monitor the water levels of Reactors 1 and 2, Fukushima Daiichi plant manager Masao Yoshida officially declared a "nuclear emergency in progress," in accordance with the Nuclear Emergency Preparedness Act. As soon as the hot core evaporated the water and exposed the fuel rods, the rods would overheat and become damaged, resulting in the phenomenon commonly labeled "meltdown."

At 7:00 p.m., the prime minister's office declared a nuclear emergency to the nation. At 8:50 p.m., around four and a half hours after the nuclear emergency had been declared by the Fukushima Daiichi plant, the Fukushima prefectural government announced that residents within a 2-kilometer radius of the Fukushima Daiichi plant should evacuate. Half an hour later, at 9:23 p.m., the central government announced a 3-kilometer radius for evacuation, ordering people to stay indoors within a radius between 3 and 10 kilometers. It was later determined that Reactor 1's core had already been exposed by around 5:00 p.m. and that increased radiation levels were detected by 5:50 p.m. in the plant.

Early Information and Communication Difficulties

As events rapidly unfolded, severe information and communications problems at all levels of decision-making plagued the recovery effort. The earthquake paralyzed telecommunications networks around the country, and in the Tokyo metropolitan area all public transportation shut down, airports were closed, and roads quickly become severely gridlocked. In the Tohoku region, many of the roads were severely damaged, with the tsunami ravaging coastal areas.

Organizationally, the locus of emergency decision-making became unclear as the nuclear crisis at Fukushima Daiichi developed. The Japanese legal framework stipulated that the power operator was in charge. However, during this initial time of crisis, neither TEPCO's chairman nor its president were at TEPCO headquarters. With the transportation infrastructure such as airports, trains, and freeways shut down, and with roads in gridlock, it took both TEPCO's chairman and president more than seventeen hours to return to headquarters, by which time the meltdowns at Daiichi had already occurred. Since telecommunications networks were down following the earthquake, it is unclear how effectively the chairman and president could communicate effectively with TEPCO headquarters, let alone the Daiichi plant operations center. The prime minister's office, overseeing the response to the broader disaster, was not aware of the leadership vacuum at TEPCO, breeding severe mistrust on the part of Prime Minister Kan Naoto. Concerned by the lack of effective communication from TEPCO, he became personally involved in the rescue effort at Daiichi.

The prime minister's office itself suffered communications problems. The government's underground emergency operations headquarters, designed for use during a terrorist attack or national conflict, lacked cellular service as a security measure. This frustrated the prime minister's attempts to orchestrate the recovery effort, leading him to move his operations up to his personal office on the fifth floor. However, his office lacked emergency telephone and fax lines, resulting in aides running up and down six flights of stairs to deliver emergency messages. The Nuclear Safety Commission (NSC) and Nuclear and Industrial Safety Agency (NISA), an agency under the Ministry of Economy, Trade, and Industry, set up a nuclear emergency headquarters within the prime minister's office, but there was no permanent or previously designated location at which it was to be set up. The office ended up being a small room in a mezzanine between the ground floor and basement emergency headquarters. The room had only one phone line, and initially no computer, fax, or information such as schematics of the Fukushima nuclear plant. With limited access to information, the head of NISA, whose function was to advise the prime minister, ended up relying on his memory of the various reactor configurations and plant layout at Daiichi. Both he and the prime minister learned of the hydrogen explosions via television during a meeting in which the head of NISA was reporting the latest—clearly outdated—information to the prime minister.

According to the law, the locus of information flows on the ground at Fukushima Daiichi should have been an off-site emergency operations center about 5 kilometers from the plant. However, transportation and communications paralysis, combined with the power outage, rendered the off-site center inoperable. Even at midnight on March 11, when a Ministry of Economy, Trade, and Industry (METI) vice minister arrived via helicopter from Tokyo, the building was still dark and unusable,[12] although it was the designated clearinghouse for managing information flows among the plant, the government, TEPCO, and local municipalities, as well as for orchestrating evacuations.

Within the Fukushima Daiichi plant itself, the loss of nearby cellular towers limited the ability to stage rescue operations, leaving the plant manager in charge, Yoshida, to work with limited information. With control panel indicators and sensors damaged in unpredictable ways, and with the plant itself lacking electricity, assessing the status of reactors required the time-consuming and potentially risky process of workers physically entering the reactor buildings and reporting back to the operations center with information.

Initial Recovery Efforts: The Direct Line and Race to Provide Electricity

Key initial recovery efforts at the stricken Daiichi plant included the creation of a direct line from which to inject water and a race to provide electricity to the plant.

Very early on in the crisis, plant manager Yoshida sent teams of men into the reactor buildings to manually open the valves to create a direct line for injecting water into the reactor. Although plant operators could normally push a button in the operations center to open valves, teams had to open multiple large valves manually within the reactor buildings in the absence of electricity. As radiation levels spiked within the reactor buildings by the late evening of March 11, the areas where the valves were located were deemed too dangerous to access. Therefore, having opened the valves in the late afternoon was critical in stabilizing the reactors later on by injecting water.

Also in the late afternoon of March 11, hours before issuing the evacuation order, Prime Minister Kan had begun to involve himself personally in the recovery effort. He directly orchestrated the dispatching of battery trucks from the Self-Defense Forces (SDF)—Japan's equivalent of a military, limited to defensive capabilities—to the plant to provide electricity for the cooling systems.

By 11:50 p.m. the power trucks had yet to be connected, because of the grid-locked traffic near the Tokyo metropolitan area, damaged roads in the Tohoku region, and technical compatibility issues, including difficulty connecting the first set of SDF battery trucks to the remaining emergency cooling system pumps owing to differences in voltage and incompatible connectors. At this time, the Fukushima Daiichi plant issued another report: radiation levels within the reactor building were rising, indicating a radiation leak. Until this time the working assumption at the plant has been that the emergency cooling system for Reactor 1 was in operation. However, it turned out that the instrument panel indicating sufficient water levels was unreliable. Water levels were low, and the exposed fuel core had damaged the containment vessel, leading to radiation leakage.

Venting the Reactor Buildings

The next step in the recovery effort was to reduce pressure within the pressure containment vessel. Around 11:50 p.m., workers at Fukushima Daiichi discovered that the pressure containment vessel in Reactor 1 had reached an internal pressure of 600 kilopascals (kPa), well exceeding its maximum design of 427 kPa. "Venting"—the process of releasing hot air from the containment vessel itself into the atmosphere in order to lower the reactor pressure and temperature—was deemed the only option, both to prevent a breach of the containment vessel, and to enable water to be injected directly into the reactor. The design of the Fukushima Daiichi reactors, lacking filters to reduce the amount of radioactive material released in the event of venting, meant that venting would release substantial radioactive material into the atmosphere.[13]

Around 1:00 a.m. on March 12, the prime minister, other political officials, and the head of NISA, along with a TEPCO liaison, all agreed that venting needed to be done to reduce pressure and avoid even bigger problems. Plant manager Yoshida had already decided to vent the reactor, and the political leadership asked Yoshida to commence venting after the government made an announcement at 3:00 a.m. After a 3:12 a.m. press conference by the chief cabinet secretary, the political leadership expected imminent news of venting—but it never came. As Prime Minister Kan waited, he suspected that TEPCO was unwilling to make, or incapable of making, the difficult choice to release radiation from Daiichi and assume blame. He was still unaware that TEPCO's top leadership had yet to arrive at headquarters, and was infuriated that top leaders had not been in touch with him. By 5:00 a.m. venting had yet to occur, and Kan decided to visit the plant himself. At 5:44 a.m., the government expanded the evacuation radius to 10 kilometers.

As it turned out, one of the problems at the plant was opening the vents. There were two types of vents in the reactors: motor operated valves and compressed air operated valves. Without electricity, neither worked. Therefore, they would need to be opened manually—but radiation levels were elevated and rising within the reactor building.

Prime Minister Kan left his office at 6:30 a.m. by helicopter, visiting Daiichi for about an hour, until 8:00 a.m. There he met the plant manager, Yoshida, who gave him answers to the questions that nobody else at TEPCO or the government had been able to provide. Assured by Yoshida's words that, if necessary, the Daiichi plant would dispatch teams willing to die in order to regain control of the situation, Kan returned to Tokyo.

At 9:04 a.m., two-man teams began to proceed to the reactor building to open the vents manually. The second team had to turn back before reaching the vent because of high levels of radiation that triggered team members' alarms. One team member received a dose of approximately 106 millisieverts (mSv), far exceeding the *yearly* limit of 1 mSv deemed safe. The others received doses of 89 and 95 mSv, respectively. It was deemed unsafe to send the third group into the reactor building. TEPCO then attempted to connect a compressor to one of the vents that could be opened with compressed air. At 2:00 p.m., TEPCO was finally able to vent Reactor 1—almost fourteen hours after the initial decision. The reactor pressure, designed for a maximum of 427 kPa, had at one point risen to over 840 kPa.

By then, the fuel core of Reactor 1 had already melted through the pressure vessel. An hour and a half later, at 3:36 p.m. on March 12, a hydrogen explosion blew away its roof and upper walls.

The Reactor Building Explosions

The explosion at Reactor 1 blew debris all over the plant, injuring two workers. It also severely disrupted operations on the adjacent Reactor 2. Falling debris damaged the cable that connected the power truck to Reactor 2. A fire truck that had been preparing to inject seawater was also damaged. Workers had been close to powering up a system that would insert a boric acid solution at high pressure to cool the reactor, but fear of high radiation kept workers away. By this time, the core fuel had melted considerably. Five months later, TEPCO revealed that radiation levels near an exhaust duct between Reactors 1 and 2 at this time read 10 sieverts (Sv), or 10,000 mSv, an hour, with 5 Sv an hour inside Reactor 1's building pipes (enough to kill a person in forty minutes).

The Reactor 1 explosion also damaged the seismically reinforced operations center. Until then, the building had been shielded from radioactive material through air filters, double doors, and workers' changing their clothes and shoes upon entry. The force of the explosion blew out the air filters and bent the outside doors so that they no longer closed properly. The entire operations center building was therefore exposed to the outside atmosphere, and radiation levels rose inside.[14]

At 6:25 p.m. on March 12, the prime minister's office expanded the 10-kilometer evacuation radius to 20 kilometers.

Injecting Sea Water

By 6:00 p.m. on March 12, Japan's political leadership and government officials began advocating the injection of seawater into the reactors. This would produce radiation-contaminated seawater and ruin the reactors. The government formally issued an order at 8:00 p.m. through the TEPCO liaison stationed in the prime minister's office. However, plant manager Yoshida had already begun injecting seawater at around 7:00 p.m., prior to receiving orders from the political leadership. In a series of events that later led to a media firestorm criticizing the political leadership's handling of the crisis, the TEPCO liaison actually ordered Yoshida to halt the seawater injections until the formal government order was issued. The press later blamed the prime minister's leadership for halting seawater injections that had already been commenced. Yet, as it turned out, Yoshida had disobeyed his own superior's orders to halt the seawater injections and had simply continued.

Fukushima Daiichi's Reactor 3 was deep into crisis as well. Officials had decided to shift the cooling method of Reactor 3 from seawater to foam water from fire engines. To inject water from fire trucks, pressure within the reactor had to be released through a safety release valve, but there was insufficient battery power to open the valve. Employees' commuter car batteries were collected to generate enough power for the operations center, opening the valve just past 9:00 a.m. on March 14. Six hours and forty-three minutes had elapsed since the high-pressure coolant injection system had stopped, and heat had risen to 2,000 degrees Celsius. At about 10:30 a.m., as TEPCO attempted to switch back to seawater, since water tanks were becoming depleted, a strong aftershock hit, delaying the switchover. As a result, there was a gap of more than an hour between the end of sending foam, and the recommencing of seawater injections at 1:12 p.m.

Reactor 3, which was later thought to have reached temperatures exceeding 2,000 degrees Celsius, had already begun to melt down around 8:00 a.m. Earlier in the morning, at 6:50 a.m., as pressure within the reactor chamber had begun to rise, all outdoor workers received evacuation orders. At 11:01 a.m., the Reactor 3 building exploded—a much stronger explosion than that of Reactor 1. The explosion injured approximately eleven people and threw the operations center into panic.

Efforts to sustain temperatures in Reactor 2 were halted, as fire trucks and hoses were destroyed. Vents had been opened approximately 25 percent, but they slammed shut again with the explosion. Just after 1:00 p.m, the battery for Reactor 2's cooling system ran out. By around 7:20 p.m., emergency workers had gathered additional car batteries to open the safety valve in order to lower the pressure and connect fire engines.

It was later estimated that Reactor 2 had experienced a meltdown about six and a half hours after the cooling system stopped. Large quantities of hydrogen were produced as a result of the zirconium shell of the fuel rods drawing oxygen from the surrounding water—which can occur at high temperatures. By 10:50 p.m., internal pressure had risen to 540 kPa, exceeding the 427 kPa maximum.

Just after 6:30 a.m., the sound of a large explosion emanated from Reactor 2. It later became apparent that hydrogen gas from Reactor 2 had leaked into Reactor 4 through a shared (and likely damaged) venting pipe. When the hydrogen gas that had accumulated in Reactor 4 ignited, the resulting explosion blew away the roof and much of the walls. Much of the Daiichi staff were evacuated to the Daini plant. At 11:00 a.m., the prime minister's office expanded the evacuation radius to 30 kilometers.

Reactor Pools: The Other Serious Danger

Reactors undergoing routine maintenance at the time of the disaster posed potentially critical problems—in particular Reactor 4, located adjacent to Reactors 1–3. The explosion that rocked the Daiichi plant at 6:00 a.m. on March 15 was not from the "live" Reactor 2, but actually from the Reactor 4 building.

Reactor 4's fuel rods had been removed from the reactor and placed in storage pools. The fuel rods still required cooling—at least several tons of water per hour to maintain temperatures that would not boil off the water. The used fuel pools in the Reactor 4 building had 1,535 fuel assemblies, each with a dozen fuel rods. These storage pools were located at the top of the reactor buildings.

Since pumps for the used fuel pools had stopped, the temperature had risen from 40 to 84 degrees Celsius. Unlike the nuclear reactor cores, which were inside multiple layers of containment vessels, the storage pools were unprotected. Once the hydrogen explosion had blown off the roof and much of the walls, the pool itself was exposed directly to the outside, which could speed up the evaporation of water in the pools.

Prime Minister Kan was concerned about various terrifying scenarios. If a meltdown began, for example, the fuel rods could burn through the bottom of the containment pools, falling all over inside the reactor building. Radiation would be so strong that cleanup and cooling activities would be highly problematic, and a vast area would need to be evacuated. This would jeopardize operations at the Fukushima Daini plant as well. Alternatively, with the roof and walls severely damaged from the hydrogen explosion, a strong aftershock could bring the entire water pool, with its fuel rods, tumbling down into the reactor building. Moreover, the heavy lids of the containment vessel and the equipment used to move it were all stored in the upper parts of reactor building 4, making it further vulnerable to structural collapse. Internal worst-case scenarios within the prime minister's office suggested the possibility of an evacuation radius of 250 to 300 kilometers. This included the entire Tokyo metropolitan area.[15]

TEPCO'S ABANDONMENT REQUEST CONTROVERSY, ESTABLISHMENT OF JOINT HEADQUARTERS

When the explosion at Reactor 3 occurred on March 14, the political leadership again first learned of it through television. The larger, black plume initially led many to fear that the reactor itself had exploded. On the ground, the seismically reinforced operations headquarters was damaged and no longer airtight—radiation levels near windows began rising. The vents in Reactor 2 to lower the pressure for water injections also slammed shut. Self Defense Force members and workers preparing for the operation were injured and pulled from the site. Reactor 2 was entering the most severe stage of crisis yet.

As the nuclear crisis entered its third night, on March 14, pressure in Reactor 2 kept building, water levels were dropping, and water injections were failing. Yoshida's team estimated the hours till a catastrophic containment vessel breach, and Yoshida began planning to evacuate all crew other than key operators—people who would die with him defending the plant.[16]

Later that night, TEPCO president Shimizu began telephoning METI minister Banri Kaieda, then Chief Cabinet Secretary Yukio Edano, numerous times, requesting to see the prime minister. In events that became the focal point of intense scrutiny in subsequent investigations, the political leadership understood Shimizu to inquire whether TEPCO could abandon Daiichi. Reading this as intent to put the responsibility on them, they stopped picking up his calls. Shimizu and TEPCO executives later insisted that they had said "retreat," rather than "abandon," implying that key personnel would stay behind to continue seawater injection operations. Kaieda and Edano dispute this view, contending that nothing was ever said about core personnel remaining. They argued that a simple "retreat" would not require Shimizu's attempts to contact the prime minister.[17]

Kan was awakened from a nap in his fifth floor office around 3:00 a.m. on March 15 by aides and political leaders informing him of TEPCO's abandonment request. Kan forcefully asserted that this could not happen, summoning Shimizu around 4:00 a.m. Shimizu arrived in twenty minutes.[18] He began talking about the rolling blackouts TEPCO had to impose, given the electricity shortage from the disaster, without bringing up anything about the explosions.

Kan finally interrupted Shimizu, asking why TEPCO had not reported personally after the explosions. Then, in response to Kan's forcefully demanding whether TEPCO intended to abandon the plant, participants were dumbfounded by Shimizu's meek reply in the negative. This seemed to undermine the purpose of his countless requests to see the prime minister and long list of missed calls to Edano and Kaieda. However, critically, his denial ensured that Shimizu left no record of explicitly requesting abandonment, and politicians rather than TEPCO were forced to decide whether TEPCO employees should risk their lives at Daiichi.[19] Kan's aide, Democratic Party of Japan (DPJ) member Goshi Hosono, had actually personally called Yoshida at the plant before waking Kan. Yoshida assured him that he had no intention to abandon the plant. Kan followed up with Yoshida, who repeated his resolve. The political leadership had felt for some time that TEPCO headquarters and the plant were not in sync.[20]

At this point, Kan took the unprecedented step of ordering a joint government-TEPCO headquarters within TEPCO. He recalls having thought about solving the information coordination problems by this means since the previous day.[21] He told Shimizu to prepare a desk for Hosono within half an hour, and that he, Kan, would visit TEPCO headquarters within the hour.[22]

It took Kan only approximately five minutes to reach TEPCO headquarters—they were that close—arriving at 5:35 a.m. He announced to the three hundred or so employees on the main floor that TEPCO would not be allowed to abandon Daiichi. He told them that they, TEPCO, were responsible, and if they fled, the company would not survive. This visit increased antagonism between TEPCO and the political leadership. However, communications flowed far more effectively with the prime minister's office. Kan's establishment of joint headquarters was later considered highly beneficial in coordinating subsequent reactor stabilization water injection operations, involving the Self Defense Forces, Tokyo Fire Department, and TEPCO.[23]

Emergency Mobilization to Cool Used Fuel Pools

A turning point in the disaster came on March 17, almost six days after the earthquake and tsunami hit. The previous day, an SDF helicopter confirmed that Reactor 4's used fuel pool contained water and that the fuel rods were not exposed. On the morning of March 17, SDF helicopters reinforced with tungsten on their lower sides to mitigate radiation flew over the reactor and dumped large buckets of water onto Reactor 3. It was not clear how effective this was as a cooling measure, but the fact that the government was finally able to orchestrate mitigation efforts was a psychological turning point.

More importantly, that evening, SDF land and air forces provided a number of SDF fire trucks equipped with aircraft-catastrophe-grade fire extinguishers. At 7:35 p.m. the trucks began dousing Reactor 3 with water, taking turns for five dousings. The following day they moved in even closer, hitting Reactor 3 and expanding to cover Reactor 4 beginning on March 20. While the effects could not be measured, given the lack of working instrumentation, this was another major psychological step toward recovery.

On that day, March 20, power from the electricity grid to the Fukushima Daiichi plant was finally restored. However, the cooling systems did not restart. Monitoring instruments were unstable, and the motor to pump water to the used fuel pools did not work.[24]

Further reinforcements for the manual hosing of the reactors and storage pools were on the way, however. A large German concrete pump truck, diverted from its destination of Vietnam as it happened to be docked in Yokohama, was deployed on March 22. Two other large concrete pumps arrived from other parts of Japan, pumping water into the 30-meter-high fuel pools. On March 23, a pump truck with an arm reaching 63 meters high arrived from China, as a gift to TEPCO. Shortly thereafter, the world's tallest pump truck, with an arm reaching 70 meters, arrived from the United States. These reinforcement measures were used until March 24, when the cooling pumps became operational.[25] On April 11, the government set a 20-kilometer radius as a no-go zone, enabling people who had evacuated from the earlier 30-kilometer radius to return if they chose.

THE OTHER TSUNAMI-STRICKEN POWER PLANTS

The Fukushima Daiichi plant was one of four nuclear power plants on Japan's eastern coast hit by the tsunami on March 11, 2011. The other three were TEPCO's Fukushima Daini plant, approximately 12 kilometers to the south; the Onagawa plant, 116 kilometers to the north, operated by Tohoku Electric Power Company; and Tōkai Daini, 112 kilometers to the south, operated by the Japan Atomic Power Company. The Fukushima Daiichi plant was the only one that experienced a meltdown, but conditions were serious at the others as well. Fukushima Daini was categorized as INES level 3, with Onagawa a level 1.[26]

At the Fukushima Daini plant, it was initially unclear whether the reactors had scrammed successfully as the earthquake hit. An indicator warned that the status of one of the control rods inserted to stop the reaction could not be confirmed. The design of Daini's BWR reactors entailed control rods inserted from below using a loaded spring-like mechanism, rather than control rods inserted from above that could be dropped down utilizing gravity. At Daini, shortly after the initial warning, it was determined that the control rod had been inserted correctly after all.[27]

The tsunami hit the Daini plant with a height of 9 meters, compared with 13 meters at Daiichi. This level was below the plant height of 12 meters, and although one section of the tsunami run-up was higher than the seawall and led to partial flooding, the seawall remained intact and damage to the plant itself was limited. However, partial flooding did destroy three out of four seawater pumps and nine of the twelve emergency diesel generators. Fortunately, one of the three off-site power lines remained, and workers were able to pull electric cables, rerouting the external power to each of the reactors to operate the emergency cooling systems for three of the four reactors in danger of melting down.

The Onagawa plant was closer to the earthquake epicenter than Fukushima Daiichi, at 70 kilometers compared with 180 kilometers, and was struck by the tsunami at the same height as Daiichi. However, the Onagawa plant was built at a height of 14.8 meters, with a seawall height of 14 meters. It was therefore largely spared from severe inundation, although four of its five external power

TABLE 1.1: Comparison of Tsunami-Stricken Nuclear Power Plants

	Tsunami Height	Plant Height	Distance from Epicenter	Maximum Gal	Surviving Off-Site Power Lines	Surviving EDGs	INES Level
Fukushima Daiichi	13m	10m	180km	550 Gal	0/6	1/13	7
Fukushima Daini	9m	12m	190km	305 Gal	1/4	3/12	3
Onagawa	13m	13.8m	70km	607 Gal	1/5	6/8	1
Tōkai	4.6m	8m	280km	214 Gal	0/3	2/3	0

lines were destroyed and two of the three backup diesel generators and seawater pumps in Reactor 2 were flooded. The plant experienced a fire in one of its turbine buildings, but the fire was extinguished without incident. In stark contrast to Fukushima Daiichi and Daini, around which evacuation radii were established, local residents of the town of Onagawa, which was largely destroyed by the earthquake, fled to the Onagawa nuclear power plant, where emergency supplies such as food and blankets were available.

The Tōkai Daini plant lost all external power in the earthquake. However, the tsunami at that point was lower than at the other plants, measuring only 4.6 meters, and was mostly contained by the 6.1-meter-high seawall. Although partial flooding occurred from a hole in a section of the seawall undergoing construction, two of the three on-site emergency diesel generators and two of the three seawater pumps remained intact, and the single reactor in operation was successfully cooled.

NOTES

1. "Final Report of the Investigation Committee on the Accident at Fukushima Nuclear Power Stations of Tokyo Electric Power Company," Secretariat of the Investigation Committee on the Accidents at the Fukushima Nuclear Power Station, Tokyo, July 2012, available at www.cas.go.jp/jp/seisaku/icanps/eng/final-report.html.

2. Executive Summary (NAIIC), in "Official Report of the Fukushima Nuclear Accident Independent Investigative Commission," National Diet of Japan, Tokyo, 2012, available at http://warp.da.ndl.go.jp/info:ndljp/pid/3856371/naiic.go.jp/en/.

3. "Independent Investigation Commission on the Fukushima Daiichi Nuclear Accident (IIC)," in *Fukushima Genpatsu jiko dokuritsu kenshou iinkai chosa/kenshou houkokusho* [*Fukushima Nuclear Accident Independent Investigation Commission Research and Evaluation Report*] (Tokyo, 2012); Kenichi Ohmae, ed., *Genpatsu Saikadou "Saigo no Jouken": "Fukushima Daiichi" Jikokensou purojekuto saishuu houkokusho* [*The "Final Conditions" for Restarting Nuclear Power Plants: Final Report of the "Fukushima Daiichi"*

Accident Investigation Project] (Tokyo: Shogakukan, 2012).

4. Tokyo Electric Power Company (TEPCO), "Fukushima Genshiryoku Jiko Chousa Houkoku sho" [Fukushima Nuclear Accident Investigation Report], Tokyo Electric Power Company, 2012.

5. International Atomic Energy Agency (IAEA), "The IAEA International Fact Finding Expert Mission of the Fukushima Daiichi NPP Accident Following the Great East Japan Earthquake and Tsunami," in *IAEA Mission Report* (International Atomic Energy Agency, 2011); Institute of Nuclear Power Operators (INPO), "Lessons Learned from the Nuclear Accident at the Fukushima Daiichi Nuclear Power Station," INPO Special Report, INPO 11-005 Addendum, 2012, available at www.nei.org/corporatesite/media/filefolder/INPO_11-005_Fukushima_Addendum_1.pdf; INPO, "Special Report on the Nuclear Accident at the Fukushima Daiichi Nuclear Power Station," INPO Special Report, INPO 11-005, November 2011, available at www.nei.org/corporatesite/media/filefolder/11_005_Special_Report_on_Fukushima_Daiichi_MASTER_11_08_11_1.pdf.

6. Yasuaki Oshika, *Merutodaun: Dokyumento Fukushima daiichi genpatsu jiko* [*Meltdown: Documenting the Fukushima Daiichi Nuclear Accident*] (Tokyo: Kodansha, 2012); Asahi, ed., *Purometeusu no wana: akasarenakatta fukushima genpatsu jiko no shinjitsu* [*The Trap of Prometheus: The Truth about the Fukushima Disaster*] (Tokyo: Gakken, 2012); Ryusho Kadota, *Shi no fuchi wo mita otoko Yoshida Masao to Fukushima Daiichi genpatsu no 500 nichi* [*The Man Who Saw the Abyss of Death: Yoshida Masao and the 500 Days at Fukushima Daiichi Nuclear Power Plant*] (Tokyo: PHP Kenkyujo, 2012); Yoichi Funabashi, *Kaunto daun meruto daun (jou)* [*Countdown to Meltdown (Part 1)*] (Tokyo: Bungei Shunju, 2012); *Kaunto daun meruto daun (ge)* [*Countdown to Meltdown (Part 2)*] (Tokyo: Bungei Shunju, 2012).

7. Makoto Saito, *Genpatsu Kiki no Keizaigaku* [*The Economics of the Nuclear Crisis*] (Tokyo: Nihon Hyoron Sha, 2011); Kenji E. Kushida, "DPJ's Political Response to the Fukushima Nuclear Disaster," in *Japan under the DPJ: The Politics of Transition and Governance*, ed. Kenji E. Kushida and Phillip Y. Lipscy (Stanford: Walter H. Shorenstein Asia-Pacific Research Center, 2013).

8. Naoto Kan, *Toden Fukushima Genpatsu Jiko: Souri Daijin toshite kangaeta koto* [*The TEPCO Fukushima Nuclear Accident: What I Thought as Prime Minister*] (Tokyo: Gentosha, 2012); Goshi Hosono and Shuntaro Torigoe, *Shougen Hosono Goushi: genpatsu kiki 500 nichi ni Torigoe Shintaro ga semaru* [*Testimony Hosono Goshi: Shintaro Torigoe Investigates 500 Days of the Nuclear Crisis*] (Tokyo: Kodansha, 2012).

9. For a more detailed English language account, see Kenji E. Kushida, "The Fukushima Nuclear Disaster and the DPJ: Leadership, Structures, and Information Challenges during the Crisis," *Japanese Political Economy* 40, no. 1 (2013).

10. Saito, *Genpatsu Kiki no Keizaigaku*, 22.

11. Saito, *Genpatsu Kiki no Keizaigaku*.

12. Kadota, *Shi no fuchi*.

13. Such filters were installed in US and European nuclear plants after the 1979 partial nuclear meltdown accident at Three Mile Island in the United States.

14. Ibid.

15. IIC, *Fukushima Genpatsu jiko dokuritsu.*

16. Funabashi, *Kaunto daun meruto 1*, 279–80; Kadota, *Shi no fuchi.*

17. NAIIC, "Official Report of the Fukushima Nuclear Accident Independent Investigative Commission."

18. IIC, *Fukushima Genpatsu jiko dokuritsu*; Asahi, ed. *Purometeusu.*

19. Oshika, *Merutodaun*; IIC, *Fukushima Genpatsu jiko dokuritsu.* DPJ member and Kan aide Hosono Goshi, however, had been in touch with plant manager Yoshida directly via cell phone a number of times. Yoshida said that there was still work they could do, and they would remain. The political leadership got the strong impression that TEPCO headquarters was not in tune with what was happening on the ground. Funabashi, *Kaunto daun meruto 1*, 307.

20. Funabashi, *Kaunto daun meruto 1.*

21. Kan, *Toden Fukushima Genpatsu Jiko.*

22. IIC, *Fukushima Genpatsu jiko dokuritsu.*

23. Ibid.

24. Oshika, *Merutodaun*, 152.

25. Funabashi, *Kaunto daun meruto 2*, 203–11.

26. For an excellent comparison across Japan's tsunami-stricken nuclear power plants, see Ohmae, *Genpatsu Saikadou "Saigo no Jouken."*

27. Oshika, *Merutodaun.*

PART II: Learning Lessons from Fukushima

2 The Accident That Could Never Happen: Deluded by a Design Basis

Gregory D. Wyss

INTRODUCTION

The nuclear accident at Fukushima Daiichi occurred when an "unthinkable" sequence of events occurred: a tsunami, caused by a massive undersea earthquake, overtopped the plant's seawall and flooded large areas of the plant. These events caused a loss of all electric power both within and external to the plant—a station blackout condition, as it is known in the industry. As a result, while the boiling water reactor (BWR) plant had many redundant systems designed to inject needed cooling water into the reactor, none of them could function, because each one was dependent on some form of electric power.

It is easy in hindsight to point to the reactor's design, and particularly that of the seawall, and say that it was inadequate. The plant was designed to withstand an assumed maximum tsunami height of 5.7 meters with a very conservative design that relied on a 10-meter-high seawall. However, no measures were provided to protect the plant from a catastrophic outcome for an event that would overtop this seawall, such as the 13-meter tsunami that occurred at the site on March 12, 2011. However, different and more conservative design assumptions about the maximum tsunami height led to very different outcomes at other nearby reactors. The purpose of this chapter is not to discuss the inadequacy of the seawall at Fukushima Daiichi, but rather to discuss the processes by which important design criteria are set, the implications of those design criteria, and how current and future systems with high consequence potential can adapt to the lessons of the Fukushima Daiichi nuclear accident.

The focus of this chapter is two fallacies that are common when system designers develop and use design bases, with eleven safety and security lessons that are derived from both the fallacies and the Fukushima Daiichi nuclear accident. However, in order for the reader to appreciate these fallacies and lessons fully, it is important to understand key foundational and historical concepts relating to how design bases are defined, formulated, and used in the engineering of high-consequence systems. Thus, the chapter begins with a discussion of these foundational concepts before proceeding through an enumeration of the fallacies and lessons. Throughout the paper, illustrative examples are drawn from the Fukushima Daiichi nuclear accident. However, examples from other disciplines are also cited, so that system designers, regulators, and operators can clearly see that these lessons apply to all types of engineered high-consequence systems and not only to nuclear power systems.

DEFINITIONS OF DESIGN BASIS

When any engineered system is designed, the design team must know the conditions, needs, and requirements that must be satisfied by the facility or product being designed. This collection of requirements, goals, and principles define what must be true of the final design in order for it to be considered acceptable.[1] Typically, "design basis" (DB) is used to refer to each high-level requirement, which the system engineering team may then further decompose into more detailed design requirements at its own discretion. For example, the design of a rocket might require that, should the rocket fly dramatically off course, it can be reliably destroyed even if any two components independently malfunction (a "two-fault tolerant" system). This is a DB for the rocket, and the details of achieving that standard are left to the design team. Other types of DBs may require that a system will operate properly for all temperatures within a specified range, or that a cutting system will be inoperable unless both of the operator's hands are removed from the dangerous cutting area, or that a security alarm will be sounded with a probability of 99 percent if the door is opened without proper authorization. Typically, an independent review is conducted to determine whether the final design of an engineered system meets all of its DBs.

Many types of DBs can find their way into the design of a system. The US Nuclear Regulatory Commission (NRC) glossary defines a design-basis accident (DBA) as "a postulated accident that a nuclear facility must be designed and built to withstand without loss to the systems, structures, and components necessary to ensure public health and safety."[2] One example of a DBA is that each US nuclear power plant (NPP) must be designed to survive the "double-ended guillotine break" of its largest single pipe. Another term, design-basis event (DBE), refers to a nonaccident event for which a DB is defined. For security purposes, the NRC glossary defines a design-basis threat (DBT) as "a profile of the type, composition, and capabilities of an adversary. The NRC and its licensees use the DBT as a basis for designing safeguards systems to protect against acts of radiological sabotage and to prevent the theft of special nuclear material."[3] Nuclear facility licensees are expected to demonstrate that they can defend against the DBT.

Finally, the NRC glossary defines "design-basis phenomena" as "earthquakes, tornadoes, hurricanes, floods, etc., that a nuclear facility must be designed and built to withstand without loss of systems, structures, and components necessary to ensure public health and safety."[4] The NRC lists many design-basis phenomena in its regulations, and a facility owner must demonstrate that the specific facility is safe with regard to these phenomena in light of each site's unique surroundings, weather, geology, and other features.

There are two typical flavors of DB. The first specifies a required characteristic of the system—for example: "The facility must have at least two diverse sources of electric power." The second specifies bounding conditions within which the system must operate. These DBs usually contain at least two features: a condition and a required response. The condition indicates bounds within which the DB is applicable, and the required response indicates what must be true of the system for any event within those conditions. In the DBA example above, the condition is a double-ended guillotine break of the largest single pipe, and the required response is "without loss to the systems, structures, and components necessary to ensure public health and safety." For example, a double-ended guillotine break of the *two* largest pipes is a very unlikely but still possible condition that would not be covered by this DB.

One additional term helps shed light on the history and important philosophical issues out of which the above definitions were born. In some circles, what is now a DBA was originally called a maximum credible accident (MCA).[5] "Maximum credible" indicates that any more severe condition need not be considered because it is, by implication, not credible. While the terms DBA, DB, and so forth are intended to remove the implication of impossibility, it is clear that the mindset of designers can and often does result in the unspoken assumption that events beyond the DB are not credible. This thinking clearly contributed to the accident outcomes at Fukushima Daiichi and is an important lesson to be learned from that event. Indeed, many accident prevention and mitigation requirements specified by the US NRC over the last few decades have sought to ensure that nuclear power plants can effectively diagnose and respond to events that are beyond the DB. Examples of and rationale for these requirements are discussed throughout the remainder of this chapter, and reinforce lessons to be learned from this accident.

FORMULATING A DESIGN BASIS

The set of DBs represents the basis upon which a product or facility will be designed, constructed, and operated. They are a necessary means of communication among those who will design, purchase, operate, regulate, and otherwise be affected by the product or facility. They act as a high-level contract among all of the stakeholders to specify the limits of acceptability for the product or facility. And as with most such high-level contracts, the process by which DBs are set can vary from a hard technical analysis to a negotiated political settlement.

Three different methods are typically used to establish DBs. First, a DB may be policy-driven. This situation results in the establishment of a qualitative or quantitative condition that must be satisfied by the design. Second, a DB can be set to correspond to an actual physical limit. Often the intent of such DBs is to represent a physical bound that is believed to be impossible to exceed. A third method for setting a DB is based on frequency arguments. For example, one might design a bridge over a river such that it should not be damaged by any flood with a depth expected to occur more often than once every 250 years (a "250-year flood").

Each method of formulating a DB has its own advantages and pitfalls. For example, a policy-driven DB imposes a specific characteristic upon the design as a policy solution to a perceived concern—a solution that may be based more on negotiation among stakeholders than on a specific technical evaluation, and which if not carefully grounded in relevant analysis, has the potential to inadvertently increase the risk for a facility or system. A DB based on a physical limit may be less conservative than intended if the selected condition fails to consider some important situation or physical phenomenon that might lead to the occurrence of a more severe condition. A frequency-based DB may be extremely uncertain for extremely rare events such as cataclysmic earthquakes because of limitations in extrapolating over time periods beyond recorded history. These limitations and their implications are described more fully in the context of the interplay between safety and security in system design near the end of this chapter.

Conservatism of Design Basis Protection

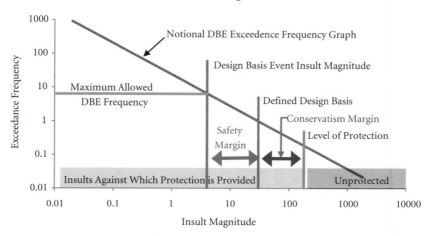

FIG. 2.1: Graphical depiction of the effect of safety margins and analytical conservatism on the level of protection provided by a DB.

A discussion of the process by which DBs are set for nuclear facilities would not be complete without a discussion of safety margins, analytical conservatism, and defense-in-depth. In general, a DB that is based on either a physical limit or a frequency argument is not set to exactly the implied insult magnitude (an "insult" is a phenomenon against which the system or facility is to be protected). Rather, the DB insult level for a DBE (including DBAs and DBTs) is considered in light of the seriousness of the potential consequences should the DB be violated. A margin of safety is applied to the implied insult magnitude from the DBE in order to arrive at the actual DB, as shown in Figure 2.1. Furthermore, for safety-related DBs, regulators often require the DB compliance arguments, including computations, analyses, experiments, and design assumptions, to be generated using conservative techniques.[6] That is, the compliance arguments are deliberately biased so that any errors that might creep into the analysis and justification process are more likely to produce a false rejection of a compliant design than a false acceptance of a noncompliant design. This combination of safety margin and analytical conservatism means that, while the facility or system is designed to withstand an insult of one magnitude, it will in many cases survive an insult of a significantly larger magnitude. This behavior was seen in the Fukushima Daiichi earthquake. The plant's response to the earthquake itself (that is, without the ensuing tsunami) indicated that safe shutdown was occurring as expected, even though the actual earthquake was significantly larger than the seismic design basis for the plant.

The concept defense-in-depth (DiD), which is pervasive throughout nuclear facility design, is also related to DBs. The NRC glossary defines DiD as follows:

> An approach to designing and operating nuclear facilities that prevents and mitigates accidents that release radiation or hazardous materials. The key is creating multiple independent and redundant layers of defense to compensate for potential human and mechanical failures so that no single layer, no matter how robust, is exclusively relied upon. Defense-in-depth includes the use of access controls, physical barriers, redundant and diverse key safety functions, and emergency response measures.

Key words in this definition include "multiple, independent, and redundant layers of defense." Some early definitions of DiD included the idea that the successive layers of defense should also exhibit increasing robustness or conservatism.[7] This design principle can be thought of as an additional criterion to be used in conjunction with the overall collection of DBs to help address "completeness uncertainty"—the possibility that the DBs might have inadvertently overlooked an issue that might lead to a system or facility that is unsafe, especially one that is unsafe in some unknown way. In this way, DiD provides some expected but unquantifiable level of protection for the resulting system or facility against the unknown unknowns to which it might be exposed during its lifetime.

USING A DESIGN BASIS

Since the set of DBs acts as a high-level contract among stakeholders to specify the limits of acceptability for the product or facility, the set of DBs is fundamentally a risk acceptance mechanism. That is, at least for high-consequence facilities and products, the DBs are set such that a system that conforms to all of the DBs is expected to pose an acceptable risk to all stakeholders, including society as a whole. For this reason, DBs generally should not be set solely by the facility or the design agent, but rather in conjunction with the other stakeholders, mediated and evaluated by independent agents (for example, regulators), and with public input.

The DBs serve as definitive high-level requirements and design constraints against which the design team must operate. Regulators take great care in specifying DBs, and designers are fastidious in following them. Designers and regulators may negotiate as to the specific meaning of particular DBs, and a final comprehensive design review occurs before high-consequence systems can operate, at which time additional safety concerns can be raised. However, a facility or product that meets all relevant DBs has a high likelihood of being built and approved for operation with only minor modifications.

Few high-consequence facilities and products are designed for one-time use. Frequently they are expected to exist for years or even decades. Such systems likely will need to be modified during their lifetimes and will evolve from their initial designs. DBs are important to system evolution in two ways. First, each change to a system must be done in such a way that it does not invalidate compliance with one or more DBs. Given the complexity of these systems and the sheer number of DBs (to say nothing of the more detailed requirements that are derived from these DBs), it is important to exercise good systems engineering practices by tracking the requirements, understanding the basis for compliance with each, and actively monitoring any system changes to ensure that compliance is maintained, which can be a Herculean task. Verifying, for example, that an electric circuit is not overloaded can easily be overlooked as one small load after another is added. However, the overloaded circuit might be discovered only during a rare DBE, when it could lead to dire consequences.

DBs are also important to system evolution in that they can be revised over time for both technical and political reasons. Compliance with new or revised DBs may be required immediately, or may be triggered by other factors such as time, license expiration, maintenance, or facility refurbishment. These changes should be expected, since the science associated with a high-consequence system may become better established over time, or stakeholder opinions may evolve. Tracking DB changes and reconciling these changes with existing DBs is an important ongoing activity for enduring systems.

DESIGN-BASIS FALLACIES

At least two common fallacies occur when system designers focus on stated DBs as the primary metrics for success of their design. These fallacies occur largely because of assumptions regarding the scope of DBs and their effect on design.

Fallacy 1: Successfully meeting the required response for a DB's stated condition implies that a successful response will occur for all lesser included conditions. This fallacy is easily illustrated in the security domain, but may be counterintuitive for safety. A security system that is designed to successfully defend against a frontal assault by a squad of five heavily armed, well-trained attackers may not succeed against the seemingly lesser attack of two persons who use stealth and deceit to sneak up to the target to accomplish their destructive objective. Thus, it is insufficient to design the security system focusing only on the worst-case condition implied in the DB (in this case, the DBT) in the belief that by covering the most severe condition one has ensured success against all seemingly lesser conditions. In this case, the attack by a lesser force may use tactics to exploit weaknesses in the system that would not be possible during the frontal assault that many system designers intuitively associate with the DBT. The designer must look across a broad spectrum of adversary tactics (including participation by insiders), attack modes, and defeat methods to ensure that the intent of the DB condition—that the facility is adequately defended against all attacks up to and including the DBT—is actually met.

This fallacy also occurs in a safety context. Nuclear power plants have long been designed to meet a DB that precludes core damage even in the event of a break in the largest pipe in the reactor's cooling system—the large-break loss of coolant accident (large LOCA). The intuitive assumption has been that by designing for success against a large LOCA, one will also be successful against all smaller LOCA accidents. Such was the conventional wisdom when the first probabilistic risk assessment (PRA) study was performed for an NPP—the WASH-1400 "Reactor Safety Study" in 1975.[8] To everyone's surprise, this study claimed that a LOCA from a small pipe, complicated by human mistakes, was much more likely to lead to core damage than a large LOCA. The study was received with skepticism in many circles because it was counterintuitive. However, the 1979 reactor accident at Three Mile Island was one instance of the small LOCA accident that WASH-1400 had warned about. The NPP was designed to be successful against a large LOCA DBA, but provided operators with confusing information about its condition during a small LOCA—a lesser accident included in the DB that designers had assumed would be mitigated by the equipment installed to address the large LOCA DBA.

A key aspect of this fallacy is that when designers focus on the worst case specified in the DB, DBA, or DBT, they often consider only a very small set of scenarios and implicitly assume that the characteristics of all other scenarios will be similar enough that the engineered solutions for the worst case will apply to these other scenarios as well. But in the security example, note how a fundamentally different attack mode renders the engineered solution ineffective. In the Three Mile Island example, the instrumentation and operating procedures were not designed to enable operators to successfully diagnose and mitigate this specific class of accidents, because the designers were focused on mitigating the large LOCA. In other situations, designers who focus on the large LOCA might design emergency cooling systems that are capable of only a low-pressure, high-volume supply of coolant under the assumption that the cooling system *must* be at low pressure because it has a large pipe break. Such a design might be incapable of compensating for a small pipe break in which the cooling system loses water and yet remains at high pressure. To combat this fallacy, designers must consider not just the most severe or limiting condition specified in the DB, but also a broad and inclusive cross-section of seemingly lesser conditions, to ensure that these conditions cannot render the engineered solution ineffective, thus violating the DB.

Fallacy 2: A DB represents the most severe condition that can credibly occur. The previous section described various means by which DBs are established. In some cases, a DB represents an actual limit that cannot be exceeded for physical reasons. In many cases, however, a DB is established based on a low estimated likelihood of exceedance rather than a physical limitation. This likelihood may be estimated statistically or heuristically, and may be driven by policy considerations. Clearly it is possible for a condition more severe than the DB to occur at some time during the life of the facility or product, but it is believed to be unlikely enough that the risk associated with its possible occurrence is acceptable. Recall that the set of DBs acts as a high-level contract among stakeholders to specify the limits of acceptability for the product or facility, and in this sense, the set of DBs acts as a risk-acceptance mechanism.

However, an interesting thing can happen as a DB is incorporated into the design process. Designers can forget that a beyond-DB event is merely unlikely, and begin to act as though it were actually impossible (that is, not credible).[9] This behavior was reinforced in past years when terms like "maximum credible accident" were used. So what happens if one of these highly unlikely events occurs? Or, what if the assessment of likelihood that supported establishment of the DB is later found to be wrong? If the designer has acted as though such events are impossible, occurrences of the event will likely lead to unpredicted scenarios and severe consequences. However, if the designer has thought about the possibility of beyond-DB events, perhaps some mitigation measures could be brought to bear that will lead to a better outcome. The US NRC defines beyond-DB accidents as follows:

This term is used as a technical way to discuss accident sequences that are possible but were not fully considered in the design process because they were judged to be too unlikely. (In that sense, they are considered beyond the scope of design-basis accidents that a nuclear facility must be designed and built to withstand.) As the regulatory process strives to be as thorough as possible, "beyond-design-basis" accident sequences are analyzed to fully understand the capability of a design.

The NRC has engaged in several activities over the years to evaluate and enhance the ability of NPPs to mitigate beyond-DB accidents should they occur, including PRA studies, symptom-based procedures, severe accident management guidelines, and most recently, mitigation strategies to include prepositioning of portable backup equipment that can be used to enable flexible response to unanticipated events,[10] as described in other chapters in this volume. Note that the NRC is compelling its licensees to analyze and prepare for events that are beyond the DB. This practice deliberately combats this fallacy.

The US nuclear weapons community took a different approach to preparing for events that might expose weapons to conditions beyond the DB. The design objective for US nuclear weapons is that the probability of nuclear yield be less than 1 in 1,000,000 given the occurrence of any credible accident environment.[11] It has been exceedingly difficult to set a DB environment that encompasses a maximum credible accident when weapons might be exposed to aircraft crashes or burning missile fuel, for example. The weapon safety community has responded to this challenge by developing a weak-link/strong-link concept in which a weak link is designed into a critical system function for the specific purpose of causing that function to fail under environmental conditions far less severe than those that the engineered strong link is designed to survive. When the weak link fails, it does so irreversibly and in a way that makes nuclear yield all but impossible. The objective is to make it impossible to achieve nuclear yield under any accident conditions, because in benign environments, the strong link keeps the weapon safe, and in severe environments, the weak link makes yield impossible. Implementation details can make it difficult to achieve this objective with 100 percent certainty, but the philosophy has changed the nature of the DBA from an upper bound (like an MCA) to merely a condition at which the fundamental behavior of the system changes in a controlled way from one safety regime to another. This is a very effective way to address this second fallacy.[12]

The key to avoiding this fallacy is to analyze and prepare for events that are beyond the DB. While the set of DBs acts as a risk-acceptance mechanism, a beyond-DB event that actually occurs may lead to severe consequences. The height of the seawall at Fukushima Daiichi is an important example of how this fallacy can be instantiated in a design and lead to severe consequences. This and other important lessons from Fukushima are discussed in the following section.

SAFETY LESSONS FROM FUKUSHIMA

The prior sections of this chapter have hinted at several safety and security lessons that can be learned from the way the treatment of DBs affected the events at Fukushima Daiichi. It is clear that, at least when the facility was designed, the DB related to tsunami height was treated as a maximum credible accident (Fallacy 2), so no consideration was given to contingencies that might be invoked to mitigate the scenario should that event actually occur. Several lessons can be drawn from this experience, most of which are designed to reduce the effects of Fallacy 2.

Safety Lesson 1: Stakeholders must ensure that the DB selected will result in an acceptable level of risk, even if the resulting design implements only the bare minimum required to satisfy the DB. Recall that the set of DBs acts as a high-level contract among stakeholders to specify the limits of acceptability for the product or facility and is fundamentally a risk-acceptance mechanism. Other chapters in this volume argue forcefully that the DB tsunami height for Fukushima Daiichi was set too low, effectively exposing the population to a much higher risk than was generally acknowledged. One reason it was set so low is that the historical record of tsunamis within 100 kilometers included only events that could be managed given a DB tsunami wave height of 5.7 meters, even though much larger tsunami waves had been observed within 150 kilometers of the site, and nothing would physically preclude a similar occurrence at this site. Especially for DBs that are based on an acceptably low frequency of occurrence, stakeholders must perform detailed analyses to ensure that the condition selected for the DB actually corresponds to the intended frequency. For other DBs, stakeholders must ensure that the selected conditions actually correspond to a case that is severe enough to encompass the events that might possibly occur. In addition, the US NRC notes that analyses related to DBs should be done using conservative assumptions. They also require that such computations be done using deterministic rather than probabilistic models and criteria to the extent that the specific DB admits such possibility. In contrast, assessments for beyond-DB events are generally carried out using realistic assumptions and are more often assessed using probabilistic criteria.[13]

It is also important to note that designers often interpret a DB as a principal requirement for the facility or product. Often, a design that significantly exceeds the requirements of a DB is significantly more expensive or otherwise less desirable than one that simply meets the DB. For example, the more capable design may impose operability constraints or additional long-term recurring costs that are not required for the minimally compliant design. Thus, this lesson brings to the forefront the fact that designers are likely to develop designs that only implement the bare minimum required to satisfy each DB, and it is up to the stakeholders to ensure that the DB will result in an acceptable level of risk even if the resulting design only minimally satisfies the DB.

Safety Lesson 2: Designers must not assume that a DB represents a maximum credible event unless a physical basis exists to preclude more severe events. This is related to Fallacy 2 above, and was particularly serious at Fukushima Daiichi. Numerous sources have stated that a 12-meter tsunami wave, which would exceed the 5.7-meter DB, was "inconceivable" to Tokyo Electric Power Company (TEPCO) personnel. Henry Willis of the Rand Corporation observes that biases and heuristics can cause analysts to be overconfident when assessing the risks associated with catastrophes, and that "overconfidence causes people to ignore what is possible."[14] A DB that represents a low-frequency event may still be possible, and Hubbard demonstrates how analysts frequently underestimate the likelihood of very rare events even when commonly accepted statistical analysis methods are employed. Thus, society may be implicitly accepting a far greater risk, in the form of both higher likelihood and higher potential consequences, than it realizes or would otherwise find acceptable.

Safety Lesson 3: Competent authorities must ensure that designers evaluate outcomes that might occur if a beyond-DB event occurs, and should understand which design characteristics are driving those outcomes. While this lesson is especially true for DBs that are based on a policy or a frequency of occurrence, it should also be followed for DBs based on a perceived physical limit. By understanding the outcome and its causes, one might not be caught by surprise if the beyond-DB event does occur. One objection to considering beyond-DB events is that merely to examine such events is to admit the possibility they could occur. A better characterization of the analysis might be that the beyond-DB analyses are intended to ensure the completeness and robustness of the design by asking the question "What if our design assumptions or requirements are mistaken?" After all, the Fukushima accident demonstrated that the operators will not just stand around, amazed and doing nothing, if the design assumptions were wrong and a beyond-DB event occurs. And if such an event has been considered ahead of time, operators are more likely to do something beneficial and timely in response to the event. Without prior consideration, operators may be reduced to uninformed improvisation, with a higher likelihood of an unfavorable outcome.

This same line of inquiry should also be pursued for events that are within the DB in order to reduce susceptibility to Fallacy 1. The question "What if our design assumptions or requirements are mistaken?" applies here not so much because the DB might have been set to the wrong level, but because the designers may have met that DB by assuming that it could be represented as a single class of event, and in so doing developed a design ill suited to handle other types of credible events within the DB. This was previously shown in the discussion of Fallacy 1.

Safety Lesson 4: Designers, owners, and operators should consider whether cost-effective modifications to the design can be made that will reduce the consequences of a potential undesired event. A key contributor to the severity of the Fukushima accident was the flooding of areas containing crucial emergency electrical components. The outcome of the accident could have been dramatically different if those areas had been designed to be watertight. Since the beyond-DB tsunami was viewed as inconceivable, this design feature was not implemented and may not even have been considered. Other design options may have also been available. Thinking through possible design options that reduce the likelihood that beyond-DB events will lead to catastrophic consequences is a key to avoiding Fallacy 2. Reduction in consequence potential for the system is also very helpful to reduce the potential seriousness of undiscovered or unanticipated events that are not beyond the DB, thus reducing the impact of Fallacy 1.

Safety Lesson 5: Competent authorities should ensure that designers and operators plan measures to mitigate the consequences of a potential undesired event, even in the face of extreme stress and challenging physical conditions with incomplete and conflicting information. Effective response to a catastrophic event is often enhanced if plans and tools are available that enable a flexible, adaptive, and robust response when situational understanding is impaired.[15] One might object that it is impossible to plan for every contingency, no matter how remote its likelihood. While that is true, consider the following. In the military, it is said that "no plan survives the first contact of battle." General Eisenhower, after becoming US president, said:

> I heard [this statement] long ago in the Army: Plans are worthless, but planning is indispensable. There is a very great distinction because when you are planning for an emergency, you must first start with this one thing: the definition of "emergency" is that it is unexpected; therefore, it is not going to happen the way you are planning.[16]

By planning, one has thought through the options and the available tools, so even if the emergency does not go according to the plan, a better outcome is much more likely. The type of planning done is also of critical importance. In particular, planning must consider communication and the chain of command. Those executing the plan must know that they have the necessary authority if communication is disrupted. This concept is sometimes known as devolution of command authority, and it is a critical feature of most successful military planning. In addition, plans can be very useful when they enable operators to respond to the symptoms of an event rather than requiring detailed root-cause diagnosis during the critical minutes of a crisis. US nuclear regulators have been developing such plans for both within- and beyond-DB events since the 1979 accident at Three Mile Island. In addition, after the terrorist attacks on September 11, 2001, US regulators and NPP operators have developed mitigation strategies to include prepositioning of portable backup equipment that would be useful for broad classes of events and accidents (such as large fires and explosions) and developing procedures for their use.[17] In so doing, they are putting action to President Eisenhower's words on planning. Such plans were not in place at Fukushima Daiichi, so both procedures and equipment had to be improvised, and there was confusion regarding the authority of the operators, as communications were hindered by earthquake damage. The importance of planning mitigation actions to be performed in the event of beyond-DB events is an important lesson from the Fukushima accident.

Safety Lesson 6: Competent authorities should ensure that operators regularly and faithfully practice implementing emergency plans. An emergency plan that has sat on a shelf for many years has lost its value. Eisenhower said that planning—thinking through the options and assessing their potential effectiveness—is the key. And the plan is worthless if those executing it are not familiar with its features. Faithful practice is important because practice familiarizes the plan to those who would be called upon to execute it, and in a sense, brings them through the planning process again. This step is critical if the benefits of planning are to be gained. Faithful practice prevents one from fooling oneself about the plan's workability. Emergency plans that work on paper often fail in practice because of unexpected or unknown realities such as outdated phone numbers, incompatible radio frequencies, and actions that take so long to accomplish that they are no longer timely. These are discovered only in faithful exercises. In the case of Fukushima Daiichi, the emergency preparedness plans were inadequate, but even those plans were exercised only as a formality. The plans were poorly known to operators, poorly executed, and their unworkable features had not been discovered.

Safety Lesson 7: Operators should learn continually from both exercises and analyses of beyond-DB events.[18] Good, faithful exercises may show flaws in emergency preparedness plans. These flaws are learning opportunities that can be exploited to improve the plan, or the training, or the system itself. It is good to ask the exercise participants, "What do you wish you would have had—or done—that would have made your response easier or the outcome better?" It is also important to learn from disciplined analyses of the plant and its surroundings. NPPs are complex machines with complex human interfaces. More can always be understood about them and incorporated into the knowledge base from which both normal and emergency operations are derived. Continual learning is a key to continual improvement and to achieving safe, secure, efficient nuclear power. When an organization stops learning, complacency often sets in, and complacency undermines all of these goals.

Safety Lesson 8: Cooperation is important to effective learning, effective operations, and effective emergency response. In the aftermath of the Fukushima accident, we saw remarkable cooperation—among nations, among disciplines, between staff and management, and even unsolicited help from citizens. This cooperation was brought about by the urgency of a common goal: prevention of a catastrophe. The cooperation had been much less significant before the accident without the urgency of the crisis. Yet cooperation is key to achieving the goal of nuclear power that is safe, secure, and economical. Even cooperation among important disciplines within a single company can be difficult in some cases because each discipline operates as a separate, inwardly focused entity. We must remember that success for the NPP does not occur unless all disciplines successfully achieve their key goals, and cooperation, communication, creative problem solving, listening, and learning are all keys to this success.

Learning from the experience of other NPP operators has also been a key to improved NPP operations and emergency response. Cooperation among operators and nuclear nations has enabled the formation of the Institute for Nuclear Power Operations and the World Association of Nuclear Operators for the sharing of insights and analyses, and has encouraged implementation of best practices by all. Sharing of emergency procedures and preparedness plans internationally has helped improve the ability of operators around the world to respond to these situations. In the case of the Fukushima accident, other papers in this volume point to missed learning opportunities from the actions of other countries that could have made the outcome of this accident much less severe.

The Fukushima accident brought home another aspect of cooperation in the outpouring of international offers of support—both technical and material—to help Japan manage or recover from the accident. While this cooperation was facilitated by the crisis, it points out how deliberately planned international cooperation for emergency preparedness and crisis management could yield great benefits. For example, in a region of the world in which several countries each have a few NPPs, a strong regional emergency management program and even regional cooperation in nuclear regulation could make possible a stronger and more technically capable emergency response program than each nation might be able to field on its own. Sharing the burden could enable this improved program to be fielded at a lower cost to each individual nation.

INTERPLAY BETWEEN SAFETY AND SECURITY IN SYSTEM DESIGN

Safety relates to the prevention of undesired consequences from the occurrence of random events (natural events, operational mistakes, and equipment failures). Security relates to the prevention of many of the same consequences caused through malevolent human intent. Thus, safety and security have many of the same objectives, and the DBs for safety and security DBs may complement one another in these cases. When safety and security are seeking to prevent the same consequences, it should not be surprising that the same design features are relied upon to achieve that goal. Thus, while safety analysts seek to ensure that these design features remain intact under various types of randomly occurring insults (such as fire, flood, drought, earthquake), security analysts seek to ensure that these same features cannot be disabled via malevolent human actions. Both must be accomplished in order to have a safe and secure design.

Security Lesson 1: Competent authorities must ensure that designers and operators pay particular attention to safety-related DBs when developing security systems and postures in order to ensure that design features important to safety are not inadvertently left unprotected to become potentially attractive adversary targets. This lesson regarding DBs and security is not specifically inferred from the Fukushima accident but is a fundamental element of the interplay between safety and security nonetheless. Since DBs represent key design acceptance criteria for a facility or product, it is logical that an adversary might want to develop an attack that deliberately causes one or more DBs to be violated in order to achieve the results or consequences the DB is designed to prevent. For example, if a DB indicates that the facility must survive a fire in one of two cable areas without significant consequences, an adversary may deliberately target both cable areas in order to cause those consequences. In other words, one form of terrorist attack on a facility is to deliberately cause the occurrence of a known safety scenario.

Issues in the Formulation of Safety and Security Design Bases

The security-specific high-level requirements for a system or facility are embodied in DBs in much the same way that DBs are used to express safety requirements. In order to understand the role of DBs in the interplay between safety and security, one must first understand how the various types of DBs are formulated for safety and security. As stated earlier in this chapter, three different methods are typically used to establish DBs. First, a DB may be policy driven. This situation results in the establishment of a qualitative or quantitative condition that must be satisfied by the design. Examples cited previously in this chapter include "two-fault tolerance" and "at least two diverse sources of electric power," while a security example might state the minimum caliber of ammunition to be used by a protective force. While such DBs may be ad hoc and prescriptive, they are often based on a qualitative if subconscious assessment of risk, such as "Failure of the rocket's self-destruct system could cause lots of damage on the ground, so we must make the event very unlikely by ensuring it does not occur without the independent failure of three highly reliable components." The key components of risk are likelihood and consequence, so a policy DB may address the likelihood of a very bad event as above, or it may seek to prevent a severe consequence by, for example, imposing a requirement for a berm of arbitrary height around a hazardous facility. The key here is that the DB imposes a specific characteristic upon the design as a policy solution to a perceived concern—a solution that may be based more on negotiation among stakeholders than on a specific technical evaluation. While it is possible that the DB solution is well founded, it is also possible for the DB's prescriptive requirements to preclude consideration of different designs that might solve the perceived problem more effectively. It is even possible for the prescriptive requirements from one DB to make implementation of another DB more difficult, or to make the resulting system excessively complex to operate or maintain. A well-meaning prescriptive policy-based DB, if not carefully grounded in relevant analysis, has the potential to increase the risk for a facility or system inadvertently—especially if it is found to be in conflict with other DBs (the specific case in which a safety DB conflicts with a security DB will be considered in some detail later in this section). Thus, such DBs should be generated and evaluated with caution.

Second, a DB can be set to correspond to an actual physical limit. For example, the DB for the pressure that must be retained by a reactor containment building might be set such that it requires the building not to leak even if all of the water from the primary coolant system were to be vaporized within the building (even with a conservative factor of safety applied to that pressure). This criterion is objective and deterministic, and can be readily evaluated by system designers and regulators. Often the intent of such DBs is to represent a physical bound that is impossible to exceed. Such DBs are not unusual in the safety context but can rarely be justified for security because it is almost always possible to postulate a larger adversary force with more capable weaponry (thus, their use in a security context would be an example of Fallacy 2). Regulators like the NRC sometimes point out that DBs of this type are based on a conservative deterministic (nonprobabilistic) analysis. In practice, however, these DBs may be less conservative than intended if those proposing the DB have selected the condition portion of the DB while failing to consider some important situation or physical phenomenon that might lead to the occurrence of a more severe condition. For example, the containment building pressure rating described above may be inadequate for an accident in which molten nuclear fuel escapes the reactor pressure vessel. In this case, the molten nuclear fuel may dump large amounts of additional heat and gas into the containment atmosphere, thus causing its pressure to increase well beyond what was envisioned when the DB was specified.

A third method for setting a DB is based on frequency arguments. For example, one might design a bridge over a river such that it should not be damaged by any flood with a depth expected to occur more often than once every 250 years (a "250-year flood"). Research into past floods can provide an estimate for the characteristics of such a flood, and specific design requirements can be derived from such a DB. These types of DBs are routinely used to describe the magnitude of natural disaster a facility or product must be designed to withstand. While these DBs are attractive in theory, they are fraught with uncertainty if the frequency specified in the DB is too low. For example, it is difficult to establish the characteristics of a 1,000-year flood at specific North American sites, since written records for many areas exist for only the last few hundred years. Extrapolation of existing data over many undocumented centuries can lead to major underprediction of the return frequency of cataclysmic events based on nothing more than the statistical distribution assumed in analysis of existing data.[19] In contrast, the failure rate data for key reactor components may be able to draw upon several thousand reactor-years of relevant operating experience across many plants when developing DBs. DBs of this type are particularly unreliable in the security context, as will be described below.

A key DB for security is often embodied in a DBT. One argument for setting a DBT is that it should represent the maximum number and capabilities of adversaries that are likely to attack a facility of this type. This basis is clearly subjective, since the likelihood of an attack depends strongly on the motivation and intent of the adversary considering the attack, and a motivated adversary may work hard to increase its capabilities in response to the facility's defensive measures so that it can increase its opportunities for a successful attack. The motivation and intent of a particular attacker can also change very rapidly in response to events unrelated to the facility itself (for example, military action against the homeland of a foreign-connected adversary). Indeed, such events can even cause previously unconsidered adversaries to begin to prepare and execute attacks!

As a practical matter, a facility cannot defend against an infinite array of possible attackers, so DBTs are frequently formulated based on the insights of law enforcement and intelligence communities, and often include judgments based on observations of threats against a wide variety of targets in locations all around the world. This assessment is generally qualitative, so a DBT set in this way may represent a heuristic assessment of the likelihood of an attack by particular types of adversaries. However, the selection of a DBT can also be molded by regulatory policy. For example, a regulatory body may decide that it would be bad public policy to require private entities to defend against highly capable state-level adversaries, asserting that defense against such adversaries is the exclusive domain of the government by means of military and law enforcement personnel. Indeed, both US and international practice is to set the DBT at the maximum adversary number and capabilities against which a site is required to defend, with the state assuming responsibility for defense against all greater threats. Thus, a DBT may be based on a combination of heuristic likelihood and policy considerations.

While DBTs themselves are not necessarily susceptible to Fallacy 1, security assessments using a DBT are particularly susceptible to it. In this context, Fallacy 1 is exposed as the mistaken belief that the ability to successfully defeat the maximum attack embodied in the DBT implies the ability to successfully defeat all lesser attacks. For example, one can easily imagine a situation in which a small stealthy attack is likely to succeed against a well-fortified facility that can readily defeat an overt attack by a large and well-armed adversary force. Successful security designs must explicitly address this fallacy.

The discussion in this section has shown that security designs are specifically susceptible to both Fallacy 1 and Fallacy 2. Recall that the eight safety-related lessons described earlier in this chapter are all derived as direct or indirect observations from these fallacies. This leads to the following security lesson.

Security Lesson 2: All eight DB-related safety lessons apply equally in the security domain. Consider how DBs and the DB-related lessons described in the previous section relate to security. Each security DB (1) must result in an acceptable level of risk even if only minimally implemented, but (2) is likely not the maximum credible event, especially when the DB is a DBT, because it is always possible that a larger or more capable adversary will attack the facility. Thus, (3) designers need to evaluate possible outcomes from attacks that are both within and beyond the DBT, and (4) consider whether cost-effective modifications to the design might reduce the consequences of an attack, whether the attack is within or beyond the DBT. Designers and operators should (5) plan mitigation measures that can be used to reduce the consequences of an attack even in the face of extreme stress and challenging physical conditions with incomplete and conflicting information, and (6) practice implementation of emergency plans regularly and faithfully. Finally, security can always be made more effective through (7) continual learning and (8) cooperation—both interdisciplinary cooperation to enable efficient operations and international cooperation to learn and implement the best practices discovered by others. Neglect of any of these lessons can lead to a security posture that is brittle toward an attack and likely to lead to severe consequences should an attack be successful.

Conflicts between Safety and Security Design Bases

Recall that the set of DBs represent an agreement among the various stakeholders regarding the requirements to which the facility or system will be designed, constructed, and operated. It would be wonderful if all of these requirements were in perfect agreement, but in practice, unintended conflicts and contradictions are frequently buried within the set of DBs, and even if the DBs themselves do not technically conflict, their implementation can cause conflicting priorities within the design team. The interplay between safety and security is one area where these conflicts are particularly common. One popular illustration of this conflict is when the safety community wants to implement DB requirements by placing several unlocked fire exits within the facility while the security community wants to implement their DB by eliminating as many access points as possible and ensuring that all remaining doors are locked at all times. In this case, the DBs themselves may or may not be in conflict, but the preferred engineering implementations of safety and security requirements are incompatible.

When DB requirements or their preferred engineering implementations are in conflict, good systems engineering practices, interdisciplinary cooperation, and design creativity are required first to recognize and ultimately to resolve the conflict. However, design processes sometimes work against these practices on account of one or more of the following tendencies.

• *Requirements and Design Bases Developed Separately for Each Discipline*— Stakeholders from each discipline develop DBs and requirements without regard to the possibility that they may negatively affect the legitimate needs of other disciplines.

• *Quasi-independent Design Activities by Discipline*—Designers from each discipline believe that *their* DBs and requirements are sacrosanct, expecting other disciplines to adjust their designs and requirements to resolve any conflict. Communication between disciplines occurs infrequently (for example, major design reviews), often after large amounts of effort and emotional energy have been invested by each discipline in the conflicting designs at hand.

• *Security and Safety as Burdensome Expenses*—Safety and security often find themselves jointly facing pressure to cut corners in order to make the design of the system or facility economically viable. This can lead to underperforming systems and expensive retrofits as the security and safety deficiencies become evident and must be remedied during construction and operation.

• *Evolving Security Requirements*—"Protect against the DBT" is a frequent requirement for the security team. Yet, the details of a DBT policy may change frequently, requiring redesign of security features.

• *Security as an Afterthought*—A security requirement such as "Protect anything that the safety team says is important" may prevent the security team from making any real design progress until it is too late to affect aspects of the facility design that may be difficult or expensive to protect adequately. Design teams from other disciplines may subconsciously treat security designers with an attitude of "Protect this! How hard can it be to put up a fence and some cameras?" They are frequently unaware that seemingly minor elements of the larger system design, such as the location of pipes, equipment, and doors, can greatly exacerbate the difficulty of providing security. The security team cannot affect these design features unless it can educate the other design disciplines early in the system design process.

These issues can combine to produce facilities whose security is at the same time onerous, expensive, and only marginally effective. In many cases the facility could be both more functional and more secure if the functional and safety designers were fully informed of the security implications of their work, and vice versa.

Recent work in systems engineering has brought new focus to the interface between safety, security, and other design requirements. Paradigms such as "Safety, Security and Safeguards by Design" (3SBD)[20,21] specify a total systems approach to design, in which the system-level objectives (including DBs and requirements) must be shared by *every* discipline within the design team. A spiral, parallel development approach is used in which each discipline explicitly considers how its decisions will affect the achievability of the design objectives for other disciplines, including both safety and security, and the various design disciplines are challenged to find synergies among their proposed designs. This can result in radical new ways of designing traditional systems where potential conflicts among requirements are recognized early, when they can be resolved much more easily, to the benefit of each discipline and, more important, the resulting system design. For example, recent advances in nuclear power plant design that have focused on replacing active electromechanical systems with passive systems appear to have resulted in designs that are safer, more secure, easier to maintain, and potentially less susceptible to insider sabotage.

When designs from different disciplines continue to conflict, it may be possible to deconflict through negotiation and compromise among the design teams. This can be fruitful when the deconflicting is facilitated by people who have the talents and expertise to act as translators and liaisons between the disciplines (such as between the safety and security design teams). In cases in which the arbiter of the conflict does not understand or value the perspective of one discipline, the conflict may be resolved such that the "loser" is left with a design that operates poorly, is unacceptably expensive, or both. These conflicts can be particularly acute when the functional designers conflict with the safety or security designers if the functional designers perceive the latter to be "just creating obstacles while we are trying to make the system work."

In some cases, unavoidable conflicts may remain among DBs or requirements. Since the set of DBs represents an agreement among the various stakeholders regarding the requirements to which the facility or system will be designed, constructed, and operated, a violation of those DBs is a violation of this agreement and must, therefore, be treated as such. Thus, it is a policy or regulatory framework issue as well as a design process issue, and stakeholders or regulators need to provide guidance as to which DBs or requirements can be relaxed, and to what extent, in order for the resulting system to be considered acceptable.

SECURITY LESSON FROM FUKUSHIMA

The Fukushima accident was not at its core a security incident, as there was no attack on the facility. However, incidents of security concern did occur during the progression and aftermath of the accident. The security implications of this event are described in detail by Kaoru Naito in a separate chapter in this volume. However, in light of the preceding DB discussions, it is important to highlight one additional security lesson derived from the events that occurred at Fukushima.

Security Lesson 3: Security must be an integral part of emergency planning. The immediate aftermath of a catastrophe frequently leads to a chaotic period in which partial information and outright misinformation flourish. In addition, limited personnel resources cause operators and officials to triage tasks and neglect those considered less important. For example, when three nuclear reactor cores are insufficiently cooled and possibly melting, as in the Fukushima accident, it is easy to view security as a less important task and focus all of the attention on mitigating the reactor accident.

During the Fukushima accident, the first several days after the tsunami were indeed very chaotic, as operators struggled to establish and maintain cooling for the three crippled reactors and to understand the condition of the spent-fuel pool in the fourth. There was an ebb and flow of persons into and out of the site bringing both materials and expertise to cope with the accident. While most of these persons were authorized, it has been reported that during the accident several unknown persons accessed the plant; these individuals may not have been authorized to do so and could not be identified or located after the fact.[22]

The key point is that the security environment is frequently compromised or even nonexistent in the immediate aftermath of a catastrophe such as a major earthquake or tsunami. Key components of the security system itself may also be damaged, as occurred during the accident at Fukushima Daiichi. If a terrorist had had the objective to cause a radiological catastrophe, such a compromised security system and environment could provide an opportunistic adversary the chance to enter the facility unnoticed and perform actions that exacerbate the ongoing accident situation or cause significant additional consequences. If such a situation were to occur at a facility that stored significant amounts of separated nuclear material, portable highly radioactive sources, or other materials that might be of interest for theft or terrorism, the catastrophe could provide an opportunity for an adversary to obtain such items more easily or with a reduced likelihood of detection. A lesson to be learned from this situation: it is important to maintain the security of high-consequence facilities and terrorist-usable materials even during a catastrophe in order to deter or prevent the activities of opportunistic adversaries.

The preceding discussion has indicated why it is important for security to be an integral part of emergency planning, but has not shown the relationship between this reasoning and DBs. Simply stated, for systems that have the potential to cause high consequences to workers, the public, or the environment, significant effort goes into the development, approval, and implementation of safety-related DBs related to emergency planning. These DBs may specify features such as emergency evacuation zones, off-site notification methods, and the presence of specific equipment to reduce the likelihood or magnitude of the consequences (see Safety Lesson 5). Yet, the formulation and implementation of these DBs often include minimal consideration of security implications, so the conditions described earlier in this section are the rule rather than the exception. Consideration of security when developing safety-related emergency plans is critical. The integration of safety and security emergency response planning would be even better. Development of complementary or integrated safety and security DBs for emergency planning could greatly aid this effort.

SUMMARY

A design basis is a high-level requirement, goal, or principle that defines what must be true of the final design for a facility or product in order for it to be considered acceptable. DBs can take many forms, including design-basis accidents and design-basis threats. Since they embody limits of acceptability, they act as a means by which the stakeholders negotiate and specify a set of limits, often heuristic, for risk acceptance. DBs can be specified based on the limits of physical phenomena, the frequency of occurrence for an operating condition or environment of concern, or a simple statement of policy that may embody some unspoken or heuristic view of risk. A DB is usually not a description of a maximum credible event, be that an accident or an adversary threat, although designers sometimes treat it that way.

The implementation of DBs in a design can be compromised by two common fallacies. First, designers may mistakenly believe that successfully meeting the required response for a DB's stated or limiting condition implies a successful response for all lesser included conditions. This assumption may not be true if the lesser conditions result in scenarios with dramatically different characteristics for which the selected design is ill conceived. The second fallacy is that the DB represents the most severe condition that can credibly occur, especially if the DB is based mainly on a low frequency of exceedance. Clearly a more severe condition is possible, but belief in this fallacy by designers can result in a facility design incapable of handling that possibility. The Fukushima Daiichi accident is an example of what can happen if this fallacy is instantiated in a system design.

Eight safety-related lessons related to DBs have been drawn from the Fukushima accident, and these have also been found applicable to security, even though Fukushima was not really a security event. These lessons were summarized as follows: each DB (1) must be properly selected to result in an acceptable level of risk even if the design implements only the bare minimum required to satisfy the DB, but (2) should be recognized as likely *not* the maximum credible event. Thus, (3) designers need to evaluate possible outcomes from events that are both within and beyond the DB, and (4) consider whether cost-effective modifications to the design might reduce the consequences of an event, whether it is within or beyond the DB . Designers and operators should (5) plan mitigation measures that can be used to reduce the consequences of an event even in the face of extreme stress and challenging physical conditions with incomplete and conflicting information, and (6) practice implementation of emergency plans regularly and faithfully. Finally, safety and security can always be made more effective through (7) continual learning and (8) cooperation—both interdisciplinary and international. Additional security-related lessons were that security must be an integral part of emergency planning, and that a facility's security posture should be designed with explicit attention to safety-related DBs, because an adversary may be able to achieve its objective simply by causing the conditions that will lead to a severe safety event. Deliberately violating specific DBs during an attack may be an attractive way to achieve that end.

Some of the insights presented in this chapter relate specifically to the design of systems, but many must be practiced continually from the earliest design activities throughout operations and even well into system retirement. In a system like an NPP, this period may be more than sixty years, and during most of that time, few if any events will occur to cause major challenges to DBs or present serious potential for major consequences. It is easy to become complacent under these conditions, and complacency allows for the slow but steady erosion of critical foundations like safety, security, and quality, often in the name of increased ease of operation or improved cost-competitiveness. The opposite of complacency might be thought of as vigilance. Thomas Jefferson has been quoted as saying, "Eternal vigilance is the price of liberty."[23] In our context, we might say, "Eternal vigilance is the price of safety." The same could be said of security, quality, safeguards, and most of the other important goals of nuclear power. But vigilance is only of value if it is directed toward activities that undergird and enable those important goals. The lessons described in this paper describe some of the activities that undergird and make possible safety and security. They are activities for which the nuclear community must remain eternally vigilant.

NOTES

The author would like to thank Scott Sagan of Stanford University and Edward Blandford of the University of New Mexico, as well as Joseph Sandoval, Felicia Durán, and several of his other colleagues at Sandia National Laboratories for their numerous contributions and insights that significantly improved this paper. Sandia National Laboratories is a multiprogram laboratory managed and operated by Sandia Corporation, a wholly owned subsidiary of Lockheed Martin Corporation, for the US Department of Energy's National Nuclear Security Administration under contract DE-AC04-94AL85000. The views expressed in this chapter are solely those of the author and do not necessarily represent the views of Sandia National Laboratories or of any agency or sponsor. This paper is approved for unlimited release as SAND2014-19730B.

1. M. P. Feher, E. C. Davey, L. R. Lupton, and M. J. MacBeth, "A Design Basis for the Development of CANDU Control Centres," paper presented at American Nuclear Society International Topical Meeting on Nuclear Plant Instrumentation, Control and Human-Machine Interface Technologies, Pennsylvania State University, May 6–9, 1996.

2. US Nuclear Regulatory Commission, "Full-Text Glossary," Washington, DC, available at www.nrc.gov/reading-rm/basic-ref/glossary/full-text.html.

3. Ibid.

4. Ibid.

5. "MCA," European Nuclear Society, Brussels, Belgium, available at www.euronuclear.org/info/encyclopedia/m/mca.htm.

6. Similar concepts exist in some security analyses. Some facilities are required to analyze security with regard to representative threats, which are included in the DBT, and sensitivity threats, which are beyond DBT threats. The facility is expected to consider whether low-cost mitigation options, changes in operations, and the like, might mitigate some or all of the sensitivity threats, even though they are technically beyond the DBT.

7. Dr. Dana Powers, former chair of the US Nuclear Regulatory Commission's Advisory Committee for Reactor Safeguards, personal communication with the author at Sandia National Laboratories, 2003.

8. Norman C. Rasmussen, et al., Executive Summary to *Reactor Safety Study: An Assessment of Accident Risks in US Commercial Nuclear Power Plants*, WASH-1400 (NUREG-75/014) (Rockville, MD: US Nuclear Regulatory Commission, 1975).

9. Daniel Kahneman and Amos Tversky, "Prospect Theory: An Analysis of Decision under Risk," *Econometrica* 47, no. 2 (March 1979): 263.

10. US Nuclear Regulatory Commission, "Order for Interim Safeguards and Security Compensatory Measures," EA-02-026 (Washington, DC: US Nuclear Regulatory Commission, February 25, 2002). See also US Nuclear Regulatory Commission, "Mitigation Strategies," available at www.nrc.gov/reactors/operating/ops-experience/japan-dashboard/mitigation-strategies.html.

11. Raymond B. Wolfgang, "Introduction to Enhanced Nuclear Detonation Safety (ENDS)," paper prepared by Sandia National Laboratories, Albuquerque, NM, for presentation at Project on Nuclear Issues Fall Conference, September 8–9, 2011, available at http://csis.org/images/stories/poni/110922_1_Wolfgang.pdf.

12. S. Drell and B. Peurifoy, "Technical Issues of a Nuclear Test Ban," *Annual Review of Nuclear and Particle Science* 44 (December 1994): 285–327, DOI: 10.1146/annurev.ns.44.120194.001441.

13. US Nuclear Regulatory Commission, "Full-Text Glossary."

14. Henry Willis, Rand Corporation, comments during symposium at Sandia National Laboratories, Livermore, CA, September 4, 2013.

15. Wolfgang, "Introduction to Enhanced Nuclear Detonation Safety (ENDS)."

16. Dwight D. Eisenhower, speech to the National Defense Executive Reserve Conference, 1957, available at www.presidency.ucsb.edu/ws/?pid=10951.

17. US Nuclear Regulatory Commission, "Order for Interim Safeguards and Security Compensatory Measures."

18. An important aspect of faithful exercises and organizational learning is to ensure that exercise participants cannot artificially predict the exact nature of the exercise. For example, a facility that always performs security drills against a DBT-level adversary may come to expect that only the DBT-level number of adversaries will ever show up. In one such exercise, the defenders came out of their secure locations when the DBT-level number of adversaries had been neutralized, assuming that the exercise was over—only to be defeated by a single extra attacker. Exercising at levels both below and above the DB introduces uncertainty into the exercise and requires realistic decision-making by exercise participants, which results in better-trained personnel.

19. Douglas W. Hubbard, *The Failure of Risk Management: Why It's Broken, and How to Fix It* (Hoboken, NJ: John Wiley and Sons, 2009), 181–87.

20. E. D. Blandford, C. Murphy, and E. Arthur, "The University of New Mexico Workshop 'Success through Safety, Security, and Safeguards by Design (3SBD): From Concept to Application,'" Institute for Nuclear Material Management Transactions, paper 318, Palm Desert, CA, July 14–18, 2013.

21. D. N. Kovacic et al., "Nuclear Safeguards Infrastructure Development and Integration with Safety and Security," proceedings of the 50th annual meeting of the Institute for Nuclear Materials Management, Tucson, AZ, July 11–17, 2009.

22. "Emergency Worker Doses," *Nuclear Engineering International*, available at www.neimagazine.com/features/featureemergency-worker-doses. It now appears that many of the workers originally reported as unknown have been located. Most were originally listed as unknown because of data entry errors in contact information. The article states: "On 16 December 2011, the names of thirteen [unknown] workers were publicized. Three more were reached. Then there were ten workers with unknown contact information.

No unknown workers appear after July 2011." The author could not determine whether these final ten unknown workers were ever identified or located.

23. Attributed to Thomas Jefferson in "The Union," *Pennsylvania Inquirer and Daily Courier*, January 4, 1838, no. 4, col. B. Similar sentiments were common in early-nineteenth-century America; see http://wiki.monticello.org/mediawiki/index.php/Eternal_vigilance_is_the_price_of_liberty_%28Quotation%29.

3 Security Implications of the Fukushima Accident

Kaoru Naito

This article focuses on nuclear security lessons that can be abstracted from the Fukushima Daiichi accident. For background, I first explain the concept of nuclear security and the potential risks involved. I then describe efforts both internationally and in Japan to ensure nuclear security. To glean nuclear security lessons from the accident, I present the sequence and cause of the accident, as well as their nuclear security implications. I then enumerate the measures taken against additional nuclear security threats identified after the accident and explain how they are being implemented in Japan. The final section covers the need for attaining synergy or closer coordination between nuclear safety and nuclear security.

NUCLEAR SECURITY AND POTENTIAL RISKS

The International Atomic Energy Agency (IAEA) has identified four categories of potential nuclear security risks: (1) the theft of nuclear weapons; (2) the acquisition of nuclear material for the construction of nuclear explosive devices; (3) the malicious use of radioactive sources including in so-called dirty bombs; and (4) the radiological hazards caused by an attack on, or sabotage of, a facility or a transport vehicle.[1]

Management of the first risk rests entirely with nuclear-weapon states, but management of the other risks rests with all states, including non-nuclear-weapon states that are engaged in the peaceful use of nuclear energy. Historically, the primary concern of the international community has been the second risk—namely, proper protection of nuclear material from theft or unauthorized transfer that might result in manufacturing nuclear weapons. The countermeasure against this risk is physical protection of nuclear materials—in contrast to radiological protection, which focuses on the fourth risk of hazardous emanations from nuclear material. Over the years, however, the fourth risk demanded increased attention because of an expansion in the inventory and transfer of nuclear material as peaceful use of nuclear energy grew worldwide. Then came the September 11, 2001, terrorist attacks in the United States, which emphasized the need for more attention on the third risk. The need for protection of radioactive materials was more strongly felt in order to prevent malicious acts, including production of dirty bombs.

The scope of protection thus expanded over the years from physical protection of nuclear materials, through protection against sabotage involving nuclear materials and their facilities, to nuclear security, which covers all radiological substances, including nuclear materials and their related facilities and transportation. Reflecting this expansion, the Advisory Group on Nuclear Security (AdSec), an advisory body of the IAEA director general, defines nuclear security as "the prevention and detection of, and response to, theft, sabotage, unauthorized access, illegal transfer or other malicious acts involving nuclear material, other radioactive substances or their associated facilities."[2] This definition clearly encompasses both nuclear and radioactive materials as well as acts of sabotage against associated facilities that handle such materials. It should be noted that nuclear security covers not only measures to prevent such acts but also responses to them, such as detection and recovery, should theft of radioactive materials occur, or close cooperation with security forces, should a nuclear security event occur.

INTERNATIONAL AND JAPANESE EFFORTS TO ENSURE NUCLEAR SECURITY

The IAEA serves as a focal point for international cooperation to establish effective nuclear security regimes both domestically and globally. The agency has conducted an extensive program to protect against nuclear terrorism by assisting countries in strengthening their nuclear security regimes. Part of this program is an international legal framework, both binding and nonbinding, that includes recommended guidelines published as "The Physical Protection of Nuclear Materials" (IAEA Information Circular 225, or INFCIRC/225),[3] the international Convention on the Physical Protection of Nuclear Material (CP-PNM),[4] and the Nuclear Security Series (NSS)[5] documents. An appendix to this chapter outlines the development of this international legal framework.

A national nuclear security regime encompasses all activities undertaken within a state, including legislation, the nuclear regulatory infrastructure, and law enforcement authorities, as well as coordination and support activities, and measures undertaken by operators—both administrative and technical—to achieve the goals of nuclear security, among others, as outlined in the relevant international guidelines.

As part of efforts to establish an adequate national physical protection regime in Japan, the Atomic Energy Commission of Japan (AECJ) established the Advisory Committee on Physical Protection of Nuclear Materials (ACPP), requesting that it make necessary recommendations with a view to international trends of physical protection. Based on the ACPP report of June 1980, the Japanese government revised the Nuclear Regulation Law in May 1988.[6] The revision included the physical protection of nuclear materials as one of its specific objectives, added physical protection provisions in line with the requirements of INFCIRC/225/Rev.1, and revised criminal law to make the offenses specified in the CPPNM punishable. Japan ratified the CPPNM in November 1988.

In December 2005, the Nuclear Regulation Law was further revised to accommodate the requirements of INFCIRC/225/Rev.4. This revision required licensees to take appropriate measures of physical protection based on design basis threat (DBT) as determined by the government in view of prevailing security conditions, to undergo annual physical protection inspections, and to protect physical protection secrets.

Amid growing international concern to expand the scope of protection from nuclear materials to that of radioactive materials, AECJ established the Advisory Committee on Nuclear Security (ACNS) in December 2006 to advise the commission on how to accommodate the requirements of ensuring nuclear security in Japan in view of international trends, including the publication of NSS documents by the IAEA.[7]

The accident at Fukushima Daiichi in March 2011 prompted ACNS to conduct further reviews of measures that could be pursued to improve nuclear security. After extensive deliberations, the committee, chaired by the author, drafted a report to the commission in September 2011, "The Fundamental Approach to Ensuring Nuclear Security" (ACNS September 2011 Report).[8] The report described the basic policy to ensure nuclear security in Japan, recognizing the fundamentals document that was in the final stage of development as the top tier document in the IAEA's NSS.[9] In its report, ACNS identified two remaining tasks: (1) to consider what additional measures should be taken in order to accommodate the requirements of IAEA's three recommendation documents,[10] and (2) to hasten deliberations on what specific measures should be taken in response to lessons learned from the Fukushima accident from a nuclear security perspective. After additional deliberations, ACNS produced its final report on the remaining two tasks in March 2012, entitled "Strengthening of Japan's Nuclear Security" (ACNS March 2012 Report).[11]

The following section describes the Fukushima accident and its nuclear security lessons, based on the ACNS reports.

REVIEW OF THE FUKUSHIMA ACCIDENT FROM A NUCLEAR SECURITY PERSPECTIVE

The earthquake and the resulting tsunami caused a total station blackout of Units 1 through 4 at the Fukushima Daiichi plant, along with the loss of cooling of these reactor cores and spent-fuel ponds. This situation led to the reactor core meltdown and subsequent hydrogen explosions, with extensive release of radioactive materials into the environment.

The ACNS March 2012 report stated the following as its basic recognition of the Fukushima accident:

1. A nuclear disaster can tremendously impact economy and society, contaminating widely the people's living environment and causing social disorder;

2. Though initiated by a natural disaster, the accident revealed the possibility that a similar incident with serious impacts to society could result from an act of terrorism against nuclear facilities. It is Japan's duty to extract lessons learned from the accident from the viewpoints of not only safety but also security and share them with the international community in order to duly reflect them in the international efforts to strengthen nuclear security;

3. It is appropriate for the licensees and the regulatory and security agencies to take relevant measures for nuclear security, assuming that sabotage against nuclear power plants (NPPs) is a plausible threat. In practice, they should enhance their measures in accordance with the September 2011 ACNS Report and establish an effective system through mutual coordination and cooperation.

Further, the report made the following observations in light of the terrorist threat to NPPs:

1. In view of the accident and associated damages, people's interest in the security threat posed by NPPs has increased, as well as terrorists' interest in NPPs as potential and effective targets.[12]

2. It is crucial to prevent total station blackout (SBO) and functional loss of cooling reactor cores and spent-fuel pools and thus it is necessary to further strengthen measures to protect these facilities/equipment.

3. It is necessary to take into account the potential risk of a terrorist attack on the facilities/equipment installed outside a protected area or an act of sabotage by an employee who has been granted access to key facilities/equipment.

4. In view of the above points, nuclear security functions should be maintained or enhanced in preparation for emergency situations, such as high radiation levels or SBOs, caused by an accident.

It should be noted that the third point above on "insider threats" was highlighted when some of the emergency workers granted entrance to the accident site could not be traced later for radiation exposure testing, because their access passes had been issued hastily without proper documentation of personal data such as registered domiciles, current address, phone numbers, or other data enabling them to be traced. The fourth point was included based on the finding that some of the peripheral fences had been damaged by severe earthquakes, and the function of intrusion monitors was lost as a result of the total SBO. Access control equipment was not functioning and peripheral intrusion monitoring had to be replaced with peripheral patrols by security guards. The number of security guards was also reduced in view of higher radiation levels at guard posts resulting from the accident.

NUCLEAR SECURITY LESSONS LEARNED

In light of the above observations, the ACNS March 2012 report proposed the following measures against additional threats identified by the Fukushima accident:

1. *Early Detection of Intrusion.* For the sake of detecting the intrusion of an adversary earlier so as to ensure enough time for notification and response, licensees should be required to shift the intrusion detection line from the present position to a site boundary. The regulatory authorities should make relevant regulations to ensure that necessary measures are put in place. Further, in view of the fact that NPP sites in Japan are normally very confined, the consideration of additional measures should be made in order to enhance the capabilities of detecting suspicious persons at the areas surrounding an NPP site, on land or at sea.

2. *Delay of Terrorist Action.* Similarly, relevant regulations should be set up

by the regulatory agencies to ensure that the licensees take appropriate measures to prevent and delay terrorist action near the detection point for intrusion—for example, by placing additional obstacles or reinforcing existing ones at a site boundary, in addition to placing fences as obstacles surrounding a protected area. In view of the particular conditions of NPPs in Japan, such as their confined sites, the licensees and the regulatory agencies should review the specific measures of such prevention and delay, and the division of their respective roles by taking into account conditions at an individual NPP site, in close consultation with security agencies.

3. *Enhancing Robustness of Protected Facilities and Equipment.* In order to increase the robustness of the facilities and equipment to be protected against a terrorist attack with explosives, relevant regulations should be set up by the regulatory agencies to ensure that the licensees take appropriate measures by, for example, encasing facilities in strong materials. Further, new measures should be installed at the place closest to the protected areas in order to facilitate stricter control measures for them.

4. *Establishment and Maintenance of an Adequate Nuclear Security Regime.* The licensees and security agencies should establish and sustain an adequate nuclear security regime so that notification and response actions can be done promptly and nuclear security functions can be maintained even in the event of emergencies. For this purpose, the licensees should be equipped with the personnel, material, and equipment resources necessary for detecting unauthorized access and notifying security forces in such an event. The same applies to security forces charged with responding to intrusions. The licensees and the regulatory agencies should review specific measures and the division of their respective roles by taking into account conditions at an individual NPP site, and in close consultation with security agencies. In this context, the licensees may be requested to provide the security forces stationed at NPPs with a stronghold or other facilities or equipment for their effective response actions.

5. *Preparation of Mitigation Measures.* In order to prepare for an event in which protected equipment is destroyed, measures for mitigating the damage caused by a terrorist attack should be taken in advance in accordance with the concept of defense-in-depth. It is important to carefully examine whether the measures concerned will fully function as designed at the time of such an act of terrorism. Contingency plans among the licensees, regulatory agencies, and security agencies should include preparations for the mobilization of additional personnel and equipment as well as for the safe evacuation of the staff mem-

bers, casualties, and neighboring residents in the event of an act of terrorism that is beyond the scope of the existing nuclear security regime. Further, it is desirable to make prearrangements for smooth communication among the organizations involved in such mobilization and evacuation.

6. *Exercises and Evaluations.* The licensees and regulatory and security agencies should collaborate more closely in conducting practical exercises and reviewing the results of these exercises in order to make the security measures more effective. In addition, the integrated exercises should be conducted at a nuclear facility, involving as many organizations as possible, including those involved in mobilization and evacuation.

7. *Measures against Insider Threat.* The 2012 ACNS report stated that a discussion should commence on a concrete institutional arrangement for introducing a trustworthiness check system in nuclear-related facilities covered under INFCIRC/225/Rev.5. INFCIRC/225/Rev.5 recognizes the risk of information leaks or sabotage by insiders, which may impair the effectiveness of a nuclear security regime. A system for checking individuals' trustworthiness was recommended as a protective measure to minimize these threats. Specifically, persons handling sensitive information on nuclear materials and nuclear power plants and persons accessing the strategic facilities and equipment should be subject to trustworthiness checks. In the United States, background checks are carried out on all potential employees to verify any criminal record, credit status, mental health issues, or history of illness, and regular drug tests are carried out on all active employees. Similar checking systems exist in Germany, the UK, and France.

At the time of the Fukushima accident and until 2015, Japan was one of the few countries with large-scale use of nuclear energy that had no established trustworthiness check system for workers in nuclear facilities. In Japan, the Nuclear and Industrial Safety Agency (NISA) had discussed the need for a trustworthiness check system but had not introduced one, because there were questions as to whether checks might infringe on individual privacy or basic human rights. Against this background, the committee recommended measures that could be taken immediately to strengthen security against insider threats. The committee recommended that licensees should ensure more thorough ID badge checking and scrutiny of personnel and their items at the time of access control. Pending the establishment of a trustworthiness reliability system, it was recommended that such measures as the "two-person rule" should be strictly adhered to as an interim alternative in order to enhance the effectiveness of measures against insider threats.

According to the nuclear security index published by Nuclear Threat Initiative (NTI) in January 2012, Japan was ranked thirtieth among thirty-two countries with weapons-usable nuclear materials in terms of "security personnel measures" because of the lack of stringent personnel vetting.[13] The 2012 ACNS report cited Japan's NTI index and recommended the establishment of legally required personnel vetting. However, as soon as the ACNS report was made public, the Japan Federation of Bar Associations (JFBA) issued a statement on December 20, 2012, opposing the creation of a legally required system of trustworthiness checks on the grounds that the effectiveness of such checks had not been proven and that trustworthiness checks would infringe on privacy and pose a high risk of discrimination as a result of personal information collected about thoughts and beliefs.

This strange reaction by JFBA could be interpreted in light of Japan's unfortunate World War II experience, when the military government was in power and infringed upon the basic rights of the public, including freedom of thought and belief, for the sake of maintaining public security and order. These memories created a unique and profound sentiment among the Japanese public that has prevented the introduction of legislation related to national secret protection until recently, and from introduction of a treason law in the past in Japan.

MEASURES TAKEN TO IMPROVE NUCLEAR SECURITY

The AECJ approved each of the ACNS reports and requested that licensees, regulatory agencies, and security agencies promptly take measures in accordance with the report and submit progress reports to the commission as appropriate.[14]

In December 2011, NISA, which at the time was the competent regulatory authority in charge of NPPs, revised relevant regulations under the Nuclear Regulation Law in order to accommodate the additional measures proposed by the reports as well as some of the new requirements identified in the INFCIRC/225/Rev.5:

• A limited access area should be established outside a protected area in order to create an additional layer of protection for detection, access control, and delay against the unauthorized removal of nuclear material or an act of sabotage. A limited access area should be partitioned by a barrier such as a fence with height and structure sufficient to prevent easy intrusion by an adversary, and equipment for warning against potential intrusions should be installed on its periphery;

• Additional structural barriers such as secure walls that are not easily breakable should be installed surrounding the equipment related to an AC power supply or cooling mechanism for a nuclear reactor or a spent-fuel storage pond that, if located outside an inner area, could be easily susceptible to acts of sabotage causing the loss of cooling of a nuclear reactor or a spent-fuel storage pool and resulting in the release of radioactivity in to the environment;

• Cyber security measures should be applied to the information system related to operation and control of an NPP as well as that of nuclear security equipment.

Another revision of relevant regulations under the Nuclear Regulation Law was made effective in the end of March 2012 in order to reflect the final report of ACNS on the basic policy on incorporating the requirements of INF-CIRC/225/Rev.5 into the Japanese nuclear security regime. The major points of the revision are as follows:

• Use of metal and nuclear material detectors to check vehicles, personnel, and packages entering a protected area;

• Fortification and redundancy of a central alarm station (CAS), including measures for maintaining monitoring and communication function required for the protection of nuclear material;

• Tamper protection against unauthorized monitoring for alarm communications;

• Emergency or uninterrupted power supplies for nuclear security equipment;

• Strict adherence of two-person rules.

To enhance their guard and alert regime, the security agencies increased the number of police officers stationed at nuclear facilities and provided them with necessary equipment and instruments required for improving response against bomb threats and terrorist attacks. In addition, other measures such as required expansion of personnel and equipment, review of guidelines for an alert, and reinforcement of interorganizational collaboration through field exercises have been implemented.

Licensees are now taking respective measures in consultation with the regulatory authority and the security force. For example, they have established stricter access control at the boundary of limited access areas (for example, security checks of vehicles, personnel, and accompanying equipment) and installed required equipment and instruments. Licensees have also pursued measures for improving nuclear security capability in the event of natural disasters, and for providing security forces stationed at NPPs with a stronghold or other means for effective response actions.

Responsive actions that have been taken by both the regulatory agency and the licensees in Japan in the context of lessons learned from the Fukushima accident are considered as thorough and comprehensive, when compared with those done in other countries. Unlike in Japan, responses in other countries were conducted mostly as measures for gaining public confidence on the safety of existing NPPs and not in fulfillment of safety and security regulations. For example, following the Fukushima accident, the European Union conducted nuclear stress tests on the NPPs in EU countries in order to assess their safety and robustness in case of extreme natural events, especially flood and earthquakes, as well as airplane crashes. Their major findings have shown the following:[15]

• Although they came to the conclusion that no closure of NPPs was warranted, they recommended numerous plant-specific improvements, recognizing that international standards and practices had not been applied everywhere;
• Lessons from Fukushima needed to be drawn, in particular, in terms of earthquake and flooding risk calculations; installation or improvement of on-site seismic instruments; and installation of containment filtered venting systems, equipment to fight severe accidents, and a backup emergency control room in some specific NPPs.

Although the EU Commission intends to follow up on the implementation status of these recommendations, it has no regulatory authority over its member states; implementation is up to the states. The requirement for these improvements is left with relevant member states for the revisions of respective national regulations.

ENHANCING SYNERGY BETWEEN NUCLEAR SAFETY AND SECURITY

A key lesson highlighted by the accident at Fukushima is the need to better synchronize efforts to enhance nuclear security and safety. In this section, I discuss Japanese leaders' inclination to view nuclear security and nuclear safety as separate spheres, and describe how this tendency led to missed opportunities to implement measures that might have helped mitigate the Fukushima accident. I then describe efforts in Japan to improve nuclear safety and security, and identify ways that nuclear safety and security organizations can work together moving forward to advance coordination between the two spheres.

The Question of B.5.b Measures

A comparison of US and Japanese nuclear communities' responses to the September 11, 2001, terrorist attacks in the United States reveals Japanese leaders' failure to recognize the overlap between nuclear security and safety efforts. Following the September 11 attacks, which used large commercial aircraft as weapons, the US Nuclear Regulatory Commission (USNRC) issued EA-02-026, "Order for Interim Safeguards and Security Compensatory Measures" (the ICM Order) dated February 25, 2002. The ICM order, which is designated as Safeguards Information (SGI), modified then-operating licenses for commercial power reactor facilities to require compliance with specified interim safeguards and security compensatory measures. Section B.5.b of the ICM order requires licensees to adopt mitigation strategies using readily available resources to maintain or restore core cooling, containment, and spent-fuel pool cooling capabilities to cope with the loss of large areas of the facility resulting from fires and explosions from any cause, including beyond-design-basis aircraft impacts.

On March 27, 2009, the B.5.b measures were codified as the regulatory requirements of Title 10 of the *Code of Federal Regulations* (10 CFR) Section 50.54(hh)(2): "Each licensee shall develop and implement guidance and strategies intended to maintain or restore core cooling, containment, and spent-fuel pool cooling capabilities under the circumstances associated with loss of large areas of the plant due to explosions or fire." B.5.b measures have been implemented steadily in the United States in the following three phases:

- Phase 1: measures using readily available materials and personnel;
- Phase 2: measures for cooling spent-fuel pools; and
- Phase 3: measures for core cooling and containment.

In addition, the Nuclear Energy Institute (NEI) prepared "B.5.b Phase 2 & 3 Submittal Guideline Revision 2" for licensees, which the NRC approved December 22, 2006.

After Fukushima, the NRC conducted a series of visits at all of the US plants to assess their implementation of B.5.b measures. While there were no detrimental findings, there were a series of issues identified at each plant. There has been considerable debate about whether B.5.b-related measures would have been sufficient to prevent the Fukushima accident, though they certainly would have helped.

Japan's Nuclear Accident Independent Investigation Commission (NAIIC) summary report pointed out that the Fukushima Daiichi accident might have been prevented had B.5.b-type measures been in place at the plant: "If NISA had passed on to Tokyo Electric Power Company (TEPCO) measures that were included in the B.5.b subsection of the U.S. security order that followed the 9/11 terrorist action, and if TEPCO had put the measures in place, the accident may have been preventable."[16] At the NRC meeting held ten days after the Great East Japan Earthquake, it was also recognized that the enhanced security measures called for under B.5.b, which had been in place in all operating NPPs in the United States, could have been effective in responding to accidents like the one at Fukushima as well:

> As a result of the events of September 11, 2001, we did a similar evaluation, and identified important pieces of equipment that, if, regardless of the cause of a significant fire or explosion at a plant, we would have pre-staged equipment, procedures, and policies to help deal with that situation. All of these things are directly applicable to the kinds of very significant events that are taking place in Japan.[17]

As pointed out above by the NAIIC summary report, NISA was informed, well before the Fukushima accident, of the fact that USNRC requested B.5.b measures to be taken as additional security measures at all operating NPPs in the United States, in view of the terrorist event of September 11, 2001. However, this information was not shared within NISA or with Japanese operators, and similar measures were never implemented in Japan, with the result being significant radiation damage.

Why was there a substantial difference in the responses of Japanese and US governments in relation to the additional threats posed by the 9/11 attacks? The difference could be attributed to the gap between the two countries' perceptions of the nuclear terrorism threat. The United States was victim of the terrorist attacks on September 11, 2001, when terrorists hijacked large airplanes and crashed them into skyscrapers and the Pentagon. At the World Trade Center the crash caused a huge fire when massive amounts of jet fuel ignited, and as a result the buildings collapsed and many lives were lost. For that reason the US government recognized that the risk (or threat) of an attack in which terrorists crash into a nuclear power plant using a hijacked aircraft was real, and therefore issued the B.5.b countermeasures to prevent such a terrorist act.

On the other hand, in Japan, measures against the theft of nuclear materials or sabotage of nuclear facilities have historically been categorized as a part of the "physical protection of nuclear materials," historically under the mandates of the AECJ, which is responsible for ensuring the peaceful use of nuclear energy. There had been no strong arguments over the years that countermeasures to prevent nuclear accidents caused by human acts should also be placed under the mandates of the Nuclear Safety Commission, even though there is no difference in terms of the radiation released if an accident is caused by natural disaster or by human acts.

This sense of compartmentalization of safety and security was so strong that the notion of achieving synergy between safety and security was almost inconceivable or nonexistent in Japan. Even when senior officials in the safety division at NISA were informed that the United States had issued the B.5.b order for the purpose of counterterrorism, they did not recognize that such measures were relevant to their own work on safety. Additionally, because of a general perception that the risk of terrorist attacks like 9/11 occurring in Japan is low, one can assume that NISA officials did not consider conveying this information to the divisions in charge of preventing acts of sabotage against nuclear facilities.

The lack of communication between NISA's safety regulation division and nuclear security division further cemented this compartmentalization. The lessons learned from a nuclear security event should be shared with the safety regulation division for further consideration of any applicability in the area of ensuring nuclear safety. The same argument holds true for the lessons learned by a nuclear safety event being shared with nuclear security regulation division for further analysis of possible applications in ensuring nuclear security. Thus, there is a need for attaining synergy between nuclear safety and nuclear security, or closer communication and coordination between them.

Efforts to Improve Cooperation between Safety and Security Spheres

The need to attain synergy between nuclear safety and nuclear security is widely recognized among countries promoting the use of nuclear power. For example, paragraph 7 of the communiqué produced at the 2012 Seoul Nuclear

Summit held March 26–27 states:

> Acknowledging that safety measures and security measures have in common the aim of protecting human life and health and the environment, we affirm that nuclear security and nuclear safety measures should be designed, implemented and managed in nuclear facilities in a coherent and synergistic manner.

Japanese prime minister Noda stated during his lunch session on March 27, 2012: "Further examination of the complementary nature of measures for nuclear security and safety is required, but there are legitimate common lessons that can be extracted regardless of what the original cause of a nuclear accident may be." He proceeded to share with the world leaders three important lessons learned. The first is the importance of preparing for unanticipated risks. After mentioning two other lessons learned, he concluded: "Whether the challenge we face is a 'natural disaster' or a 'terrorist attack,' the 'wisdom' of the human race is tested. We must all cooperate closely and combine our wisdom, so as not to make light of nature or lose this 'battle of wits' against terrorists."

The need for attaining synergy between nuclear safety and nuclear security is also recognized by the World Institute for Nuclear Security (WINS). On May 12, 2012, WINS hosted a one-day roundtable discussion focused on the early lessons emerging from the Fukushima accident. The summary finding of the roundtable emphasizes the importance of integrating safety, security, and emergency arrangements:

> Safety and security have traditionally been regulated and managed in isolation from each other. . . . This situation must change. The complex, interconnected nature of safety, security and emergency management requires convergence; without it, serious gaps in capability and response will persist. . . . It is neither efficient nor effective to consider nuclear safety cases, security vulnerability assessments, and financial and reputational risk separately.[18]

These are just a few examples of the widespread international will to strengthen the relationship between nuclear safety and security.

Following the nuclear accident at the Fukushima Daiichi power plant, countries had to revisit the safety of their respective nuclear fleets in order to ensure safe operation and allay public fear. To a far lesser degree, these countries have tried to learn how the Fukushima Daiichi accident can improve the physical protection posture of their respective fleets. It can also be said that the converse is true: regulators and operators rarely investigate improvements to plant safety following security events. Principally, the distinction is made because safety events such as Fukushima are the result of stochastic events, while security events involve strategic interactions between adversary and defender.

The resultant operator actions and plant performance during the severe accident conditions experienced at Fukushima illustrated the tremendous challenges plant personnel had in restoring backup power to critical cooling equipment, as well as in establishing an ultimate heat sink for key safety systems to reject heat. The lack of instrumentation to get online plant diagnostic measurements during the accident added greatly to the confusion during the accident response and drove misinformed decision-making. These conditions of severe operational confusion and decision-making under deep uncertainty would also be present during a coordinated security attack in which plant consequence mitigation and emergency response strategies would be initiated.

In light of the Fukushima accident, it was resolved that safety and security groups should establish a dialogue to share their mutual experiences and lessons learned through a major event to enhance the synergy among these two camps. Based on this recognition, the ACNS report and its provisional English version have been made available to the public. Further, the outlines have been presented at international forums such as the 2012 Seoul Nuclear Security Symposium and the 53rd Institute of Nuclear Material Management (INMM) Annual Meeting in Orlando, Florida, in July 2012.[19]

Recognizing the need for closer coordination between the two spheres, Japan has already taken important steps to integrate nuclear security and safety efforts. The Japanese Diet passed a bill in June 2012 for regulatory reforms prompted by the Fukushima accident. The bill created a regulatory body as an independent organization, separate from the Ministry of Economy, Trade and Industry (METI), tasked with promoting nuclear energy as well as controlling it through NISA. The function to coordinate counter–nuclear terrorism measures among relevant government agencies in Japan, which had so far been under the AECJ, was consolidated under this new body, the Nuclear Regulation Authority (NRA), and its secretariat. The NRA began operation on September 19, 2012, as an affiliated organization under the Minister of Environment with centralized authority over nuclear safety, safeguards, and security. Under the new organization, mistakes like the one made by NISA with regard to the B.5.b order should not be repeated.

The Fukushima accident emphasized the need to facilitate better integration of security and safety infrastructures. The report by the Advisory Committee on Nuclear Security pointed out that "a terrorist attack on a nuclear power plant should be considered as plausible" and stressed that countermeasures against terrorist attacks should be implemented. In addition, as Japan's equivalent of the B.5.b., NISA has requested that all electric power companies implement countermeasures to deal with the total loss of power supply—a lesson learned from the Fukushima accident. In view of the Fukushima accident, the NRA also reviewed former safety design review criteria for NPPs and published its revision on July 8, 2013. It includes provisions against the threat of sabotage, including intentional airplane crashes. This revision is indeed a sign of expected improvements.

In December 2013, the newly created Nuclear Regulation Authority established the Committee on Nuclear Security to follow up the recommendations made in the final report of the ACNS. At its first meeting, the committee identified the following high-priority items to be addressed immediately:

• Establishment of a legally required system for trustworthiness check of workers at nuclear power plants;
• Codification of physical protection requirements for transportation of nuclear materials contained in INFCIRC/225/Rev.5;
• Codification of nuclear security requirements for radioactive materials contained in the IAEA recommendation, Nuclear Security Series no. 14.

The committee conducted follow-up meetings to address these high-priority items. In light of the first item, the committee established the Working Group on Trustworthiness Checks to explore the best check system for Japan. On October 19, 2015, the group presented the committee with its report on the outline of the scheme for trustworthiness checks of certain workers at Japanese nuclear facilities. The report was approved by the committee and presented to the NRA on October 21, 2015.

Within its authority of facility management, a nuclear facility licensee is to establish trustworthiness of workers at its facility, including those of subcontractors, before authorizing their access to protected areas and inner areas without escorts, or their access to information related to protection of prescribed nuclear fuel materials. The authorization should be based on the application by an individual worker.

In establishing trustworthiness of workers, to the extent necessary for the prevention of theft of and sabotage against prescribed nuclear fuel materials, the applicant is requested to provide a set of limited personal data, such as his/her name, address, date of birth, educational history, vocational history, record of rewards and punishments, legal ability to fulfill responsibilities, and relationship with organizations such as criminal or terrorism organizations that may have a potential to conduct an act of sabotage. Some of these data are to be substantiated with accompanying documents to prove his/her declarations. In addition, personal interviews and some fitness tests should be conducted before issuing authorization.

It is appropriate to provide these measures based on the Nuclear Regulation Law and the rules under it as part of required physical protection measures.

The NRA immediately approved these recommendations and started to develop detailed rules and regulations to implement the proposed scheme. It took over four years after the accident to get a plan for trustworthiness checks approved. But the October 2015 decision marks a milestone in the difficult effort to learn from Fukushima and to change traditional organizational security practices.

Another working group was created in July 2013 to address codification of physical protection requirements for transportation of nuclear materials. The working group had met twice as of April 2014 for fact-finding sessions. The third working group has been established for codification of nuclear security requirements for radioactive materials, while some preliminary discussions were held on this topic at a meeting of the Committee on Nuclear Security. Identification of these high-priority items is a sign of progress, though the lack of concrete measures to address these issues thus far suggests that much work remains to be done in these areas.

Moving forward, the hope is that the international community will make full use of the findings contained in the ACNS report to enhance the effectiveness of nuclear security regimes of respective countries. It is also important for the international community to share best practices in the area of nuclear security, especially the synergy between nuclear safety and nuclear security.

In this context, WINS is an important international forum that promotes best practices in the field of nuclear security. It has published a best-practice guide for an integrated approach to nuclear safety and nuclear security.[20] Further, the IAEA convened the "International Conference on Nuclear Security: Enhancing Global Efforts" at its headquarters in Vienna, Austria, July 1–5, 2013, with ministerial sessions on the first day. This conference reviewed the international community's experience and achievements to date in strengthening nuclear security. It aimed to enhance understanding of current approaches to nuclear security worldwide and identify trends, and to provide a global forum for policy-makers and senior officials to formulate views on future directions and priorities for nuclear security. One technical session addressed the topic of safety-security interface. The hope is that the nuclear security lessons learned from the Fukushima accident as well as best-practice experiences in integrating security and safety will continue to be shared internationally through similar venues.

APPENDIX

The Development of Physical Protection Recommendation (INFCIRC/225) and NSS Documents by the IAEA

The IAEA Physical Protection Recommendation, INFCIRC/225, constitutes a special document in the nuclear security framework. It was for several years the sole internationally recognized guidance document addressing physical protection of nuclear material and nuclear facilities. It was developed by IAEA member states and published by the IAEA as an information circular document.

Though a nonbinding document, the circular achieves a formal, legally binding position when referenced in bilateral agreements and multilateral regimes. For example, Article 7 of "Agreement for Cooperation between the Government of Japan and the Government of the United States of America concerning Peaceful Use of Nuclear Energy" (signed on November 4, 1987, and entered into force on July 17, 1988) stipulates:

> Adequate measures of physical protection shall be maintained with respect to nuclear material transferred pursuant to this Agreement and special fissionable material used in or produced through the use of material, nuclear material or equipment so transferred, at levels, as a minimum, comparable to those set out in Annex B of this Agreement.

In its Annex B, the levels of physical protection are set out by quoting the same categorization of nuclear materials and corresponding physical protection measures as recommended in IAEA's INFCIRC/225.

The development of physical protection recommendations began in 1972 when the IAEA director general convened a panel of experts for the development of recommended levels of physical protection of nuclear material, to address the threat that nuclear material may be stolen and possibly used by nonstate actors to construct an improvised nuclear device (IND). This effort resulted in the publication, in 1972, of "Recommendations for the Physical Protection of Nuclear Material" ("the Grey Book"). These recommendations were

TABLE 3.1: Formulation and Revisions of INFCIRC/225

Published in	Title	Remarks
September 1975	The Physical Protection of Nuclear Material (INFCIRC/225)	These are the first physical protection recommendations made by IAEA.
June 1977	The Physical Protection of Nuclear Material (INFCIRC/225/Rev.1)	Categorization of nuclear material was revised.
December 1989	The Physical Protection of Nuclear Material (INFCIRC/225/Rev.2)	Scope of protection was expanded to cover the sabotage against nuclear reactor facilities and quality assurance provisions were included.
September 1993	The Physical Protection of Nuclear Material (INFCIRC/225/Rev.3)	Categorization of nuclear material was revised and the level of protection for vitrified high-level wastes was considered sufficient when protected after prudent management practices; additional provisions were made for the control of transportation information.
June 1999	The Physical Protection of Nuclear Material and Nuclear Facilities (INFCIRC/225/Rev.4)	Improved the structure and clarity of the previous versions, as well as reflected the progress in international and national practices. The obligations of a state are added to set out design basis threat (DBT) and present it to the licensees to take appropriate protection measures to cope with DBT, to conduct a periodic inspection to check if these measures are effective, and to make legal provisions with sanctions to protect sensitive information related to physical protection. In addition, a chapter providing specific recommendations related to the protection against sabotage of nuclear facilities was included. As a result, the title was changed to "The Physical Protection of Nuclear Material and Nuclear Facilities," implying that nuclear facilities are also the objects of protection in addition to nuclear materials.
January 2011	Nuclear Security Recommendations on Physical Protection of Nuclear Material and Nuclear Facilities (INFCIRC/225/Rev.5)	Further revised and published as a Nuclear Security Series document in order to reflect the prevailing threat environment, which changed dramatically after 9/11, and to ensure that it supports and provides implementing guidance for the amended CPPNM, UNSCR 1540,[a] and UNSCR 1887,[b] as well as to provide guidance to newcomers on nuclear power programs.[c]

[a] UN Security Council Resolution 1540, "Nonproliferation of Weapons of Mass Destruction," April 28, 2004.
[b] UN Security Council Resolution 1887, "Maintenance of International Peace and Security: Nuclear Nonproliferation and Nuclear Disarmament," September 24, 2009.
[c] Melissa Krupa, "Combating the Nuclear Terrorist Threat: A Comprehensive Approach to Nuclear Security," *Journal of Nuclear Materials Management* 38, no. 4 (Summer 2010): 32.

then published as INFCIRC/225 in 1975 and subsequently revised in, 1977, 1989, 1993, 1999, and 2011, as summarized in Table 3.1.

It should be noted that the agency's role in developing international consensus guidance for nuclear security is recognized in both the International Convention for the Suppression of Acts of Nuclear Terrorism (Nuclear Terrorism Convention),[21] and the Amendment of the CPPNM,[22] which is still undergoing ratification. Both legal instruments refer, in their operative paragraphs, to the role of the IAEA in the development of *guidance* for the implementation of the conventions.

As a part of this effort, the IAEA began publishing the NSS documents as guidelines for member states to establish and maintain effective nuclear security regimes. This series comprises four tiers of publications, the primary one being the fundamentals document, followed by three recommendation documents, implementing guides, and technical guidance publications. The key fundamentals document, "Nuclear Security Fundamentals: Objective and Essential Elements of a State's Nuclear Security Regime," was published in February 2013, while the three recommendation documents were published in January 2011,[23] and some twenty documents had been published as implementing guides as of March 2013.

NOTES

1.   Mohamed ElBaradei, "Nuclear Terrorism: Identifying and Combating the Risks," in *Nuclear Security: Global Directions for the Future,* proceedings of an international conference, London, March 16–18, 2005 (Vienna: IAEA, September 2005), 4.

2.   "Nuclear Security: Measures to Protect against Nuclear Terrorism," IAEA General Conference, forty-ninth regular session, report by the director general, GC(49)/17, Vienna, September 23, 2005.

3.   IAEA, "The Physical Protection of Nuclear Material," Information Circular 225 (INFCIRC/225), Vienna, September 1975, available at www.iaea.org/Publications/Documents/Infcircs/Others/infcirc225.pdf.

4.   "Convention on the Physical Protection of Nuclear Material," March 3, 1980, Vienna and New York. It is the only international legally binding undertaking in the area of physical protection of nuclear material, though it obliges states to protect nuclear material only during international transport. It establishes measures related to the prevention, detection, and punishment of offenses relating to nuclear material.

5.   This series is composed of four tiers of publications, the primary one being the fundamentals document, followed by three recommendation documents, implementing guides, and technical guidance publications.

6. Law on the Regulation of Nuclear Source Materials, Nuclear Materials and Nuclear Reactors, Law no.166 of June 10, 1957.

7. Kaoru Naito, "Ensuring Nuclear Security in Japan: Policy and Activities of Japan Atomic Energy Commission," paper presented at the forty-ninth annual meeting of the Institute of Nuclear Materials Management, Nashville, TN, July 14–17, 2008.

8. "The Fundamental Approach to Ensuring Nuclear Security," report of Advisory Committee on Nuclear Security, Japan Atomic Energy Commission, September 5, 2011, available at www.aec.go.jp/jicst/NC/senmon/bougo/kettei110905.pdf.

9. "Objective and Essential Elements of a State's Nuclear Security Regime" (fundamentals document) was formally adopted by the IAEA's board of governors in September 2012.

10. "Nuclear Security Recommendations on Physical Protection of Nuclear Material and Nuclear Facilities (INFCIRC/225/Revision 5)," *Nuclear Security Series* 13; "Nuclear Security Recommendations on Radioactive Material and Associated Facilities," *Nuclear Security Series* 14; "Nuclear Security Recommendations on Nuclear and Other Radioactive Material out of Regulatory Control," *Nuclear Security Series* 15 (Vienna: IAEA, 2011).

11. "Strengthening of Japan's Nuclear Security," report of Advisory Committee on Nuclear Security, Japan Atomic Energy Commission, March 9, 2012, available at www.aec.go.jp/jicst/NC/senmon/bougo/kettei120309.pdf.

12. Despite the report's assertion, there have been no terrorist attacks on nuclear power plants reported to date, though there have been cases of antinuclear activists who managed to intrude into French NPPs in December 2011 and May 2012, the US Y-11 plant in July 2012, and Swedish NPPs in October 2012, in order to publicize the risk of nuclear facilities.

13. NTI Nuclear Materials Security Index, Nuclear Threat Initiative, January 2012.

14. "Strengthening of Japan's Nuclear Security," decision of Japan Atomic Energy Commission, March 21, 2012, available at www.aec.go.jp/jicst/NC/senmon/bougo/kettei120321.pdf.

15. "Communication from the Commission to the Council and the European Parliament on the Comprehensive Risk and Safety Assessments ('Stress Tests') of Nuclear Power Plants in the European Union and Related Activities," EU Press Release IP/12/1051 (COM [2012] 571 final), Brussels, October 4, 2012.

16. "Official Report of the Fukushima Nuclear Accident Independent Investigative Commission," National Diet of Japan, Tokyo, 2012, available at http://warp.da.ndl.go.jp/info:ndljp/pid/3856371/naiic.go.jp/en/.

17. Nuclear Regulatory Commission, "Briefing on NRC Response to Recent Nuclear Events in Japan," transcription of proceedings, public meeting, March 21, 2011, 15.

18. World Institute for Nuclear Security (WINS), "Time for an Integrated Approach to Nuclear Risk Management, Governance and Safety/Security/Emergency Arrangements," May 2011.

19. Kaoru Naito, "Lessons Learned from the Accident at the Fukushima Daiichi Nuclear Power Station: Nuclear Security Perspectives," *Journal of Nuclear Materials Management* 41, no. 1 (Fall 2012): 16–20.

20. WINS, "A WINS International Best Practice Guide: An Integrated Approach to Nuclear Safety and Nuclear Security, Revision 1.1," January 2011.

21. The convention details offenses relating to unlawful and intentional possession and use of radioactive material or a radioactive device, and use or damage of nuclear facilities. It is designed to promote cooperation among countries through the sharing of information and the providing of assistance for investigations and extraditions. It entered into force in July 2007 and requires all "states parties to make every effort to adopt appropriate measures to ensure the protection of radioactive material, taking into account relevant recommendations and functions of the agency."

22. A diplomatic conference in July 2005 was convened to amend the convention and strengthen its provisions. The amended convention makes it legally binding for states parties to protect nuclear facilities and material in peaceful domestic use, storage, and transport. It also provides for expanded cooperation between and among states regarding rapid measures to locate and recover stolen or smuggled nuclear material, mitigate any radiological consequences of sabotage, and prevent and combat related offences.

23. *Nuclear Security Series* 13, 14, and 15.

4 Political Leadership in Nuclear Emergency: Institutional and Structural Constraints

Nobumasa Akiyama

The Fukushima nuclear accident revealed serious problems in Japanese response mechanisms against a complex megadisaster. Facing unprecedented severe accidents involving the simultaneous meltdown of multiple reactors, various response and mitigation measures were attempted. Some of these measures worked, but other efforts turned out to be in vain.

Governing risk and responding to crises pose two major challenges: generating and collecting knowledge about the risk, for which the government, companies, and other stakeholders must prepare (assessment phase), and making decisions about how to mitigate, control, or manage risk (decision and implementation phase).[1] During the Fukushima nuclear accident there were major failures of governance and response suffered during both phases. Emergency responses to the Fukushima nuclear crisis revealed a lack of preparedness, associated with inappropriate risk assessment, and a rather disorganized command and control mechanism for disaster response. Crises can be viewed as extended periods of elevated threats, high uncertainty, and high politics that disrupt a wide range of social, political, and organizational processes.[2] During crises, leaders are responsible for collecting information, making decisions, and executing responses, as well as learning from experience.[3] In short, the quality of political leadership matters.

Over the course of identifying and implementing emergency responses, the Japanese government and the Tokyo Electric Power Company (TEPCO), two primary actors in crisis management, were exposed as being unprepared not only in terms of equipment for mitigation but also in terms of human resource capacity for crisis management. As the crisis unfolded, various actors in government, social, and corporate sectors became involved but failed to establish a proper chain of command among themselves. The decision-making process during the emergency response was plagued by miscommunication among responders within TEPCO and government emergency headquarters, revealing the vulnerability of command and control structures. Poor information compounded communications problems.[4] In addition, conventional crisis management manuals did not provide useful guidelines for communications between responders, as they did not properly address a crisis of this magnitude.

Analyzing disaster response raises the question of whether catastrophic outcomes resulting from nuclear accidents are really unavoidable. In other words, with the 9.0 magnitude earthquake and tsunamis at the "unprecedented" height of 15 meters, was there any way of preventing meltdowns at Fukushima Daiichi Units 1, 2, and 3 and mitigating the severe consequences of those meltdowns? How much did organizational factors such as mismanagement of the crisis worsen the situation by preventing more effective responses?

It is true that operators and staff on site as well as first responders including the Japan Self-Defense Forces (SDF), police forces, and firefighters did remarkable work while operating in such a severe environment. The fact-finding mission of the International Atomic Energy Agency (IAEA), which made one of the earliest assessments of the Fukushima nuclear accident, issued the following statement after their investigation and research in Japan: "Given the extreme circumstances of this accident the local management of the accident has been conducted in the best way possible."[5]

Despite heroic efforts by responders, the measures taken on site were clearly haphazard as a result of lack of preparedness. For example, following the station blackout and the loss of emergency generator functions, TEPCO operators first used the automobile batteries from employees' cars in the station. They then tried to procure automobile batteries from a repair shop in the neighborhood. Because they did not have enough cash, TEPCO's Tokyo headquarters flew their staff with cash to Fukushima the following day. But the neighborhood surrounding the plant had been evacuated by then, and no one could procure batteries on March 13. Staff of Fukushima Daiichi then went to Iwaki City, located approximately 60 kilometers away, and purchased eight batteries. More batteries were finally delivered to Fukushima Daiichi on March 14, a short-term, temporary solution.[6]

Skepticism about the conduct of the emergency response by the government and TEPCO has grown as various pieces of information have been revealed through extensive media reporting and reviews commissioned by the government of Japan and the Diet, as well as private review initiatives including a project by the Rebuild Japan Initiative Foundation.[7] These investigations looked into mitigation and damage-minimizing actions and measures taken by TEPCO; first responders, including the SDF, police, and firefighters; regulatory agencies, including the Nuclear and Industrial Safety Agency (NISA) of the Ministry of International Trade and Industry (METI), Nuclear Safety Commission of Japan (NSC), and Atomic Energy Commission of Japan (AECJ); as well as political leadership, including the prime minister and his office (*Kantei*). All raised questions about why confusion, a series of errors, and negligence in decision-making occurred during the response.

These investigations commonly pointed out three things in assessing responses to the crisis. First, lack of preparedness both in terms of emergency equipment and the operational capacity of responders and operators was a cause of confusion in responses to reactor meltdown and the spent-fuel pool crisis, as well as in evacuation of residents.

Second, the magnitude of potential nuclear disasters was underestimated. Groundless confidence in the safety of nuclear facilities, described as the "myth of absolute safety" (*Zettai Anzen Shinwa*),[8] prevailed among the stakeholders in nuclear energy, which inevitably created situations "beyond assumption" (*Souteigai*),[9] leaving some critical issues unaddressed in the planning of responses to and mitigation of nuclear disasters or severe accidents.[10]

Third, poor communications during both the decision-making and implementation phases during the crisis worsened the situation. Confusion surrounding command and control has been attributed to Japan's political leadership; incompetent regulatory authorities such as NISA and NSC, which were supposed to support leaders' decision-making; as well as the personal style of Prime Minister Naoto Kan.

All three of these factors came to the fore during the crisis, producing ineffective leadership and command and control. Because of the inadequacy of assessments made in predicting severe events, caused by the dominance of the myth of absolute safety (*Zettai Anzen Shinwa*), crisis management manuals were not so useful, and responses prescribed in those manuals could not be implemented. When TEPCO, a primary responder to on-site reactor crises, had to deal with situations beyond assumption (*Souteigai*), the role of political leadership became even more important. But people in the *Kantei* had not familiarized themselves with crisis management manuals and the legal system in place

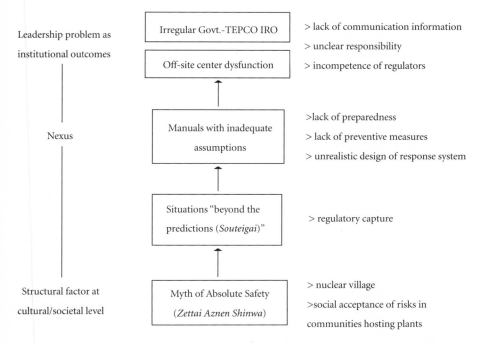

Leadership problem as institutional outcomes

Irregular Govt.-TEPCO IRO

> lack of communication information

> unclear responsibility

Off-site center dysfunction

> incompetence of regulators

Nexus

Manuals with inadequate assumptions

>lack of preparedness

> lack of preventive measures

> unrealistic design of response system

Situations "beyond the predictions (Souteigai)"

> regulatory capture

Structural factor at cultural/societal level

Myth of Absolute Safety (Zettai Aznen Shinwa)

> nuclear village

>social acceptance of risks in communities hosting plants

Fig. 4.1: Consequential relationship among *Zettai Anzen Shinwa*, *Souteigai*, and the leadership problem.

for responding to a nuclear disaster. Predictably, confusion dominated during the emergency response, and the resulting leadership deficit led to the establishment of an ad hoc decision-making organ, Government-TEPCO Integrated Response Office (IRO), which was not prescribed in crisis management manuals of the government. Figure 4.1 shows how *Zettai Anzen Shinwa*, a structural and cultural factor, led to a leadership deficit as an institutional outcome. The leadership deficit in turn led to the establishment of an ad hoc decision-making organ, the Government-TEPCO IRO, which was not prescribed in crisis management manuals of the government.

In a way, crisis management in an unprecedented event depends to a large extent on leadership. But the capacity of leadership is largely shaped by the organizational capacity that supports leaders, including skills, capabilities, and assets, and the network among stakeholders that facilitates communications. But organizational capacity and the nature of the network among stakeholders are structurally imbedded in political and social culture including regulatory culture.[11]

Ideally, any emergency response should be conducted through an effective, cohesive command-and-control mechanism with clear lines of communication and well-defined areas of responsibility. As the International Risk Governance Council describes: "Communication is particularly important for the involvement of stakeholders in participative risk-related decision making and conflict resolution and for ensuring that they can make informed choices about the risk, balancing factual knowledge about it."[12] Ideally, an effective, cohesive command-and-control mechanism with clear lines of communication and well-defined areas of responsibility would help leaders respond to a crisis effectively. Leaders, bureaucrats, and responders must know who has decision-making authority, for example, as well as who is responsible for providing timely information to actors involved and to the public. In reality, what we witnessed in Fukushima was an example of the contrary: the miscommunication and distrust between Japan's political leaders, bureaucracy, and TEPCO. The case showed that "crisis operations are multiorganizational, transjurisdictional, polycentric response networks. They demand lateral coordination, not top-down command and control."[13] The lack of effective communications among stakeholders led political leadership to choose to take control over all responses to the accident.

Some of the decisions made by political leaders at Fukushima were astute. For example, Kan demonstrated critical leadership with his decision to establish the Government-TEPCO IRO, which was not prescribed in the emergency manual of the government but eventually worked somewhat effectively to make communications between the government and TEPCO smoother. However, an irregular mechanism of crisis management largely amplified uncertainties, increasingly unpredictability and creating more room for political considerations to override scientific and technical considerations, which could create a greater risk.

This chapter will discuss the structure of the failure of leadership during the crisis based on the examination of factors such as organizational and regulatory cultural background that contributed to troubled leadership during the crisis, including the myth of absolute safety, a failure to imagine scenarios beyond assumption, and organizational factors of poor communications. I then examine, using lessons drawn from the Fukushima accident, what form of incident command structure is the most effective for dealing with nuclear emergencies and provide suggestions on how training can be improved.

INSECURE LEADERSHIP IN THE ABSENCE OF
SOUND PREPAREDNESS AND A PROPER INFRASTRUCTURE

According to the Japanese Act on Special Measures concerning Nuclear Emergency Preparedness (hereafter, Nuclear Emergency Act, or NEA), nuclear operators are primarily responsible for "taking full-scale measures" for prevention of nuclear disaster, the prevention of the progression of disaster, and recovery from the disaster (Article 3). In the wake of the Fukushima accident, the plant management was supposed to communicate with the government, primarily with NISA, through the off-site Emergency Response Center (ERC, or "off-site center"), which was set up at a location outside of, but not so far from, the plant to be a hub of crisis communications among various stakeholders including the utility, various government organs including the prime minister (or the head of the prime minister's Nuclear Emergency Response Head Quarters, NEHQ), and local governments and fast responders. In other words, the original emergency plan expected plant operators and NISA staffers at the off-site center to handle matters related to nuclear reactors.

The emergency communications protocol in the case of nuclear crisis was stipulated in the NEA.[14] The command structure outlined in the NEA is designed with an off-site center playing a central role in information gathering and communications between Tokyo and the on-site response team. The off-site center receives information from on-site plant operators and conveys information to TEPCO in Tokyo and NISA. And in Tokyo, the NEHQ, with its secretariat office to be set up in NISA's ERC, is supposed to delegate authority to the Regional Nuclear Emergency Response Team established in the off-site center, with staff members dispatched from NISA Emergency Response Center in Tokyo. The off-site center then instructs, commands, supervises, and advises operators who are directly dealing with on-site situations. In principle, the Regional Nuclear Emergency Response Team at the off-site center is expected to play a central role in any response to a severe accident.

In the case of the Fukushima nuclear accident, the crisis management mechanism outlined in the NEA did not work, as a result of dysfunction of the off-site center and the incompetence of the Emergency Response Center in NISA, causing poor initial communications between the site and Tokyo (TEPCO headquarters and government organizations). It was not well protected against radiation and lost electricity and communications infrastructure. The off-site center's central decision-making function for crisis management in the case of the Fukushima nuclear accident was replaced with the ad hoc Govern-ment-TEPCO IRO, which was established in the Tokyo headquarters of TEP-CO on March 15 after a few days of confusion in communications among the *Kantei*, regulatory agencies, on-site operators, and the headquarters of TEPCO.

The dysfunction of the crisis management mechanism as outlined in the NEA could be attributed to two aspects of crisis management—namely, the personality or characteristics of leaders, and institutional settings in which the leadership stands. Although personal factors play an important role in shaping the leadership in crisis, the leadership is supported by institutions, and per-sonal elements of the leadership are more or less constrained by institutional surroundings.

Because of Prime Minister Naoto Kan's strong personality and the media's attention on him, the public tended to focus on his leadership style. Howev-er, his behavior was also shaped by institutions of crisis management deci-sion-making—or their absence. Therefore, in order to learn lessons from the Fukushima nuclear accident for more resilient preparedness, it is more appro-priate to examine the problems of institutions and policy instruments as fac-tors that affected leadership effectiveness in the crisis.

Kan as the leader, and bureaucratic institutions as channels of information and implementation, failed to establish proper lines of communication and respect the prescribed chain of command between them. On the leader's side, there was mistrust of bureaucracy, which had been imbedded in Kan's mindset before the accident,[15] and was reinforced by the bureaucracy's failure to provide sufficient and appropriate information for decision-making during the early stages of the crisis. On the bureaucracy's side, NISA and NSC were unable to demonstrate their competence as agencies to collect information on-site and provide appropriate mitigation advice to TEPCO and evacuation information to the public. The loss of the off-site center prevented NISA from executing these functions. The off-site center lost electricity and communication from earthquake damage, which made it impossible for the center to perform its assigned role. But bureaucrats were also frustrated that political leaders did not respect (or simply did not have sufficient awareness of) the NEA crisis manage-ment protocols and did not listen to them.[16] Kan's mistrust of bureaucracy and his perception of NISA's incompetence led to the establishment of an irregular crisis management dynamic, and creation of the Government-TEPCO IRO at TEPCO headquarters, along with the appointment of six external experts as his advisors by March 29.

Prime Minister Kan's Leadership Style

In the case of the Fukushima nuclear accident, the management style of Prime Minister Naoto Kan had a considerable impact on shaping the emergency response to the Fukushima accident. He strongly preferred to take the initiative in decision-making. As Goshi Hosono, special advisor to the prime minister, described, Kan's leadership style was "top-down," and he tried to involve himself in collecting information, even details, and then making his own decisions rather than listening to bureaucrats.[17] His involvement in information gathering and decision-making ranged from major crisis management decisions such as the rejection of TEPCO's proposal to retreat on-site personnel,[18] and the establishment of an ad hoc crisis management headquarters, the Government-TEPCO IRO, to micromanagement of issues such as inquiry about the size of batteries necessary for restoring electricity on the site, the dispatch of power generator trucks, and when to start spraying water into heated reactors.

His proactive attitude brought him to Fukushima Daiichi by helicopter in the early morning of March 12, in the midst of crisis escalation when on-site operators were struggling to find a method for manual venting at Unit 1, whose pressure was rising. Kan, who had already become frustrated with ineffective communication with TEPCO headquarters and the TEPCO executive who had been dispatched to the *Kantei* as liaison, reflected that he was relieved to have found someone to communicate with directly who knew the situation.[19] It was the plant manager, Masao Yoshida. On one hand, direct communication between the plant manager and the *Kantei*, or politicians at IRO, smoothed the flow of information on the ground until it reached the highest layer of the decision-making hierarchy. On the other, direct interventions by political leaders in on-site decisions such as the timing of crisis mitigation measures like venting and sea water injection brought confusion to experts on the site, who, grasping the situation better, may have had better ideas.[20]

For Kan, the first priority was the establishment of channels through which he could directly obtain firsthand information. With his distrust of bureaucracy, he wished to control the whole process through the Government-TEPCO IRO, specifically through his aide, Hosono, whom he stationed there.

The establishment of an unorthodox, ad hoc command-and-control structure between the *Kantei* and TEPCO certainly contributed to smoothing the flow of information and more effective decisions at the leadership level. Ironically, it could be said that Kan's unusual leadership was beneficial, as it facilitated closer communication between the government and TEPCO. It also brought about the extensive intervention in the emergency response by the government, which was not stipulated in prepared manuals. Such intervention can result in better responses but also poses a risk of mismanagement: in a complex and high-consequence disaster such as a nuclear accident, strong political leadership cannot guarantee appropriate decisions because many dynamic, situation-specific, and urgent problems that require highly technical judgments arise simultaneously at different places. In such cases, on-site operational leaders with sufficient mandates should make decisions.[21] The establishment of ad hoc headquarters showed that existing crisis management planning and manuals were not useful in establishing a proper response mechanism in the wake of the crisis.

Institutional Problems

Responses to complex disasters such as the Fukushima nuclear accident require lateral coordination among various stakeholders in the various nodes of a response network. The nature of the disaster dictates the style of leadership required, but there are key skills that all leaders overseeing multiorganizational, transjurisdictional responses must possess. These include the ability to make sense of new developments while also executing decisions in a highly uncertain environment that features complex flows of information.[22] To help leaders fulfill their roles, institutional or organizational capacities to support leadership decisions are important.

The loss of function at the off-site center rendered the planned chain of command and the information-gathering system unusable, which partly brought about the irregular leadership protocol during the crisis. This section describes how an irregular decision protocol was established and operated during the nuclear crisis, from the establishment of an informal core group of political leaders shaped by the dysfunction of Crisis Management Center (CMC) and other official channels, to the formation of the Integrated Response Office between the government and TEPCO (Government-TEPCO IRO), through which political leaders took control of TEPCO's internal flow of information and decision-making.

Typically, the Crisis Management Center is a gateway and hub for the flow of information from other governmental agencies to the *Kantei*. Located in the basement of the *Kantei*, it provides screening and filtering of information between the sources and the political leaders in the *Kantei*. If that screening does not function effectively, necessary and proper information cannot be transmitted to decision-makers in a timely fashion.

Intelligence and other relevant crisis information was supposed to be gathered and analyzed there and then sent to the prime minister and other relevant leaders, such as the chief cabinet secretary in the *Kantei*, who are involved in decision-making. Before establishment of the Government-TEPCO IRO, information gathering for decision-making was poor, as the Crisis Management Center in the *Kantei*, which was supposed to be the core of information gathering for political leaders, was unable to function as expected. When the Fukushima nuclear crisis was reported, the Crisis Management Center was overwhelmed by the flood of information on earthquake and tsunami damage.

Having viewed the CMC's inability to handle the nuclear disaster, Kan invited Chief Cabinet Secretary Yukio Edano; Minister of Economy, Trade, and Industry Banri Kaieda; Special Advisor Goshi Hosono; and a few other politicians in his inner circle—as well as limited senior members of NISA, NSC, the Japan Nuclear Energy Safety Organization (JNES), the Atomic Energy Commission (AEC), and TEPCO—to his office on the fifth floor. Kan sought information and expert opinions from this informal circle for decision-making; official channels of information and advisory functions, including the Crisis Management Center, were not utilized. Kaieda, Hosono, and other political figures in an inner circle received reports by phone from various sources in TEPCO, NISA, and other organizations in different formats. As a result, information gathered at this informal group at *Kantei*'s fifth floor was rather fragmented, and systematic analyses for decision-making were not properly made. The liaison of TEPCO stationed in the fifth floor group was not able to effectively communicate with Kan, failing to inform him of the status and data of reactors, measures that were being taken, and advice based on technical expertise.

Poor coordination between the political leaders and bureaucracy was also seen in the handling of the System for Prediction of Environmental Emergency Dose Information (SPEEDI), a system operated by the Ministry of Education, Culture, Sports, Science and Technology (MEXT). Had there been relevant information available for policy-makers, the evacuation plan, which was based on information from SPEEDI, could have been different in timing and pattern. However, although information from SPEEDI was certainly conveyed to the Crisis Management Center, an organ with bureaucrats dispatched from various ministries and agencies to support crisis management of the leadership, it was not conveyed to the fifth-floor core team of political leaders in the *Kantei*. In other words, the operation of SPEEDI and reporting of data were conducted routinely as the manual described. Nevertheless, such information was pooled

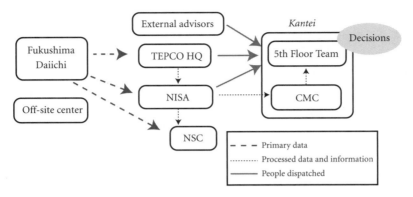

F IG . 4.2: Flow of information before the establishment of Government-TEPCO IRO.

at an organization (Crisis Management Center) where the information was gathered and integrated, and not utilized in decision-making. Similarly, at the start of seawater injection into Unit 1 on March 12, the fifth-floor core team was not informed, although the Crisis Management Center received information from NISA that TEPCO had started water injection at 7:04 p.m.

These cases show that communications between the Crisis Management Center and the fifth-floor core team, the central decision-making organ, were not efficient. Furthermore, experts invited to the fifth-floor core team from NISA, NSC, and TEPCO also could not provide information and advice in a timely fashion.[23] The information gap that the fifth-floor core team faced would become a constraint on prompt, accurate decision-making.

Aware of communications problems between TEPCO and political leaders and bureaucratic organizations charged with supporting decision-making, Kan decided to establish the Government-TEPCO IRO and put Hosono in charge. The Government-TEPCO IRO made a tremendous contribution, as it reduced the number of layers through which information passed before it reached the ultimate decision-makers. The political leaders (dispatched by Kan), NISA officials, and TEPCO executives were gathered in the operation room in TEPCO headquarters, which was directly connected by video conference channel with the Fukushima Daiichi power plant. METI minister Kaieda and others testified that the establishment of the IRO improved the information-gathering and decision-making processes, as all relevant players shared the same information and discussed response measures based on these shared perceptions.[24]

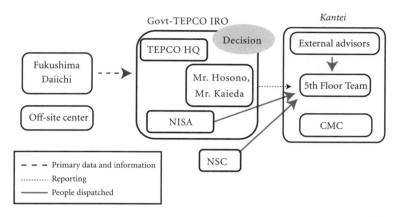

F IG . 4.3: Flow of information after the establishment of Government-TEPCO IRO.

However, it also increased the likelihood that political considerations would influence responses to technical or scientific matters, as *Kantei*'s intention was directly transmitted to the accident site. An exemplary case of a distorted chain of command and the political intervention problem was seen in the divide between the Government-TEPCO IRO and plant manager Yoshida over the decision on pouring seawater into Unit 1.[25] Yoshida was ordered to hold up the operation of seawater injection until the prime minister approved it. In communication with the TEPCO headquarters, he said "Yes" to Tokyo, and vocally declared the suspension of the operation. On the side, he issued a different order to his staff, unheard by the headquarters, to continue seawater injection. It turned out to be the right decision to override the politically driven decision of headquarters'. However, it also indicated a collapse of the chain of command and trust in leadership.

FAILURE OF FAMILIARIZATION WITH
THE EMERGENCY PROCEDURE

In addition to confusion surrounding various on-site mitigation measures, the lack of preparedness was seen in ineffective severe accident instruction manuals, and lack of expertise and practical wisdom (*phronesis*) in applying measures to never before experienced situations.[26]

By design, according to Karl Weick and Kathleen Sutcliffe, contingency plans "influence perception and reduce the number of things people notice."[27] The planning is to set a frame of reference, which could stipulate what decision-makers should pay attention to, and what they would not. Plans also undercut organizational functioning because they specify contingent actions through restricting attention to what to expect and focusing views on capabilities in possession. In short, contingency plans preclude extensive improvisation.[28] In the case of the Fukushima crisis, as seen above, the crisis management manual did not provide effective guidance to establish a proper chain of command that supported the leadership during the crisis. Ironically, the crisis management manual's shortcomings provided room for political leaders to improvise, which led to the establishment of the Government-TEPCO IRO.

Nevertheless, the importance of familiarization with manuals should not be discounted. Weick and Sutcliffe (2007) emphasize the importance of a concept of containment rather than anticipation in the preparedness. Organizations need not prevent unexpected events, but do need to prevent unwanted outcomes after unexpected events occur. In the wake of crises that are not predicted, organizations are inevitably reactive. Better responses to crises require organizations to prepare for being mindfully reactive.[29] That is why the ability to make sense and meaning of developments while executing decisions is required for leadership in a highly uncertain situation.

The experience of Fukushima yields two important lessons for effective leadership with regard to emergency preparedness and preparation of crisis management manuals. First, adequate preparedness and well-drafted crisis management manuals should narrow the margin of ambiguity in action, and thus reduce the reliance on the individual quality of leaders in charge of decision-making at the time of crisis. The manual provides leadership with the basis for sense-making and decision-making. Second, familiarization with the manual both in terms of what is included in the manual and what is excluded is an important procedure for leaders and organizations that support leaders in a crisis. The case of Fukushima reveals an incorrect approach to crisis preparedness, as crisis management manuals did not establish conditions or procedures that would have allowed leaders to react flexibly to uncertain situations.

The responses and responsibilities of nuclear operators and the government are stipulated in the NEA and the manual that the government prepared based on the NEA, the Nuclear Accident Response Manual (NARM). Lack of familiarity with the procedures of the NEA and NARM in response to nuclear disaster was symbolically seen in the delay in issuing the Declaration of a Nuclear Emergency Situation. According to the NEA, the prime minister was expected to declare the state of emergency at the outset of the severe accident so that the government institutions would activate their crisis management machines. However, Kan was not fully aware of the necessity for issuing the declaration in order to launch the emergency response, and was surrounded by aides who did not know the details of how to launch the government response. So it took two hours to issue the declaration after TEPCO notified officials of the situation at Fukushima Daiichi under Article 15 of the NEA.[30]

On-Site Response and Coordination

On site, similar "never-happened-before" responses were required. Actions taken by plant operators and first responders and coordination between them should provide a useful case for the review of political leadership. While on-site actions for mitigation of reactor accidents by first responders such as the Self Defense Forces, the fire department, and the police department demonstrated their ability to achieve their individual missions, which were originally *not* mandated in the NEA or in their operation manuals, only political leadership could overcome the difficulty of coordinating the operations of diverse implementation arms under a single command structure.

According to Article 3 of the NEA, controlling reactors is primarily the responsibility of nuclear operators (in this case, TEPCO). No local first responders had been preassigned any on-site activities during a nuclear crisis in the NEA or in their operation manuals. They were originally expected to fill only supportive roles for the local communities' safety and off-site evacuation of the residents.

However, TEPCO did not have sufficient personnel or equipment for cooling down reactors when the situation on site deteriorated. As instructed by the NEHQ at the *Kantei*, the SDF, police, and firefighters were dispatched for controlling the nuclear reactors in trouble on-site. They were engaged in the injection of water into reactor buildings to cool down reactors. Obviously, these departments had not been adequately prepared for such operations in terms of expertise, staff, materials, and equipment.

The coordination between these departments and with TEPCO during water injection operations provided some lessons on the command and control of operations and the relationship between central leadership organs and on-site responders. Despite the absence of pre-event planning, coordination among implementation arms went well, following the *Kantei*'s instruction to designate SDF as central to coordination among them, with the issuance of a document titled "Basic Policy for 18 March Water Injection Operation" and instruction under the NEA on March 20. The role of these documents was to authorize and legitimize the local de facto chain of command. It must be noted that the on-site chain of command had already functioned mainly as a result of the superior capacity of the SDF over other responders, which induced spontaneous cooperation of on-site responders to the SDF leadership.

Prior to the incident, each organization had its own plans based on guidelines in existing manuals, and this external instruction was performed irregularly outside the manuals and without proper consultation and coordination with headquarters of these organizations. However, political leadership facilitated the mobilization of various organizations and made smooth the coordination among them for unplanned objectives and mandates. Responders conducted unexpected on-site water injection under instruction by the *Kantei*. In this case, since the on-site situation had moved beyond the level that TEPCO alone could handle, the judgment of the *Kantei* to order the establishment of a chain of command on-site beyond the NEA and nuclear accident response manual was understandable and appropriate. However, a question remains. Although the *Kantei*'s involvement helped establish a clear chain of command among responders on site and eventually provided useful mitigation responses, this centralized command system (on direct order from Tokyo) was not suited to properly and quickly establishing control of the situation in a rapidly changing state of emergency in the stricken area. To what extent should this kind of emergency protocol of command be prescribed, in order to help leadership decision-making?

Another legal issue that would have required decisions by leadership to overrule existing laws was the sharing of security information among responders. On-site operations to cool down reactors had to be conducted under the limited information available. Information sharing between responders and TEPCO was not sufficient, in terms of plant layout, the purpose of water injection, various potential risks, and other details necessary for conducting operations. Despite the rules in the NEA for reporting and communications by nuclear operators, responders were not provided detailed information, including a map indicating locations of various equipment. A potential reason for TEPCO's failure to share required information with responders could be a restriction under the design-basis threat (DBT) requirement, to which only limited number of TEPCO staffers had access, and a violation of which constitutes a criminal act.[31] Because of inadequate planning at TEPCO headquarters and failure to coordinate thoroughly with the *Kantei*, these legal issues might not have been resolved. The failure of existing manuals to clearly define the chain of command and responsibilities for different responders hampered cooperation between responders and TEPCO. It is easy to imagine how, in another disaster scenario, the mandate given to these responders might have had serious consequences.

Missed Opportunity: Significance of Drills

Lack of familiarity with emergency procedures was seen in many other instances. Politicians involved with decision-making, including Kan, criticized bureaucrats for failing to inform them of SPEEDI data (and even of SPEEDI's existence), which prevented them from using the information for evacuation planning.[32] But Kan had the opportunity to be acquainted with SPEEDI before the accident. In October 2009, Kan, then a minister in charge of science and technology policy within the prime minister's office, participated in a comprehensive exercise for nuclear emergency at Hamaoka Nuclear Power Station that featured a scenario that included the use of SPEEDI.[33] Although it may not be realistic for a leader of a state to have perfect knowledge of all necessary response procedures for every kind of crisis, policy institutions, which support leadership, should have closer acquaintance with procedures.

At Fukushima Daiichi, a comprehensive nuclear emergency exercise was held in 2008, the first since 1999. The assumptions of the accident scenario were far more optimistic than what actually happened in Fukushima in 2011. In that scenario, the NEA Article 10 event was assumed to occur ten hours after the accident happened, and twenty-five hours later, an Article 15 event, with the abnormal leakage of radioactive materials to the environment. Furthermore, the scenario envisioned an accident at a single unit, not multiple units.[34] In reality, the Article 10 report was made by TEPCO to NISA at 3:42 p.m., approximately one hour after the earthquake, and at 7:03 p.m., four and a half hours later, the Article 15 report was made. The situation actually deteriorated much faster.

This example indicates two principles. First, political leaders alone are not well positioned to take control over the whole process of crisis management in a nuclear accident, as it is not realistic that they would become experts on crisis management by mastering necessary procedures in a manual. Tetsuro Fukuyama, deputy chief cabinet secretary at the time of the accident, later stated that the political leaders in the *Kantei* did not know the detailed manuals and did not receive any briefing on them.[35] As a result of the separation of the nuclear crisis response core team from the Crisis Management Center (or bureaucratic mechanism for crisis response), which was preoccupied with response to the earthquake and tsunami, the political leaders lost the effective support of bureaucrats with expertise in crisis management. A better mechanism to mobilize existing resources and expertise in the bureaucracy would be extremely important to let political leaders exercise their leadership in guiding and directing responses without being preoccupied with detailed micromanagement.

Second, drills in Japan are not designed to build capacities and practical wisdom among responders, operators, and leaders. In a sense, it is inevitable that someone unfamiliar with crisis management procedures would become prime minister, and political aides for prime ministers are relatively inexperienced. Therefore, human resource development in crisis management, accumulation of expertise among these human resources, and the establishment of trust between these experts and political leaders are essential tasks that must be addressed to increase the *Kantei*'s crisis management capacity. Building trust between experts in bureaucracy and the political leadership would avoid confusion on site by excessive political intervention in technical and operational decisions.

Emergency response drills should also be used to improve preparedness, upgrade manuals, and build capacity among responders. But the nuclear community avoided the "failure" of response even in the drill. Such a mentality was derived from a fear that such failure would draw public attention to the risk of nuclear power plants. Government officials wanted to avoid such an outcome because it could affect the promotion of nuclear energy policy—in particular, public acceptance in siting nuclear power plants.[36]

However, it is extremely rare in Japan to conduct blind scenario drills, which would be expected to increase the capacity of decision-makers and responders to handle unknown situations. While drills with ready-made, preknown scenarios may not help responders and decision-makers accumulate practical wisdom, they do familiarize responders with routine procedures. In situations beyond assumption, decision-makers and responders are required to take actions that are often unwritten in accident management manuals. Even the division of labor among organizations and individuals would become ambiguous. In such situations, shared norms and principles of conduct, rather than detailed descriptions of procedures, are more useful.

BEYOND ASSUMPTION (SOUTEIGAI): STRUCTURAL FACTORS OF UNPREPAREDNESS

The nuclear emergency manual was drafted based on overly optimistic assumptions. It did not envision a complex emergency combining an earthquake (which caused station blackout), a tsunami (which caused damage to emergency generators and cooling systems), and a nuclear accident on multiple reactors. Certainly, the Fukushima nuclear accident was an extremely rare situation, in terms of the sheer scale of the natural disaster, which would have been difficult to imagine. However, individual phenomena such as the station blackout or loss of backup power supply, as well as the consequent loss of communications, were not unpredictable incidents. In light of the overly optimistic assumptions made in the manual, the actual situation emerged literally "beyond assumptions" of responders and decision-makers.

In the early days of response to this complex disaster of triple shocks (earthquake, tsunami, and nuclear disasters), the government and TEPCO emphasized that this scale of natural disaster was so enormous that it was *Souteigai*. This characterization implies that it was inevitable and almost "accidental" that planned measures and prepared equipment for crisis management and mitigation could not match the magnitude of the disaster.

It is, however, important to review why such a case of *Souteigai* happened. The previous part of this chapter argued the importance of institutional infrastructure for the effective political leadership in a case of *Souteigai*, and the importance of effective crisis management manuals for such a leadership, which were missing in the case of Fukushima. In the following part of this chapter, a root cause of such an absence of effective preparedness will be discussed by focusing on failing to properly address precautionary information on the tsunami risk and station blackout (SBO) scenarios in setting a safety guideline.

Setting a Loose Antitsunami Standard: Regulatory Capture

Official and private investigations and reviews of the accident revealed problems related to the lack of preparedness in severe accident management and the shaping of responses at the decision-making level, as well as insufficient capabilities of plant operators and responders on the site. The lack of preparedness was a major cause of problems in the government's response, as well as TEPCO's. Factors contributing to poor preparedness included poor disaster risk assessment and failure to consider how to manage residual risk, or the risk remaining after treatment of reasonable risk.[37] If risk assessment is faulty, residual risk, which requires mitigation, would not be correctly identified.

In the case at hand, the prediction of the level of risk of a natural disaster such as a tsunami was inappropriate. The size of the tsunami on March 11 was *not* unprecedented. Geological archeologists and historians, before the earthquake, had found remnants of an even greater tsunami with the Jogan earthquake at Sanriku in 869.

To be fair, since the adoption of the NSC's revised Anti-Seismic Design Guidelines in September 2006, NISA requested that utility companies perform a so-called back-check, a reevaluation of provisions for earthquake safety and protections. Indeed, in June 2009, a joint working group within the Advisory Committee for Natural Resources and Energy discussed whether the assessment of the Jogan tsunami should be included in a back-check report, which would have required that existing reactors be examined based on new criteria. However, the risk of a tsunami turned out to be insufficiently addressed in the process despite the fact that tsunami safety evaluation constitutes part of the evaluation of preparedness for earthquake, as a tsunami is among the events accompanying earthquake. In the end, the interim report was accepted without reference to the Jogan tsunami.[38]

TEPCO also conducted an assessment of tsunami risk based on a report titled "Tsunami Assessment Technique for Nuclear Power Plants," developed by the Japan Society of Civil Engineering in 2002. TEPCO calculated the maximum size of tsunamis at the Fukushima Daiichi and Daini nuclear power plants and concluded that the height at Fukushima Daiichi would be 5.4 to 5.7 meters, and 5.1 to 5.2 meters at Fukushima Daini. TEPCO took countermeasures against tsunami based on this assessment. In May and June 2008, TEPCO made another calculation about tsunami risk based on an assumption that a great earthquake equivalent to the Meiji-Sanriku earthquake (M8.3, in 1896) could happen offshore Fukushima. The calculation showed that tsunami size could be as high as 9.3 to 15.7 meters. Another assessment by other experts, which was based on the Jogan tsunami (M8.4, in 869), indicated that an 8.6- to 9.2-meter-high tsunami could hit Fukushima Daiichi.[39]

An in-house TEPCO study on the risk of a tsunami causing damage to a reactor with the method of probabilistic risk assessment, which was presented at an international conference, had also showed that the probability that a 15-meter tsunami would hit the Fukushima Daiichi was at a level that would require immediate response.[40]

TEPCO, however, did not consider these assessments as serious warnings, but rather viewed them as merely indications of possibilities. Instead of taking immediate measures to cope with the risks identified by the assessments, TEPCO made a request to the Japan Society of Civil Engineers for further investigation.

Responses by regulators were also incomplete. With regard to Fukushima Daiichi, TEPCO submitted an interim antiseismic back-check report on Unit 5 in March 2008, deemed acceptable by NISA and NSC in 2009. Although TEPCO was required by a new guideline to make new reinforcements to upgrade antitsunami measures, and NISA was responsible for implementing such reinforcements, neither TEPCO nor NISA took action.

Although in recent years there has been much progress in research on tsunami science and tsunami risk assessment, tsunami risks still may not be properly recognized by the nuclear safety community. NISA received reports on tsunami assessment from TEPCO in September 2009, May 2010, and on March 7, 2011 (four days before the East Japan great earthquake), but none of these reports led to concrete actions to strengthen antitsunami measures at nuclear power plants.[41]

Shunsuke Kondo, chairman of the Atomic Energy Commission of Japan (until December 2012) and a leading expert on nuclear safety, recognized that nuclear safety experts, who are, in general, not keen on conducting probabilistic safety assessments (PSA),[42] had not communicated with tsunami researchers to seek the information necessary for addressing tsunami risks.[43]

Regulators were reluctant to incorporate new findings and advancements in technology, and ultimately safety designs were made based upon an insufficient level of risk assessment. Clarifying safety performance would serve as a guideline for assessing the effectiveness of severe accident measures and residual risk. Unlike the United States, which adopted this notion as policy in 1986,[44] Japan has not updated safety performance metrics for tsunamis.

An issue of greater concern is that, despite recognition of the need to reinforce antitsunami safety regulations, TEPCO unilaterally decided to postpone submission of the report without NISA's consent. Furthermore, in the process of drafting a report slated for release in October 2011 on the assessment of long-term trends for seismic activities in the Sanriku area, TEPCO submitted a request to the drafting committee of the MEXT's secretariat of the promotion of earthquake research and investigation. In this March 3, 2011, request, TEPCO called for revision of the descriptions of the Jogan earthquake to prevent interpretations that earthquakes happened repeatedly in the offshore Sanriku region, on the basis that the epicenter of the Jogan earthquake had not been clearly identified.[45] Such requests should not be seen as promoting sincere scientific debate on assessment, but should instead be interpreted as an attempt to avoid further investment in countermeasures against tsunami and to avoid charges of negligence.

The case of tsunami risk assessment clearly depicted regulators' lack of competence and their dependence on TEPCO in drafting safety standards.[46] The improper relationship between the regulators and the regulated also led to the marginalization of NISA in emergency planning, which prevented NISA from fulfilling its role as a node of communication during the crisis.

Ignorance of Severe Crisis Scenarios in SBO Guidelines: Consequences of the Myth of Absolute Safety (Zettai Anzen Shinwa)

A similar dynamic between NISA and power companies can be observed in the adoption of guidelines for response to station blackout in 1990. The guideline (Regulatory Guide for Reviewing Safety Design of Light Water Nuclear Power Reactor Facilities) specified steps to be taken in case of SBO triggered by internal causes but did not address the risk of external events causing SBO. Furthermore, the guideline required operators to consider only short-term SBO, and did not require operators to consider possibilities of long-term SBO, as "in such cases it may be expected that power grids will be recovered or emergency power generators will be restored." According to Yoshihiko Sasaki, the first director general of NISA, the power companies had strong voices in drafting the guidelines.

Since then, there have been occasions to revisit the practice of considering only short-term SBO cases caused by internal events. In 1993, NSC's subcommittee discussed the probability of SBO and the endurance time of batteries and cooling water supply by comparing Japanese regulations with the US Nuclear Regulatory Commission's SBO regulations.[47] The US regulations required operators to assume the possibility of external events as causes of SBO, while Japanese regulations did not require operators to do so. Other opportunities for review came in 2001 when NSC discussed the case of SBO at Taiwan's Maanshan nuclear power plant, which was caused by the breakdown of an external power supply, and a near-SBO case at Kashiwazaki Kariwa nuclear power plant during the Chuetsu earthquake in 2007.

Why were regulators unable to assimilate new knowledge or technology into their regulations? The cases mentioned above illustrate a relationship between the regulators and the regulated agency (TEPCO) in which the regulated agency had considerable influence over regulatory politics, a situation that can be characterized as "regulatory capture." In 2007, Barack Obama, then a presidential candidate, said that the Nuclear Regulatory Commission had become "captive of the industries that it regulates."[48] In Japan, too, the regulatory side was inferior to the side regulated in terms of knowledge or expertise and power in the nuclear policy community.

According to the IAEA's Fundamental Safety Principle no. 1, the primary responsibility for safety resides with license holders—namely, in the case of Japan, utility companies. The institutional design in the NEA therefore reflected IAEA guidelines. The IAEA's Fundamental Safety Principle no. 2 states that the role of the regulator is to establish an effective legal and administrative framework for safety, including independent regulatory institutions. Operators and regulators are in a complementary relationship in reinforcing safety regulations, which are also to be set through the interactions between these two. The state of the relationship between regulators and utilities can be shaped by their balance of power, in terms of technological expertise and information; bargaining power derived from access to politics; and scale of the power companies.

In the case of the relationship between TEPCO and NISA, TEPCO was far superior in nuclear safety expertise and knowledge, as it is a large enterprise with extensive experience in building and operating reactors and possesses the in-house capacity to conduct research and collect data on nuclear safety onsite. It was a huge repository of data and scientific knowledge. On the other hand, NISA, as a part of METI's bureaucratic system, had a limited number of experts, and the job rotation system within the organization often put generalists and specialists in inappropriate positions. This practice did not help the organization build institutional memory based upon technical expertise or technological knowledge. The agency's implementation arm, JNES, which was expected to function as the government's repository of technical expertise and knowledge, also lagged behind industry in proficiency.[49]

A follow-on question is whether the situation in Fukushima could have been better managed had residual risk been properly addressed in the planning of mitigation measures. Attitudes toward the acceptance of risks, which were constituted by the so-called myth of absolute safety, might be a cause for the lack of preparedness. It is not simply a cultural tendency of the Japanese society. It was rather a combination of culture and structural problems within the Japanese nuclear community.

The myth of absolute safety has prevailed in the so-called nuclear village, an inner circle of the nuclear energy community, consisting of the nuclear regulatory agencies (NISA, JNES, MEXT), industrial organizations (power companies and their industrial organization, *Denjiren*), Japan's nuclear energy policy organization (METI's Agency of Natural Resources and Energy), and local communities that hosted nuclear power stations. Despite differences in the rationales among stakeholders, the dynamic among these stakeholders in the nuclear village allowed all parties to avoid publicly acknowledging the existence of risks, including residual risk, in nuclear power plants.

As described above, power companies had a strong influence in shaping regulatory guidelines, as they possessed greater technical expertise than NISA with regard to nuclear safety. The *Kokkai Jikocho* reported that regulators were captive to the power companies.[50] According to the report, since 2006, NISA and TEPCO had shared information on the possibility of SBO in the case of a tsunami exceeding a certain level of height, as well as the possibility of a seawater cooling system breakdown in the case of a tsunami exceeding the prediction made in the official guideline. But this information was not disclosed to the public. TEPCO was reluctant to accept the result of risk assessment by a method of PSA, and also delayed countermeasures for a tsunami, arguing that PSA was a methodology with significant technical uncertainties. Had there been a safety culture firmly embedded in TEPCO management, the company would not have hesitated to take further countermeasures for a tsunami. Meanwhile, NISA did not reprimand TEPCO for its delay in taking tsunami countermeasures and chose to overlook the risk of tsunamis. The excessively optimistic attitudes of NISA and TEPCO had no clear scientific foundation but were rather based on TEPCO's manipulated risk level. TEPCO's lack of acknowledgment of the risk was representative of how the myth of absolute safety dominated the decision-making process.

Approaches toward safety influenced by the myth of absolute safety led to a lack of preparedness and the production of crisis management manuals that lacked imagination with respect to possible severe accident situations. These factors affected the predictability of the crisis, creating a situation believed to be beyond the realm of assumptions. In the absence of effective support from regulators and a clear command-and-control mechanism, these factors ultimately produced leadership failures.

CONCLUSION

It is true that many crises will happen in a way not predicted or assumed. During crises, leaders may have to make decisions regarding situations that are not predicted in crisis management manuals. Therefore, leaders should not be overwhelmed by situations "beyond assumptions" at the onset of a crisis. Crisis management manuals will not be able to tell decision-makers everything that must be done to cope with the crisis.

When facing crises, leaders must rely on technical expertise and practical wisdom that crisis management experts can provide, since political leaders are not necessarily well acquainted with crisis mitigation methods. Crisis leadership is not all about decision-making but also involves sense-making and meaning-making, as well as learning following crisis resolution.[51]

In the case of the Fukushima nuclear accident, the tenuous relationship between political leaders and technical experts in bureaucracy and scientific and technical communities drove political leaders to dominate the processes of information gathering and decision-making at every level, without relying on expert advice.

In the early stages of the Fukushima crisis, organizations that were to support decisions by leaders failed to function as effective liaisons between on-site responders and the *Kantei,* and also failed to provide appropriate and plausible accounts of the situation and communicate with decision-makers in language understood by nonscientific policy-makers, in turn reducing confidence in the nuclear community.

Confusion within leadership was not a product of chance. It had profound structural causes, too. Regulators failed to nurture their competence under regulatory arrangements that were dominated by the power companies being regulated (that is, regulatory capture). Regulatory capture in turn led to risk assessments distorted toward overly optimistic assumptions, based on faith in the absolute safety of Japan's nuclear plants (that is, the myth of absolute safety: *Zettai Anzen Shinwa*). In the end, the dynamic created during the formulation of regulatory standards shaped the standing relationship between the regulators and the regulated. Because regulators that supported political leadership were subordinated to the regulated, it was impossible to establish an effective chain of command with candid and thorough information exchange.

The myth of absolute safety also appeared in the ways in which drills were conducted. Japanese emergency exercises did not help to build capacity and practical wisdom in regulators, responders, and leadership. Encountering a disaster beyond the realm of assumptions was a product of the myth of absolute safety and regulatory capture, which constituted the structural fragility of the leadership.

One staff member of the *Kantei* described his feeling after the critical moment had passed, that he "felt in [his] heart that God is with this country after all."[52] This statement implies how lucky Japan was to avoid an even more catastrophic consequence, and sheds light on the degree of uncertainty that the decision-making community faced during the Fukushima crisis. To reduce uncertainty in uncertain environments moving forward, the Japanese nuclear community will need to reform institutions—both the organizations themselves and the operational procedures and rules they maintain—and challenge cultural norms that have contributed to nuclear safety and security liabilities.

NOTES

This paper is indebted to research and investigation conducted by the Independent Commission on the Investigation of the Fukushima Nuclear Accident, organized by the Rebuild Japan Initiative Foundation. The author participated in the project as a core member of the planning team and a coteam leader of the working group responsible for investigation of the incident. Facts, observations on the events, and interviews quoted in this paper are based on this investigation, unless otherwise stated. The author is solely responsible for analyses and arguments in this paper.

1. Andreas Klinke and Ortwin Renn, "Risk Governance: Contemporary and Future Challenges," in *Regulating Chemical Risks: European and Global Perspectives*, ed. J. Eriksson, M. Gliek, and C. Ruden (Berlin: Springer, 2010), 13.

2. Arjen Boin and Paul 't Hart, "Public Leadership in Times of Crisis: Mission Impossible?" *Public Administration Review* 63, no. 5 (2003): 544–553, esp. 545.

3. Compare Arjen Boin, *The Politics of Crisis Management: Public Leadership under Pressure* (Cambridge: Cambridge University Press, 2005).

4. A special advisor to the cabinet later described the situation thus: he was supposed to be invited to help crisis management, but in reality, he was observing the management crisis. Special advisor to the cabinet, interview by the author, August 30, 2011.

5. "Mission Report of the IAEA International Fact Finding Expert Mission of the Fukushima Daiichi NPP Accident following the Great East Japan Earthquake and Tsunami," IAEA, 2011, available at www-pub.iaea.org/MTCD/meetings/PDFplus/2011/cn200/documentation/cn200_Final-Fukushima-Mission_Report.pdf.

6. From videotape that recorded video conversations between Fukushima Daiichi and TEPCO Headquarters in Tokyo, http://photo.tepco.co.jp/date/2012/201210-j/121005-01j.html. See also TEPCO, "Fukushima Gensiryoku Jiko Chosa Hokokusho" [Report on

the Investigation of Fukushima Nuclear Accident], Tokyo Electric Power Company, 2012, 242–47, available at www.tepco.co.jp/cc/press/betu12_j/images/120620j0303.pdf.

7. "Final Report of the Investigation Committee on the Accident at Fukushima Nuclear Power Stations of Tokyo Electric Power Company," Secretariat of the Investigation Committee on the Accidents at the Fukushima Nuclear Power Station, Tokyo, 2012, available at www.cas.go.jp/jp/seisaku/icanps/eng/final-report.html; "Official Report of the Fukushima Nuclear Accident Independent Investigative Commission" (hereafter "Official Report"), National Diet of Japan, Tokyo, 2012, available at http://warp.da.ndl.go.jp/info:ndljp/pid/3856371/naiic.go.jp/en/; "Report of the Independent Investigation Commission on the Fukushima Daiichi Nuclear Accident," Rebuild Japan Initiative Foundation, Tokyo, February 28, 2012, available at http://rebuildjpn.org/en/project/fukushima/. The Atomic Energy Society of Japan has organized a review commission, and undertook the review of the accident. Nihon Genshiryoku Gakkai, *Fukushima Daiichi Genshiryoku Hatudensho Jiko Sono Zenbo to Asunimuketa Teigen: Gakkai Jikocho Saishu Hokokusho* [*The Fukushima Daiichi Nuclear Incident: Final Report of the AESJ Investigation Committee*] (Tokyo: Maruzen, 2014).

8. For a more comprehensive discussion of the myth of absolute safety, please refer to Suzuki's chapter in this volume.

9. "Beyond assumption" does not simply mean that the magnitude of risk is too large because the size of an event, or the event itself, cannot be predicted. It further implies that such a situation beyond prediction could be created by setting the limit of assumptions for preparedness by deliberately excluding data or observations that could require measures to cope with such risks.

10. For a further discussion of this phenomenon, see Greg Wyss's chapter in this volume on the design-basis criteria. In the case of Fukushima, the myth of absolute safety created a social context in which emergency contingencies beyond assumption (or *Souteigai*) were not considered seriously.

11. International Risk Governance Council (IRGC), *An introduction to the IRGC Risk Governance Framework* (Geneva: International Risk Governance Council, 2008), 20.

12. Ibid., 6.

13. Boin and 't Hart, "Public Leadership in Times of Crisis," 547.

14. See "Official Report," 35.

15. Compare Kan Naoto, *Daijin* [*Minister*] (Tokyo: Iwanami Shoten, 1998) (in Japanese).

16. "Report of the Independent Investigation Commission on the Fukushima Daiichi Nuclear Accident" (in Japanese), Rebuild Japan Initiative Foundation, Tokyo, February 28, 2012, 100–101 (hereafter RJIF)

17. Goshi Hosono, interview with author, November 19, 2011.

18. It is still a subject of controversy whether TEPCO actually asked for the with-

drawal of all staffers on site, which meant abandoning the entire station, or a partial withdrawal, leaving necessary staffers to control reactors. And it was an exemplary case of miscommunication between TEPCO and the government, which escalated mistrust by the political circle in the *Kantei* against TEPCO. This event, amid other cumulative mistrust, led to the establishment of the Government-TEPCO IRO.

19. RJIF, 79–80.

20. The gap of perception between the on-site response team led by Yoshida and Tokyo was symbolically seen in the case of Yoshida's decision to continue water injection against the order from Tokyo HQ.

21. Compare Rhona Flin, *Sitting in the Hot Seat: Leaders and Teams for Critical Incident Management* (Chichester, UK: John Wiley and Sons, 1996).

22. Compare Boin, *The Politics of Crisis Management.*

23. They might simply add another layer that information had to pass through.

24. Banri Kaieda, interview with author, October 1, 2011; Masaya Yasui, Agency for Natural Resources and Energy, interview with author, February 9, 2012.

25. RJIF, 82–83. This scene was widely reported by various media.

26. On practical wisdom, see Bent Flyvbjerg, *Making Social Science Matter: Why Social Inquiry Fails and How It Can Succeed Again*, trans. Steven Sampson (Cambridge University Press, 2001), 56–57.

27. Karl E. Weick and Kathleen M. Sutcliffe, *Managing the Unexpected: Resilient Performance in an Age of Uncertainty*, 2nd ed. (San Francisco: John Wiley and Sons, 2007), 66.

28. Ibid., 67.

29. Ibid., 65.

30. RJIF, 74–77.

31. Ibid., 163–64.

32. Ibid., 174.

33. Deputy Chief Cabinet Secretary (in charge of crisis management), Director-General for Policy Planning (disaster response), Ministry of Education, Culture, Sports, Science and Technology, and Ministry of Economy, Trade and Industry, "Heisei 21 nendo gensiryoku sogo bosai kunren jisshi yoryo" [2009 Comprehensive Exercise for Nuclear Emergency, Summary of Response Guidelines for Implementation], October 2010, available at www.meti.go.jp/committee/summary/0004125/019_01_02_00.pdf.

34. Deputy Chief Cabinet Secretary (in charge of crisis management), Director-General for Policy Planning (disaster response), Ministry of Education, Culture, Sports, Science and Technology, and Ministry of Economy, Trade and Industry, "Heisei 20 nendo gensiryoku sogo bosai kunren jisshi yoryo" [2008 Comprehensive Exercise for Nuclear Emergency, Summary of Response Guidelines for Implementation], October 2009, available at www.meti.go.jp/committee/materials2/downloadfiles/g81006b02j.pdf.

35. Tetsuro Fukuyama, interview with author, October 29, 2011.

36. It should be pointed out that avoiding failure in training sessions or drills is commonly seen in other areas, including earthquake emergency exercises.

37. The Japanese NRC's seismic design guideline defined seismic risk as "the risk that a facility will be impacted by seismic motion in excess of design predictions in such a way as to provoke (1) events resulting in serious damage to a facility, (2) events resulting in the release of large quantities of radioactive material from a facility, and/or (3) the possibility of harmful radiation exposure to the surrounding population as a result of such an event" (Revised Seismic Design Guidelines, Section 1: Basic Policies, subsection "Discussion"); "On Reviewing Seismic Safety at Existing Nuclear Reactor Facilities for Electricity Generation Seeking Inspections under the Revised Anti-Seismic Design Guidelines," NSC Decision no. 60, available at www.nsr.go.jp/archive/nsc/anzen/sonota/kettei/20060919-2.pdf (in Japanese).

38. RJIF, 272–74.

39. "Investigation Committee on the Accident at Fukushima Nuclear Power Stations of Tokyo Electric Power Company, Final Report," July 23, 2012, 495–96 (hereafter "Government Investigation Committee"), available at www.cas.go.jp/jp/seisaku/icanps/eng/final-report.html.

40. Makoto Takao, "Tsunami Assessment Method for NPP in Japan and Recent Studies," presentation drafted in 2008. The author obtained this presentation material from an anonymous American scientist who was in a public position at the time of the Fukushima nuclear accident.

41. "Government Investigation Committee," 495–96.

42. According to the IAEA, the objectives of PSA are "to determine all significant contributing factors to the radiation risks arising from a facility or activity, and to evaluate the extent to which the overall design is well balanced and meets probabilistic safety criteria where these have been defined." And it may "provide insights into system performance, reliability, interactions and weaknesses in the design, the application of defense-in-depth and risks, that it may not be possible to derive from a deterministic analysis." IAEA, *Safety Assessment for Facilities and Activities*, IAEA Safety Standard Series, GSR-Part 4 (2009).

43. Shunsuke Kondo, "Where Japan Is and Where Japan Will Go: Update of the Fukushima Accident and the Deliberation of Post-Fukushima Nuclear Energy Policy in Japan," Japan Atomic Energy Commission, December 2, 2011, available at www.aec.go.jp/jicst/NC/about/kettei/111202b.pdf.

44. USNRC, "Safety Goals for the Operation of Nuclear Power Plants," Policy Statement, 51FR 28044, August 4, 1986.

45. "Government Investigation Committee," 495–96.

46. See Executive Summary, "Official Report."

47. US Nuclear Regulatory Commission Regulation, Title 10, Code of Federal Regulations (10 CFR), Sec. 50.63, Loss of All Alternating Current Power, 1988.

48. Justin Elliott, "Ex-Regulator Flacking for Pro-Nuke Lobby," *Salon.com*, March 17, 2011, available at www.salon.com/2011/03/18/jeff_merrifield_nuclear_energy_institute/.

49. JNES was established in 2003, integrating three semigovernmental entities handling nuclear safety regulatory operations. Upon the revelation of false reporting by utilities on safety records of nuclear reactors, JNES was launched six months earlier than originally planned. To strengthen its capabilities, JNES recruited technical experts (to be appointed as inspectors) from outside the organization. However, those who were recruited were not necessarily sufficiently competent. Author interview with an anonymous NISA inspector, January 18, 2012.

50. See "Official Report," 27–28.

51. See Boin, *The Politics of Crisis Management.*

52. Interview with an anonymous staff member of the *Kantei*, January 19, 2012, conducted by a member of the working group for RJIF *Minkan Jikocho.*

5 Radiation Protection by Numbers: Another "Man-made" Disaster

Toshihiro Higuchi

The Fukushima nuclear accident triggered one of the world's most serious environmental radiological disasters. According to the UN Scientific Committee on the Effects of Atomic Radiation (UNSCEAR), the total atmospheric release of iodine-131 (^{131}I) and that of cesium-137 (^{137}Cs)—two of the fission products of concern from the bioenvironmental point of view—ranges between 100 to 500 petabecquerels (PBq) and 6 to 20 PBq, respectively. The magnitude of each radionuclide release is estimated to have been lower than that from the Chernobyl accident by a factor of about 10 for ^{131}I and 5 for ^{137}Cs.[1] Still, as of October 2013, areas of nearly 250 square miles registered annual air doses of 20 mSv and above, with approximately forty-eight thousand residents still displaced from this heavily contaminated region.[2] Land is not the only part of the environment affected by radioactive fallout. A substantial portion of radionuclides also entered the Pacific Ocean. The latest UNSCEAR estimates show that the amount of ^{131}I and ^{137}Cs discharged into the surrounding seas was approximately 10 percent and 50 percent, respectively, of those released into the air.[3] Given the scale of radioactive contamination, the International Nuclear Event Scale (INES) ranked the Fukushima accident at its highest Level 7, on a par with the Chernobyl accident.

Radiation protection is one of the most important dimensions of any nuclear disaster—be it a nuclear explosion or reactor accident. Indeed, it has proved decisive in changing the historical trajectory of nuclear uses for both military and peaceful purposes. The Partial Test Ban Treaty, concluded in 1963 as a landmark agreement in nuclear arms control, was spurred in no small part by the growing worldwide demand to "put an end to the contamination of

[the] environment by radioactive substances."[4] The frightening specter of serious exposure following a reactor accident, coupled with the heated debate on the effects of low-dose radiation, have also contributed to the growing opposition to nuclear power.[5] Concerns about the leakage of fission products have similarly hampered the search for a site for nuclear waste. The 2012 report of the US Blue Ribbon Commission is just one of the latest testaments to the continuous predicament for the back end of the nuclear fuel cycle.[6] Despite its historical significance, radiation protection is still among the missing subjects in our learning from Fukushima. Both the Japanese Diet and independent reports spare relatively little space for the problem of radiation protection, compared with that for a series of events leading to the reactor meltdown.[7]

To learn from the troubled experience of radiation protection following the Fukushima accident, this paper will focus on its most prominent feature: the use and abuse of the so-called reference levels by the Japanese government. To put the politics of numbers in perspective, it is essential to first ask what the reference levels actually mean. The concept originally comes from the International Commission on Radiological Protection (ICRP), a nongovernmental organization in operation since 1928. According to the ICRP, data have failed to show statistically significant difference in cancer effects in a range of doses below 100 mSv. Seeing that the lack of evidence does not mean the absence of damage, the ICRP has adopted the so-called linear nonthreshold (LNT) hypothesis, assuming that doses smaller than 100 mSv contain a corresponding degree of cancer risk (Figure 5.1). As this model postulates no threshold of damage, the ICRP has proposed that radiation protection should be situation-dependent—namely, when the exposure to be dealt with is (1) planned and routine, (2) unexpected and serious, or (3) already existing. Seeing cases like Fukushima as falling into the latter two categories, the ICRP has recommended that the reference levels are to be chosen to guide protection measures in such a manner as to "do more good than harm" and also to keep the magnitude of exposure "as low as reasonably achievable, taking into account economic and societal factors."[8] Various stakeholders have challenged the scientific and ethical underpinnings of the ICRP's past and current recommendations.[9] For the purpose of our discussion, it is sufficient to note what the reference levels are *not* intended to be: the numbers mark neither a threshold of safety nor that of action.

Once transferred to the realm of public administration, however, the reference levels tend to lose their original intention and become the only basis for radiation protection. Instead of serving as a flexible decision-making aid, the

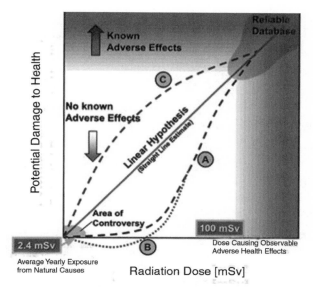

FIG. 5.1: Dose-Response Models Below 100 mSv. Lines marked as A, B, C represent alternative models to the linear hypothesis. Source: Alan E. Waltar, *Radiation and Modern Life: Fulfilling Marie Curie's Dream* (Amherst, NY: Prometheus Book, 2004).

numbers now act as a cutoff line for a wide range of practices from evacuation to decontamination, food control to financial compensations. This startling transformation in the meaning and function of the reference levels can be explained as a classic example of what historical sociologist Donald MacKenzie calls the "certainty trough." According to MacKenzie, the producers of knowledge understand its limits and nuances. Perceived uncertainty is therefore reasonably high. The users of knowledge, however, feel more confident of it, while people affected by it feel much less so.[10] The certainty trough can be extreme if the users are government offices and agencies. Sociological inquiries into formal organizations have shown that administrative criteria, intended as means to an end, often wind up becoming ends in themselves.[11]

Radiological management by the stringent application of reference levels, however, is more than a bureaucratic mishap: it is a new form of power that the Japanese government has been exerting over its citizens. In explaining the operation of a state-run welfare system in Ukraine for the victims of the Chernobyl disaster, anthropologist Adriana Petryna has shown how the post-Soviet state seeks to dictate what counts as suffering solely based on what its experts define as the verifiable facts of damage.[12] Likewise, the Japanese government has been using the reference levels to monopolize knowledge and decision-making—a key element in the political centralization of modern Japan.[13] As a result, people at risk have been given no choice but to suffer from sweeping actions on the one hand and gross inaction on the other.

Before tracing the politics of numbers and its disastrous outcomes, I would like to make it clear that I am not arguing against the use of the reference levels in radiation protection. The question is rather how to use them. As will be shown in this chapter, the Japanese government relied on the reference levels in such a way as to exclude all backup plans at the time of crisis. Even after the immediate threat of serious exposure had passed, it continued to use the reference levels in a rigid manner so that residents and consumers found it difficult to make timely, informed choices. The most ironic consequence of all is that the Japanese government suffered from the inevitable consequences of overreliance on numbers. As government agencies planned and implemented radiological management solely on the basis of reference levels and official monitoring, experts and citizens responded by scrutinizing their scientific and nonscientific underpinnings. To restore public trust, the Japanese government was forced to lower reference levels, only to realize that its administrative and technological capacities could not deliver the promised results. In this sense, radiation protection following the Fukushima reactor accident was another man-made disaster, whose political implications might ultimately prove even larger than the reactor meltdown.

EMERGENCY EVACUATION

The Japanese government stepped into the field of radiation protection in the late 1950s when the Diet passed a series of legislative actions to promote the use of radioactive materials for medical and industrial purposes, including but not limited to nuclear power plants. While Tokyo drew on dose levels in radiological management from the outset, it deepened its reliance on numbers when a computer-based decision support system called SPEEDI was introduced in 1985. SPEEDI was designed to make real-time predictions of up to seventy-two hours about the diffusion of a radioactive plume and dose rates within up to a 100-kilometer radius from ground zero.[14] This system, however, had a critical flaw. Its predictions hinged on whether real-time radiological data at a troubled power plant were available. As it turned out, the earthquake and tsunami knocked down all power sources and communications. SPEEDI started its calculations as early as 4:40 p.m. on March 11, roughly one day before the first explosion happened, but the system was forced to use a dummy value. Judging that the predictions were too uncertain, officials in Tokyo simply ignored them and decided to implement evacuation in a concentric distance from ground zero. At 9:23 p.m. on March 11, evacuation was ordered within a distance of 3 kilometers from the plant. Next morning, at 5:44 a.m., the mandated evacuation zone was extended to 10 kilometers. Five hours later, at 10:17 a.m., venting started at Reactor 1, followed by the other damaged facilities. At 6:25 p.m., shortly after the first explosion, Tokyo was forced to expand the evacuation zone once again, from 10 kilometers to 20 kilometers.

Postdisaster reports have gone to great lengths to explain why SPEEDI failed to work. The fundamental problem, however, lay in Tokyo's vested interest in using reference levels as a chief trigger for early response. In fact, Japan was the only country in which evacuation was planned according to the computer-generated prediction of dose rates. The International Atomic Energy Agency (IAEA) and other authorities adopted the zonal approach, assuming that it was difficult to predict radiological situations and manage them accordingly. In that spirit, the IAEA modified its safety guidelines in 2005. It recommended that areas within 5 kilometers of the reactor be designated as precautionary action zones (PAZ), where evacuation and other protective measures must be promptly implemented, and that areas between 5 kilometers and 30 kilometers of the reactor be designated as urgent protective action planning zones (UPZ), where protective measures must be prepared in advance. Some Japanese officials favored this proposed approach. In 2006, the Nuclear Safety Commission of Japan (NSCJ) started its work to incorporate the IAEA's revised manual into its own guidelines. Those in charge of nuclear disaster countermeasures also began to question the usefulness and reliability of SPEEDI.[15]

Despite the growing tide of support for the zonal approach, the Japanese government continued to rely on SPEEDI to activate protective measures. Part of the reason was scientific. As variable winds, weather, and topography result in a strikingly uneven spread of contamination, real-time dose calculations would help the authorities to implement protective measures most effectively. While the dose-based approach was technically sound, it did not explain why Tokyo adamantly excluded the zonal approach as a backup. The real reason lay in the politics of nuclear power. The Japanese government always guarded against providing a broad mandate to local authorities, but the zonal approach posed a danger of allowing the municipalities to make judgments and take action without instructions from Tokyo. In fact, the Japanese government's official guidelines contained no zone like PAZ, where residents were asked to evacuate promptly. The Japanese equivalent to UPZ, called EPZ (emergency planning zones), were also much more narrowly defined, as 8 to 10 kilometers instead of 30 kilometers as recommended by the IAEA. In Japan, towns within the EPZ usually demanded the right to inspect and intervene with reactor operation. This local assertion of power was politically dangerous because antinuclear forces and local residents managed to stage some successful NIMBY ("not in my backyard") resistance to not only the construction of a new plant but also the national plan to complete the nuclear fuel cycle.[16]

In this politically delicate atmosphere, the Japanese government fiercely resisted the zonal approach. The Nuclear and Industrial Safety Agency (or NISA) under the Ministry of Economy, Trade, and Industry pressured the NSCJ not to adopt the IAEA guidelines, arguing that the expansion of evacuation zones would increase anxiety and confusion among local residents near power plants and turn them against the government's plan to introduce plutonium-containing mixed-oxide (MOX) fuel. In the end, the NSCJ agreed to postpone adopting the new zone classification pending further investigation.[17] As a result, NSCJ's 2011 guidelines continued to base evacuation decisions upon dose levels predicted by SPEEDI: 50 mSv for whole-body exposure (or 500 mSv for thyroid).[18] The behind-the-scenes bargaining between the NISA and the NSCJ strongly suggests that Japan's disastrous overreliance on SPEEDI for mass evacuation stemmed less from the Japanese government's naive confidence in science than from its vested interest in retaining administrative power and also in promoting nuclear power.

Once the tsunami hit the Fukushima Daiichi station and destroyed the real-time monitoring infrastructure, the Japanese government was forced to improvise with the zonal approach that it had strongly resisted until then. Evacuation based on the distance from ground zero, however, had its own problems. The radioactive cloud drifted out of the 20-kilometer zone and created numerous "hot spots" to the northwest. More important, the sheer lack of prior planning and preparation for zone evacuation created a chaos on the ground. As evacuation orders were quickly extended from 3 kilometers to 10 kilometers, and then to 20 kilometers in a matter of twenty-four hours, a total of about seventy-eight thousand residents were suddenly asked to leave areas. Those living outside the EPZ (10 kilometers) had no preparation for prompt evacuation, while some of those from within the EPZ were forced to move farther after reaching their original destinations. In the middle of this confusion, many elders and patients were left behind with no medical or food supplies. Thirty-five patients from Futaba Kosei hospital, located 4 kilometers northwest of ground zero, were reported missing until March 15, when it was discovered that they were staying at a nursing home just 1 kilometer outside the initial 10-kilometer evacuation zone.[19]

As the improvised zone evacuation proved unworkable, government officials in Tokyo turned to reference levels once again. On April 11, one month after the earthquake, the Japanese government announced the plan to evacuate people in areas outside the 20-kilometer zone where the annual doses measured outdoors were expected to exceed 20 mSv based on radiological measurements conducted by the Ministry of Education and Science (MEXT). On April 6, MEXT started measuring radiation with the aid of the US Department of Energy and Japan's Self-Defense Forces. Its aerial surveillance measured external radiation doses at 1 meter above the ground, the map with a mesh down to 1 kilometer.[20] This schematic sketch was then compared with ground air and soil samples taken at approximately twenty-two hundred sites within a 100-kilometer radius. On August 2, MEXT released the air dose rate map, followed by the soil concentration map at the end of the month.

This centralized effort to monitor radiation, however, had a fateful outcome when it was coupled with the 20-mSv cutoff line. A good example is Iitate village in the central region of Fukushima, located between 25 and 45 kilometers from ground zero. From the beginning of its monitoring program, MEXT was well aware that this small village contained seriously contaminated areas. Its public reports, however, did not disclose the locations where measurements were taken. Those whom the ministry sent to the village to measure radiation also refused to share data with local residents. MEXT later defended this secretive practice as a sincere effort to contain "groundless rumors" until all measurements were completed and processed in Tokyo.[21]

The villagers finally realized the seriousness of contamination at the end of March, when a team of scientists led by Tetsuji Imanaka from Kyoto University visited Iitate. Assisted by village officials, these experts measured radiation at 130 points and sampled soil from five places.[22] It was soon discovered that part of the village was contaminated twice as much as the IAEA's reference levels for evacuation.[23] The residents became restless but still received no instructions from Tokyo. Government experts visited Iitate on April 6, claiming that the village was a safe place to live.[24] Less than a week later, however, the national government announced a plan to evacuate all six thousand residents in Iitate within two months. The villagers greeted this sudden announcement with mistrust. When a town hall meeting was held following the official notice, the participants complained about housing, cattle-raising, medical care, and communal life. One of them stood up, loudly wondering why he must leave the village that experts had just recently declared as safe.[25]

Those who found themselves outside the official 20-mSv zone faced the opposite problem. When the reactor buildings exploded, residents in the city of Iwaki, located 30 kilometers south of the damaged station, were asked to take shelter or leave areas voluntarily. This order was lifted on April 11, as the government's monitors found no place with projected annual doses above 20 mSv. The coverage of surveillance, however, was thin and uneven. Fewer than ten monitoring posts were installed in Iwaki, and most of them were concentrated in the city center. One of the neglected rural communities was Shidamyo, where about 130 people lived. One day, Kiyoko Ohkoshi, a sixty-two-year-old lifelong farmer, bought a personal dosimeter online and began to check her surroundings so that her grandchildren, temporarily evacuated in Hiroshima, could come back. Soon she discovered a number of highly contaminated spots around her house. Ohkoshi and her neighbors reported this alarming finding to the city office. Local officials, however, dismissed the report as amateurish, insisting that the national and prefectural authorities should take charge of surveillance.[26]

The hot spots finally moved out of the blind spots created by the government's monitoring program when a local councilman known for his antinuclear activism recruited a radiation expert, Shinzo Kimura.[27] From May 16, Kimura and other scientists drove a monitoring car throughout Iwaki, while thirteen residents used four radiation recorders to collect data at 713 sites with a mesh of as small as 10 meters. Soil was sampled with special care, because local people worried about farmland, which was at the heart of community life. While the prefectural samplers had taken out all soil to 15 centimeters deep and mixed it together, Kimura's team, aided by local farmers, measured radioactivity at every 5 centimeters down to 30 centimeters from the surface. As Kimura later explained before the Lower House of the Diet, this grassroots project produced "the only contamination map in the world that local residents made for themselves."[28]

Contrary to what government officials in Tokyo had feared, the local production of knowledge did not trigger a mass panic or inappropriate action. In fact, the independent monitoring in Iwaki helped local residents to take far more nuanced and pragmatic protective measures than an all-or-nothing approach based on the magic number of 20 mSv. For example, the detailed soil survey discovered that most contamination still remained within the first 5-centimeter layer, showing radioactivity three times as much as the official value. This finding not only revealed the limits of formal knowledge but also helped local people focus on quickly removing the thin top layer by themselves.[29] The same held true for the problem of evacuation. The map created by Kimura's team showed that some areas were indeed heavily contaminated, more than those within the evacuation zone around Chernobyl. In response, the district's forty-eight households held a town meeting on June 28. While twenty-two of them expressed their desire to evacuate, twenty-three families chose not to do so.[30] Despite this divergence of opinions within the community, the grassroots surveillance effort made a genuine difference for all residents. Officials in Tokyo were forced to recognize the hot spots in Iwaki and pledged public assistance to the choices made by its residents to address the problem of contamination.

The inelastic use of the 20-mSv guideline was most evident in the case of school contamination in Fukushima. In Japan, a new school year begins in April. The nuclear disaster that happened on March 11 thus raised a question as to whether school should open as scheduled. The first attempt to measure contamination at school was made by a network of antinuclear, environmental, and consumer activists. Shortly after the nuclear meltdown, the Association against Old Nuclear Power Plants in Fukushima, Green Action, and the Consumers Union of Japan joined forces and shipped monitoring devices to their local partners in Fukushima. One of them was the Fukushima Conference for Recovery from the Nuclear-Earthquake Disaster led by Seiichi Nakate and two other parents. Well aware of deep concerns about the health of children, Nakate's group decided to measure radiation levels at and around schools.[31] Discovering that some of the schoolyards were heavily contaminated, it issued a public appeal at the end of March, demanding that the schools not be opened until further investigation. In response, the prefectural government surveyed more than fourteen hundred schools during the period from April 5 to 7. These measurements confirmed the allegations made by Nakate, showing that approximately 76 percent of the facilities registered external radiation levels higher than those designated as radiation-controlled areas (0.6 μSv, or microsievert, per hour).

For MEXT, however, the situation was not a "planned exposure situation" that defined the radiation-controlled areas, but an "emergency exposure situation" that justified additional exposures for children. On April 9, MEXT consulted the NSCJ about its plan to adopt 3.8 μSv per hour for the use of schoolyards. This number was based on a projected annual external radiation dose of 20 mSv, assuming an eight-hour continuous period of exposure each day. MEXT pointed out that actual doses were likely to remain well below 20 mSv.[32] Once MEXT publicized the 3.8-μSv-per-hour standard on April 19, however, this number triggered a public uproar. Parents in Fukushima complained that MEXT's guidelines led some schools to suspend or relax their decontamination efforts.[33] More important, the top-down decision to open school based on a single number created a situation in which students had no choice but to go to school. This denial of potential alternatives enraged local communities and parents striving to minimize children's exposures by all means.

MEXT grossly misread the situation by mechanically adopting 20 mSv from the manual without looking into whether it was actually justifiable and optimum in the case of schools. On April 22, the Japan Federation of Bar Associations publicly criticized the guidelines, followed by a similar protest from the Japan Medical Association. The most powerful statement against MEXT came from Toshiso Kosako, a leading radiation protection expert. On April 29, Kosako resigned his post as an adviser to the cabinet secretariat in protest against the 20-mSv guidelines. At a press conference, he argued that MEXT's reference to the "emergency exposure situation" more than a month after the accident was a "complete mistake." Pointing out that few radiation workers were allowed to receive exposure up to an annual dose of 20 mSv, Kosako declared that it was "difficult to force this number on babies, children and pupils not only from an academic point of view but also based on my humanistic ethics."[34]

The public dissent from experts like Kosako seemed to vindicate the outrage among parents in Fukushima against the imposition of the 3.8-μSv-per-hour reference. On May 1, shortly after Kosako's resignation, about 250 parents in Fukushima, including antinuclear activists, held a meeting and created the Fukushima Network for Saving Children from Radiation. This local campaign lobbied Tokyo, with the help of Diet members, to replace 20 mSv with 1 mSv, defined by the ICRP as a "normal" radiological situation. It also demanded the "rights to evacuate" that MEXT's guidelines denied.[35] This demand not only asked for compensations for voluntary evacuation but also spoke to a multitude of administrative, social, and psychological problems with which children temporarily leave school or move to a different school.[36] In the end, the national government bowed to the mounting pressure from parents in Fukushima. On May 27, MEXT announced its formal commitment to reduce exposures at school to 1 mSv through financial and technical assistance to those facilities that registered radiation levels above 1 μSv per hour.[37] By the end of August, when schools no longer showed levels over 3.8 μSv per hour, MEXT officially lowered the reference level down to 1 μSv per hour. MEXT's about-face, however, came too late to restore the lost trust among concerned parents. On July 12, the National Network of Parents to Protect Children from Radiation was formed, with its local affiliates increasing to over three hundred within the first year since the accident. MEXT's top-down radiological management based on one number thus turned concerns about children into a new antinuclear focus nationwide.

NUMBERS FOR FOOD AND WATER CONTROL

The rigid application of reference levels by the Japanese government was also evident in the case of water and food management. Soon after a radioactive plume appeared in the air, flora and fauna in Fukushima began to show concentrations of radioactive materials that were much higher than those cited in the NSCJ's 1998 guideline. The task of determining reference levels for food and drink control fell to the Ministry of Health, Labor and Welfare (MHLW). The 2003 Food Safety Basic Act provided that MHLW must consult an independent expert committee under the cabinet, the Food Safety Commission (FSC), before establishing a tolerable daily intake for any food item. The unfolding disaster, however, forced the health ministry to skip this procedure and name numbers. On March 17, with consent from the Nuclear Disaster Control Headquarters, MHLW issued an official notice that adopted the NSCJ's 1998 guideline as the "provisional regulation values": concentrations of radiocesium equivalent to an annual dose of 5 mSv (200 Bq per kilogram for milk and drinking water, 500 Bq per kilogram for all other items) and those of radioiodine equivalent to an annual dose of 50 mSv (300 Bq per kilogram for milk and drinking water, 2,000 Bq per kilogram for all other items). It was ordered that an entire lot of drinking water or food should be destroyed as a violation of the Food Sanitation Act if any sample from it exceeded the provisional values.[38]

When later consulted by the health ministry about the provisional limits, the FSC faced a serious dilemma. On the one hand, some members proposed to revise the reference value for radiocesium upward from 5 to 10 mSv. In fact, the latest ICRP recommendations regarded 10 mSv as an action-trigger line for one food item. Epidemiological studies cited by the ICRP also found no positive evidence of cancer risks in the range of 10 to 20 mSv. On the other hand, the FSC had to take into account a legal principle allowing no exposure to cancer-inducing genotoxins in food. While the US Food and Drug Administration has adopted a probabilistic risk concept (called a "virtually safe dose") since the 1990s, food control in Japan has been based on the concept of a tolerable intake. If chemicals like genotoxins fail to show a discernible cancer-inducing threshold, the tolerable intake is set at zero, which is equal to nondetectable levels defined by a standardized method of measurements. The ICRP model indicates, however, that the provisional value for food control, 5 mSv, represents not a zero cancer risk but 1 in 10,000.[39] Faced with this unprecedented situation, the FSC decided to postpone a final decision. In its interim report published on March 29, the FSC endorsed MHLW's provisional restriction limits as "standing on the safe side." It warned, however, that these limits took into account a "special and critical social situation," and that the provisional values "should not be used as a basis for risk management under normal circumstances."[40]

Despite the FSC's reservations about the provisional limits, these numbers became entrenched through the administrative control of food distribution. On March 21, the Nuclear Disaster Control Headquarters announced that the shipping of an agricultural product should be banned if a sample showed radioactivity above MHLW's provisional limits. This ban was initially applied to an entire prefecture, even when a contaminated item might be found in only part of the prefecture. This sweeping measure was in part intended to reassure consumers. But it also reflected the severe limits of administrative knowledge of the food market. The Japanese Agricultural Standard Law provided that a product label must show a prefecture of origin. This requirement made it difficult to control food shipping at subprefectural levels. The prefecturewide restriction order threatened to ruin the business of numerous farmers even far away from the disaster region. Soon the national government was forced to revise this draconian restriction. A new directive published on April 4 allowed the subprefectural designation of a shipping restriction area. It also laid out a procedure to lift the ban. If a banned product passed screening for three consecutive weeks, it would be reintroduced to the market.[41]

While food producers managed to escape the worst effects of the sweeping application of the provisional limits, consumers faced the opposite problem: the lack of choice. While food and drink contaminated above the provisional limits were to be impounded, those less contaminated were guaranteed free access to the market. This application of the provisional limits as a cutoff line was crucial not only for the normalization of food supplies but also for the reconstruction of Fukushima, where agriculture was a leading economic sector. Soon after the disaster, the "eat and support" campaign spontaneously arose as one of the grassroots relief initiatives for farmers in Fukushima. The Japanese government immediately jumped on the bandwagon, and the Ministry of Agriculture (MOA) orchestrated an official program called "Let's Support East Japan by Eating." To manage a potential clash of interest between consumers and producers, the Japanese government turned to the provisional limits as the sole standard, insisting that all food that passed an official test was practically "safe."

A singular emphasis on the government's screening program as the only basis for consumer choice unwittingly raised the stakes for its effectiveness in preventing a violation. The actual operations of food control, however, were far from ideal. In a directive dated April 4, the national government asked Fukushima and thirteen other prefectural authorities in East Japan to monitor food and drink.[42] This request initially accompanied no further assistance or guidelines required to standardize the inspection procedures. Each prefecture was forced to improvise its inspection planning, which widely varied from place to place. By early June, Fukushima prefecture had sampled 137 food items, while its neighboring Ibaraki prefecture had sampled only 24.[43] Only in June did the national government establish the timing of sampling for seafood (weekly), milk (biweekly), fresh produce (monthly), and others, unless an unusually contaminated sample, such as that exceeding 500 Bq per kilogram, was found.[44] What also hampered the performance of the official food inspection was Japan's severely limited capacity for radiological analysis. Only a few dozen officially certified laboratories for this purpose existed in Japan. Processing of samples was also slow in order to detect low-level radiation with precision. For example, it took more than one hour for a germanium-semiconductor detector to complete the analysis of one sample.[45] As a result, a backlog rapidly grew, and so did chances of overlooking unusually contaminated products.

Despite the alarming divergence between the ostensible and actual effectiveness of the official food-screening program, the Japanese government refused to take a more decentralized approach, such as aiding in additional screening by retailers and consumers. Public administrators might have feared that such an action would create a panic, but consumers worried for precisely the opposite reason: there was no means by which to know risks other than the official inspection. A poll taken during the period from May 30 to June 5 showed that, even before a series of major violations rocked the public's confidence in the government's food control, only 41.4 percent of respondents believed that food in the market was safe. In the same poll, 43.8 percent voiced concerns about whether regulation was fully enforced, and 45.9 percent suspected that the official inspection was inadequate to prevent contaminated food exceeding the provisional limits from reaching the market.[46]

As suspected by consumers, violation indeed happened. One of the most famous examples was beef contaminated with radiocesium. The source of contaminants was one that government officials in Tokyo had entirely overlooked: rice straw. The undetected spread of radiocesium through this cattle-fodder food chain was as much social as ecological. On March 19, MOA asked Fukushima and other prefectural authorities to ensure that no fodder harvested following the accident should be used. MOA, however, failed to mention rice straw in this instruction because it assumed that all straw had been stored indoors at the time of harvest. In fact, many farmers had left rice straw on fields over the winter. Laid on the ground, the straw absorbed considerable amounts of radioactive fallout. The top-down chain of command failed to correct MOA's erroneous assumption. Farmers in Fukushima, desperate to keep their cattle fed after the accident, collected the straw and used it as part of the fodder.[47] On July 8, about four months after the accident, the first cesium-contaminated beef was discovered. For the next few months, beef processed from some forty-seven hundred cattle fed on the contaminated fodder appeared in the market nationwide, except for Okinawa.[48] Unsure about the actual extent of contamination, anxious consumers stopped eating domestic beef. On July 21, MOA made a public announcement with the promise to buy up all contaminated cattle for destruction.

The "cesium-beef" scandal eventually subsided. But this incident, with other cases of violation, vindicated the suspicion among consumers that the government's food inspection program was highly inadequate. Expert critics lent further support to their conclusion. On July 27, Tatsuhiko Kodama, head of the Radioisotope Center of Tokyo University, testified in the Diet. With visible anger, he mentioned the beef problem, arguing that the government's screening program could not deal with the complex-system dynamic in which the uncontrolled release of radioactive materials in an enormous volume spread sparsely but led to high concentrations in some sites and foodstuffs. Kodama concluded his testimony by demanding that a massive "assembly line" be installed for screening all agricultural products from contaminated areas.[49] His criticism reflected the dilemma that the Japanese government created for itself: a singular emphasis on the official screening program as the only legitimate means of food control raised the bar for its expected performance impossibly high.

MAKING OF A MAGIC NUMBER

So far we have seen how government officials in Tokyo turned numerical guides for radiation protection into an administrative cutoff line that stifled local initiative and informed choice on the part of residents and consumers. The overreliance on the reference levels in radiological management, however, had a serious consequence for the Japanese government. As the numbers dictated all top-down decisions, all sides came to scrutinize their actual meaning. In a desperate attempt to restore public confidence, the expert reviews commissioned by the national government found it inevitable to lower the reference levels for decontamination and food control down to 1 mSv—the number purported to represent a "normal" situation.

The first full review was done about the provisional limits for food control. After issuing the interim report on March 29, the FSC created a working group about the health effects of radioactive materials in food. From April 21 to July 27, the group met nine times and drew up a draft report. This first reevaluation by the FSC was strongly influenced by its institutional mission as an independent scientific committee. Chairman Yasushi Yamazoe repeatedly stressed the principle of separation between scientific assessment and administrative management. "Rather than arguing whether it is OK or not," he said, "we must first ensure the assessment of risk . . . and provide reliable numbers. It is the task of an administrative office to decide, based on those numbers, what kind of countermeasures to take."[50]

This sense of mission led the working group to faithfully follow the established rule of food assessment—that is, to evaluate the cancer risks of chronic and internal exposures to each radionuclide. Radioactive elements, however, radically differed from chemicals. Estimates of radiation-induced cancer risks were based not on a specific type of radionuclide or mode of exposure but instead on a cumulative effective dose. Moreover, epidemiological data cited by the ICRP failed to prove statistically significant correlations between the range of doses below 100–125 mSv and cancer effects. To overcome this limit of scientific knowledge, the ICRP adopted the LNT hypothesis so that it could extrapolate the cancer risks of low-dose and chronic radiation exposures from the data of high-dose and instant exposures among the atomic survivors in Hiroshima and Nagasaki. One of the working group members, Chiharu Toyama, advocated a similar approach, proposing that the working group should calculate cancer risks at 100 mSv according to the LNT model. With this calculation, he said, it was possible to establish food restriction limits at an optimum balance between radiation risks and various other risks.

Yamazoe, however, opposed deviating from the established principle of food safety evaluation. The chairman maintained that the scientific basis remained too weak to legitimate the calculation of a "virtually safe dose" based on the LNT model.[51] As a result, the draft report, released on July 26 for public comments, determined intake limits only for uranium, because of its well-known chemical toxicity. While the report confirmed the scientific consensus that a cumulative effective dose of 100 or more millisieverts, excluding that from natural background, would pose health risks, it refused to calculate risks at or below 100 mSv. It was "difficult based on the evidence available," the report concluded, "to elucidate the health effects of added radiation exposures lower than 100 mSv."[52] This reticence, however, triggered a public uproar, because no reference to theoretical risks below 100 mSv created the impression that the FSC regarded 100 mSv as a threshold. The FSC received more than three thousand comments from members of the public, most of whom were highly critical of the draft report.[53] The FSC, however, refused to revise its conclusion before the final report came out on October 27.

Strong reactions to the FSC created irresistible pressure on health officials to lower the provisional limits without waiting for a formal expert review. On October 28, the day after the FSC's report was released, Health Minister Yoko Komiyama held a press conference following a cabinet meeting. She announced that the ministry had decided to cut the allowable amount of radiocesium in all foodstuffs after April 2012 from the provisional 5-mSv limit to 1 mSv (or 100 Bq per kilogram). The new guideline proposed to halve 1 mSv for milk and baby food (0.5 mSv, or 50 Bq per kilogram) and also to divide the number by a factor of 10 for drinking water (0.1 mSv, or 10 Bq per kilogram).[54]

The chief reasons for MHWL's proposal were twofold. First, 1 mSv had been long cited by the Codex Alimentarius for world food trade.[55] The ICRP and other bodies have long regarded this value the normal radiological situation: 1 mSv was thus taken to mark the lowest level below which no food control was justified. Indeed, any country refusing food that showed radioactive concentration below that based on 1 mSv would be liable for prosecution by the World Trade Organization. Adopting 1 mSv from the Codex, in short, would not only reassure consumers with a stricter standard but also allow the government to balk at a demand for further reduction.

Second, health officials were willing to embrace 1 mSv based on their belief that it would be feasible without causing much trouble. Their optimism was based on the reassuring finding reported by a subcommittee on radioactive materials under MHLW's food sanitation council. Based on the data of food inspection until the end of August 2011, the subcommittee estimated that the median value in the actual distribution of annual effective doses via food was approximately 0.1 mSv, with that number expected to decline further over time. The past inspection records also indicated that increases in violation resulting from the new 1-mSv guideline would be small. Of 8,258 samples taken from Fukushima, for example, 764 (9.2 percent) would have exceeded the proposed limits. The expected violation cases were limited to seafood, mushrooms, and wild meat. Of 52,693 samples taken outside Fukushima, only 594 (1.1 percent) would not have passed the inspection.[56]

When Minister Komiyama made an announcement about the new food inspection guideline based on 1 mSv, she denied that her remarks were intended to influence the expert review.[57] Despite her disavowal, the public reference to 1 mSv set the ground for the subsequent deliberation. On October 31, when the subcommittee on radioactive materials held its first meeting to review the proposed guidelines during a joint meeting with the committee on food sanitation, most members supported the adoption of 1 mSv without much discussion. The experts met twice more before approving the proposal on December 22. Within a week, the approved numbers were referred to the Radiation Council under MEXT. The council members were upset when mass media discussed 1 mSv as if it were decided. Their review proceeded under strong pressure, as the proposal was simultaneously open to public comments. The review received 1,877 comments during a one-month period from January 6, 2012, and an overwhelming portion, 1,449, called for even more stringent standards.[58]

A few members of the Radiation Council tried to resist the tremendous pressure for 1 mSv. Izumi Umeda argued that it was not enough to name numbers without considering actual operations. He recalled that the Radiation Council had recently approved the Ministry of Environment's number, 0.23 μSv per hour (based on an annual dose of 1 mSv) as a reference value for government assistance to decontamination. According to him, this number had already been treated in some regions as a line to defend at all costs. "Numbers have wings," he said.[59] Another member, Michiaki Kai, also complained about the trend to reduce limits as a panacea to restore public trust in the government. The proposed guideline, however, seemed to offer only a marginal effect in the actual reduction of radiation exposures. Calculations done by MHWL showed that the reduction of the food control limit for radiocesium from 5 to 1 mSv would shift the median value of the estimated actual exposures via food from 0.051 to 0.043 mSv per year.[60]

In addition to the dubious health benefit from the new number, members of the Radiation Council also pointed out that the use of 1 mSv would cause a serious problem by prolonging the time required to detect very small amounts of radionuclides. Indeed, the proposed reduction of radiocesium concentrations from 500 to 100 Bq per kilogram had the effect of lowering the screening level from 250 to 50 Bq per kilogram, with the detection limit to be halved from 50 to 25 Bq per kilogram.[61] Food inspection was far from prepared for this stringent detection standard. The Japanese government, for example, possessed only 216 germanium semiconductor detectors at the end of 2011, capable of screening a daily average of only about 660 samples during the October through November period.[62] Kai explained that the new 1-mSv standard would reduce the number of samples to be processed in a given time, which he feared would raise the risk of overlooking heavily contaminated food.[63] Indeed, as seen before, the inadequate state of inspection was responsible for the cesium-beef scandal and other violations. "In this sense," Kai argued, "1 mSv has really become a magic number. This is very unfortunate for Japan."[64]

To counter the momentum toward a lower number, the Radiation Council unsuccessfully sought to underline the principle of optimization. Chairman Otsura Niwa, who was also a key ICRP member, pointed out a serious impact that 1 mSv might have on food producers and community life. He complained that the government seemed to be changing numbers solely to create peace of mind. "Such a response leads to a vicious circle, creating the situation in which it was considered enough to lower numbers."[65] A health official who briefed the council, however, pointed out a different legal principle in operation for food safety. He explained that the Food Sanitation Act had no concept of promotion, and that its risk assessment could not take into account the interest of producers. To ensure whether the new guideline was "reasonably achievable," he continued, the health ministry was consulting with the agriculture ministry as well as the general public, including both producers and consumers.[66] "We tried hard to call for optimization, but unfortunately our advice was not taken," Niwa said in his concluding remarks at the end of the review. "When the national government uses this reference value, it has a very wide impact."[67] On February 16, 2012, with much hesitation, the Radiation Council endorsed the new food restriction limits. The guideline went into effect on April 1.

In the case of food control, the FSC, eager to defend its scientific nature, refused to name numbers for food control, only to force health officials to come up with their own. A parallel review about decontamination in the latter half of 2011 differed from the food case in that the NSCJ readily embraced a pragmatic approach and turned to the ICRP for advice. Its July 19 statement included a proposal to find an optimum level for decontamination in the lower range of 1 to 20 mSv, as recommended by the ICRP for the "existing exposure situation." The NSCJ also declared that 1 mSv should be an ultimate goal.[68] The NSCJ's proposal was then forwarded to the newly created Liaison and Coordinating Council on Contamination by Radioactive Materials. Its Working Group for the Management of the Risks of Exposure to Low-Dose Radiation held its first meeting on November 9 and conducted an intensive review until December 15. The cabinet's working group was unusual in that it included Diet members, including nuclear minister Goshi Hosono, a young and energetic figure. The working group also invited dissenting experts to the discussion. The group's openness to political concerns and expert disagreement determined the way in which it reviewed the existing 20-mSv level used for evacuation and decontamination.

At the outset, the experts in the working group were eager to discredit all allegations about biological effects of low-dose radiation not accepted by the UNSCEAR and other mainstream bodies. For example, Yoshisada Shibata, a leading radiation epidemiologist, dismissed various reports of health effects around Chernobyl as anecdotal. He declared that no health effect other than thyroid cancer among children was "scientifically proven."[69] Kazuhiko Maekawa, cochair of the working group, nodded to Shibata, arguing that what was at stake was whether to "look at things with a scientific attitude."[70] Their arguments, however, triggered harsh criticisms from Diet members in the working group. For them, the lack of positive evidence from a statistical point of view alone did not justify the outright dismissal of alarming findings as unscientific. Otohiko Endo, for example, pointed out the limits of scientific knowledge, calling upon the scientists to be "humble."[71]

The working group also invited Kodama as an expert witness. Since his highly publicized attack on the government's food inspection, Kodama had become a well-known critic. Kodama challenged the consensus among the expert members of the working group that the epidemiological method was the most "scientific" approach to the low-dose problem. Kodama, a molecular biologist, spent much time discussing DNA repair errors and other molecular-level effects of ionizing radiation. He insisted that the lack of epidemiological evidence did not mean the absence of risks.[72] Endless debate ensued between Kodama and other experts, but it had a definite effect of underlining the incomplete state of scientific knowledge. The Diet members in the committee interpreted this highlighted fact as a sufficient reason to lower a reference level out of precaution. A key figure behind this maneuver was Minister Hosono. When a draft report prepared by the cochairing experts simply noted an "opinion" calling for preventive actions to reduce exposures to low-dose radiation, Hosono insisted that such a call was not a mere opinion but consensus. "If we do not assume that everything is known in today's science," the nuclear minister said, "I think that it is reasonable to take preventive measures against low-dose exposures."[73]

Hosono's strong leadership moved the reluctant expert members toward adopting a lower number than the original 20 mSv guideline. Cochairman Maekawa agreed that scientific knowledge was not enough to dictate the government's management of low-dose radiation. Decontaminating toward an ambitiously low reference level, he said, was based on an "administrative judgment . . . beyond the reach of science."[74] In its final report issued on December 22, the cabinet committee in part echoed the FSC's conclusion that it was difficult to prove increases in cancer risks at doses less than 100 mSv. Unlike the FSC, however, the committee went further, declaring that the government should take measures to reduce risks resulting from exposure to doses less than 100 mSv based on the "safe side" of the LNT hypothesis. Based on this ICRP model, the working group declared 1 mSv as an ultimate goal for decontamination. At the same time, it proposed interim reference levels that would gradually decrease in unison with progress in the government's decontamination plan, which aimed to halve annual doses to the general public each year.[75]

CONCLUSION

The reactors have been stabilized. Reconstruction is in progress. The Fukushima accident as a radiological disaster, however, has just started, with no end in sight. If there is a lesson to be learned from this earliest stage, it is that radiation protection by numbers will backfire if national authorities abuse them as a political tool to control knowledge and decision-making. As this chapter has shown, the Japanese government consistently deployed reference levels in such a manner as to exclude backup plans and stifle local initiatives. There was no early action plan other than that based on real-time forecasts of dose levels; when SPEEDI failed, officials in Tokyo were forced to improvise, the result of which was a chaos on the ground. Even after the immediate threat of serious exposure had passed, the Japanese government continued to ground counter-measures on a combination of reference levels and centralized monitoring. The sudden announcement of planned evacuation, based on an annual projected dose of 20 mSv, forced local communities to face a stern choice of either in-definite evacuation or no assistance. The same lack of choice angered parents over the opening of schools, and also consumers over food and drink control. The most serious outcome of all, however, was that the Japanese government became a victim of its own overreliance on numbers. In their elusive quest for public trust, central officials found themselves trapped in a spiral of lowering reference levels despite severely limited capacities in radiation protection. Re-cent news reports on little progress in decontamination underline a serious mismatch between the public pledge and actual outcomes.

To avoid the peril of overreliance on numbers in a nuclear disaster, we must downscale radiation protection from the state to the regional levels and reas-sign the role of national authorities from a decision-maker to a coordinator. After all, it is what Japan routinely does regarding natural disasters. In the case of tsunami, the central government focuses on providing warnings and advi-sories, while municipal authorities take immediate actions without waiting for instructions from Tokyo. In this sense, the designation of a zone of prompt evacuation is a move in the right direction. The experience of Fukushima, however, has demonstrated the obvious: the radioactive plume never respects administrative boundaries. It is thus essential to take a regionwide approach in order to cover communities both near and far from nuclear facilities.

The tragic failure of early responses in Fukushima has also underlined the pressing need for formulating backup plans and flexible actions that do not necessarily require radiological information. While this chapter is not a place to exhaust the discussion of all possible options, one of the understudied mea-sures that local communities can readily take is public sheltering. In fact, if done at the earliest time of a crisis, it would make mass evacuation easier and speedier, while making it possible to monitor and reduce radiation exposure in the most critical phase. Sheltering, however, requires careful studies, as does evacuation. The Cold War experience with the fallout shelter has shown that the mode and degree of sheltering in each nation reflected political culture as much as financial resources and technical problems. The fallout shelter also had a cultural impact reinforcing the militarization of social space.[76] The point that I wish to make here is that we must take stock of the checkered past of nuclear disaster preparedness in order to be guarded against hidden obstacles to, and unintended consequences of, each countermeasure.

The need for decentralization also holds true for postdisaster radiological management. The success of grassroots radiological measurements in Fukushima strongly suggests that experts and citizens must work together in collecting relevant data, discussing local concerns, and exploring a range of options to choose regarding where to live and what to eat. Unlike the top-down management style, this bottom-up and interactive approach can turn people at risk into active partners to whom experts can turn for scientific information, value judgment, and resource mobilization during the postdisaster period. The experts also do not necessarily always come from the center: science teachers and college researchers in or near a disaster-stricken region, if trained, equipped, and networked, can serve as a local reservoir of expertise for municipal authorities.

The administrative reform suggested above will change little, however, unless we reconfirm the original meaning of reference levels. Facts of radiation effects at low doses are not certain enough, and values not consensual enough, for any single number to serve as a trigger for draconian action or an excuse for serious negligence. The purpose of reference levels is strictly pragmatic: a decision-making aid toward the ultimate goal of keeping radiation exposure "as low as reasonably achievable." Since what is "reasonably achievable" is a political question, the principal user of reference levels—national authorities—must be held politically accountable for justified exposure, residual risks, potential errors, and, above all, its promotion for nuclear power without preparations for a severe accident. Reference levels must not be abused to make this political decision appear purely technical—and thereby to allow those responsible for a radiological disaster to be off the hook. Only when we embrace this basic principle of justice will we be able to avoid another "man-made disaster" in the future.

NOTES

1. UN Scientific Committee on the Effects of Atomic Radiation (UNSCEAR), *Sources, Effects and Risks of Ionizing Radiation,* UNSCEAR 2013 Report to the General Assembly, vol. 1 (New York: United Nations, 2014), 6.

2. Naikakuhu Genshiryoku Hisaisya Seikatsu Shien Chiimu, "Kikan konnan kuiki ni

tsuite" [The Difficult-to-Return Zone], October 1, 2013, available at www.mext.go.jp/b_
menu/shingi/chousa/kaihatu/016/shiryo/__icsFiles/afieldfile/2013/10/02/1340046_4_2.
pdf.

3. UNSCEAR, *Sources, Effects and Risks,* 6.

4. Treaty Banning Nuclear Weapon Tests in the Atmosphere, in Outer Space and Under Water, US-UK-USSR, August 5, 1963, Preamble, available at www.state.gov/t/isn/4797.htm#treaty.

5. J. Samuel Walker, *Permissible Dose: A History of Radiation Protection in the Twentieth Century* (Berkeley: University of California Press, 2000); Spencer R. Weart, *Nuclear Fear: A History of Images* (Cambridge, MA: Harvard University Press, 1988), 312–20.

6. Blue Ribbon Commission on America's Nuclear Future, "Report to the Secretary of Energy," Washington, DC, January 2012. Also see Jacob Darwin Hamblin, *Poison in the Well: Radioactive Waste in the Oceans at the Dawn of the Nuclear Age* (New Brunswick, NJ: Rutgers University Press, 2008).

7. Fukushima Genpatsu Jiko Dokuritsu Kenshō Iinkai, *Chōsa kenshō hōkokusho* [*Research and Investigation Report*] (Tokyo: Nippon Saiken Initiative Zaidan, 2012), 44–67, 171–96; Kokkai Jikochō, *Hōkokusho* [*Report*] (Tokyo: Government of Japan, 2012), 349–79, 411–24, 431–86.

8. "ICRP Publication 103: The 2007 Recommendations of the International Commission on Radiological Protection," *Annals of the ICRP* 37, nos. 2–4 (2007): 13–14.

9. A seminal historical work on radiation protection is Walker, *Permissible Dose.* See also Soraya Boudia, "Global Regulation: Controlling and Accepting Radioactivity Risks," *History and Technology* 23, no. 4 (2007): 389–406; Gilbert F. Whittmore, Jr., "The National Committee on Radiation Protection, 1928–1960: From Professional Guidelines to Government Regulation," Ph.D. diss., Harvard University, 1986. A leading historical critique of the ICRP in Japanese is Yasuo Nakagawa, *Hōshasen hibaku no rekishi: Amerika genbaku kaihatsu kara Fukushima genpatsu jiko made* [*History of Radiation Exposures: From the Development of the American Atomic Bomb to the Fukushima Nuclear Reactor Accident*], rev. ed. (Tokyo: Akashi Shoten, 2011).

10. Donald MacKenzie, "The Certainty Trough," in *Exploring Expertise: Issues and Perspectives,* ed. Robin Williams, Wendy Faulkner, and James Fleck (Basingstoke, UK: Macmillan, 1998), 325–29.

11. Peter M. Blau and W. Richard Scott, *Formal Organizations: A Comparative Approach* (Stanford: Stanford University Press, 2003 [1962]), 228–31.

12. Adriana Petryna, *Life Exposed: Biological Citizens after Chernobyl* (Princeton: Princeton University Press, 2002).

13. For the quantification of public administration that came with the rise of a centralized state, see Theodore M. Porter, *Trust in Numbers: The Pursuit of Objectivity in Science and Public Life* (Princeton: Princeton University Press, 1995).

14. Kokkai Jikochō, *Hōkokusho,* 412.

15. Ibid., 392–93.

16. For community resistance to nuclear power in Japan, see Daniel P. Aldrich, *Site Fights: Divisive Facilities and Civil Society in Japan and the West* (Ithaca, NY: Cornell University Press, 2008), 119–51.

17. Kokkai Jikochō, *Hōkokusho*, 395–96.

18. Genshiryoku Anzen Iinkai, *Genshiryoku shisetsu tō no bōsai taisaku ni tsuite* (Bōsai shishin) [*On Measures to Prevent Accidents at Nuclear Facilities and Others (A Guide for Disaster Prevention)*] (11-03-06-01) (Tokyo: Nuclear Safety Commission of Japan, 2011), 22, 90–92.

19. "Shinwa no hateni, dai 2 bu: Meisō (4)" [After the Myth: Volume 2: Astray (4)], *Kahoku Shinpō Nyūsu*, April 22, 2012. Also see Kokkai Jikochō, *Hōkokusho*, 365–68, 380–85.

20. "Monitoring Information of Environmental Radioactivity Level," Nuclear Regulation Authority of Japan, available at http://radioactivity.nsr.go.jp/ja/.

21. Tokushū Shuzaihan, *Hotto supotto: Nettowaaku de tsukuru hōshanō osen chizu* [Hot Spot: Networked Radiation Contamination Map] (Tokyo: NHK ETV/Kōdansha, 2012), 106–9.

22. Ibid., 132–33, 158–61.

23. "Iitatemura, hinan jōken ni gaitō" [Iitate Village Qualified for Evacuation], *Asahi Shimbun*, March 31, 2011.

24. Asahi Shimbun Tokubetsu Hōdōbu, *Purometeusu no wana* [The Prometheus Trap] (Tokyo: Gakken Paburisshingu, 2012), 81.

25. "Jūmin ra tomadoi, hanpatsu: Iitate, arata ni hinan kuiki ni" [Confusion and Anger among Residents: Iitate Now Designated as Evacuation Zone], *Asahi Shimbun*, April 12, 2011.

26. "Doubting Assurances, Japanese Find Radioactivity on Their Own," *New York Times*, August 1, 2011.

27. Ibid.

28. Minutes, Teisenryō hibaku no risuku kanri ni kansuru waakingu gurūpu [Working Group on Risk Management of Low-Dose Radiation Exposure] (thereafter LCC WG), 2nd session, 16–17.

29. Asahi Shimbun Tokubetsu Hōdōbu, *Purometeusu no wana*, 78–80.

30. "Hōshasenryō takai 2 chiku setsumeikai" [Town Meetings Held at 2 Districts with High Radiation Levels], *Asahi Shimbun*, June 29, 2011.

31. Takeshi Sakagami, "Fukushima no kodomotachi o hōshanō kara mamoru tameni: '20 miri shiiberuto' tekkai o motomeru konoaida no undō" [To Protect Fukushima Children from Radioactivity: Digests on Our Campaign for the Cancellation of '20 millisievert'], n.d., available at www.jca.apc.org/mihama/News/news112/news112fukurou.pdf; Memo, "Fukushima genpatsu shinsai 28: Kōsenryo chiiki no nyūgakushiki enki o yōsei: Hōshanō sokutei purojekuto" [Fukushima Nuclear Power

and Earthquake 28: Request for the Postponement of School Entrance Ceremonies in Areas with High Radiation Levels], March 30, 2011, available at http://fukurou.txt-nifty. com/fukurou/2011/03/post-754e.html; Tokushū Shuzaihan, *Hotto supotto,* 185–86.

32. Monbukagakushō, "Hōshasen o tadashiku rikai surutameni: Kyōiku genba no minasama e" [To Understand Radiation Correctly: For Educators], April 20, 2011, available at www.mext.go.jp/component/b_menu/shingi/giji/__icsFiles/afield-file/2011/06/15/1305459_2_1.pdf.

33. "Fukushima no kodomotachi ni taisuru 20 miri shiiberuto mondai" [The 20 mSv Problem for Children in Fukushima], Fukushima Network for Saving Children from Radiation, press release, May 23, 2011, available at http://kodomofukushima. net/?page_id=81.

34. Toshiso Kosako, "Naikaku kanbō sanyo no jinin ni atatte (jii hyōmei)" [On My Resignation as an Adviser for Cabinet Secretariat (Official Resignation)], April 29, 2011, available at www9.nhk.or.jp/kabun-blog/200/80519.html.

35. "Fukushima no kodomotachi ni taisuru 20 miri shiiberuto mondai."

36. Fukushima rōkyū genpatsu o kangaeru kai and FoE Japan, "'Hinan no kenri' ni kansuru ankeeto (chūkan matome)" [Opinion Surveys Regarding "Rights to Evacuate" (Interim Summary), July 25, 2011, available at www.foejapan.org/energy/news/pdf/110725.pdf.

37. Monbukagakushō, "Fukushima-ken nai ni okeru jidō seito tō ga gakkō tō ni oite ukeru senryō teigen ni muketa tōmen no taiou ni tsuite" [On Tentative Measures for Reducing Radiation Exposure of Schoolchildren and Others at School and Other Places in Fukushima Prefecture], May 27, 2011, available at www.mext.go.jp/a_menu/saigaijohou/syousai/1306590.htm.

38. Kōseirōdōshō, "Hōshanō osen sareta shokuhin no toriatsukai ni tsuite" [On Handling Radioactively Contaminated Food], March 17, 2011, available at www.mhlw. go.jp/stf/houdou/2r9852000001558e-img/2r9852000001559v.pdf.

39. Shokuhin Anzen Iinkai, "Hōshasei busshitsu ni kansuru kinkyū torimatome" [Urgent Recommendations regarding Radioactive Substances], March 29, 2011, page 14, available at www.fsc.go.jp/sonota/emerg/emerg_torimatome_20110329.pdf.

40. Ibid., 24.

41. Kokkai Jikochō, *Hōkokusho,* 452; Genshiryoku Saigai Honbu, "Kensa keikaku, shukka seigen tō no hinmoku, kuiki no settei, kaijo no kangaekata" [Guidelines on Planning for Inspection, Items and Areas Subject to Shipping Restriction, and Its Termination], April 4, 2011, available at www.mhlw.go.jp/stf/houdou/2r98520000017tmu-att/2r98520000017ts1.pdf.

42. Kōseirōdōshō, "Nōchiku suisanbutsu tō no hōshasei busshitsu kensa ni tsuite" [On the Inspection of Radioactive Substances in Crops, Livestock, Seafood and Others], April 4, 2011, available at www.mhlw.go.jp/stf/houdou/2r98520000017txn-img/2r98520000017ze4.pdf.

43. "Hōshasen risuku o yomitoku" [To Decipher Radiation Risk], *Asahi Shimbun Globe* 65, June 19, 2011.

44. Asahi Shimbun Tokubetsu Hōdōbu, *Purometeusu no wana*, 155.

45. "Hōshasen risuku o yomitoku."

46. Shōhishachō, "Shoku no anzen ni kansuru shōhisha no ishiki chōsa kekka hōkokusho" [Report on the Investigation of Consumer Opinion Regarding Food Safety], July 2011, available at www.caa.go.jp/jisin/pdf/110715press.pdf.

47. Kokkai Jikochō, *Hōkokusho*, 457; "Shasetsu: Inawara osengyū, Nōsuishō no shissaku no tsuke" [Editorial: Cows Contaminated by Rice Straw as a Consequence of the Ministry of Agriculture's Failed Policy], *Asahi Shimbun*, August 8, 2011.

48. Kokkai Jikochō, *Hōkokusho*, 457.

49. The Lower House Committee on Health, Labor and Welfare, July 27, 2011, available at http://kokkai.ndl.go.jp/SENTAKU/syugiin/177/0097/main.html; Minutes, LCC WG, 4th session, 7.

50. Shokuhin Anzen Iinkai Waakingu Gurūpu [Working Group in the Food Safety Committee] (SAI WG), Minutes, 4th session, 26.

51. SAI WG Minutes, 9th session, 16–17.

52. Shokuhin Anzen Iinkai, "Shokuhin ni hukumareru hōshasei busshitsu no shokuhin kenkō eikyō hyōka ni tsuite" [On the Food Safety Evaluation of Health Effects Due to Radioactive Substances in Food], October 27, 2011, page 51, available at www.fsc.go.jp/sonota/emerg/radio_hyoka_detail.pdf.

53. Shokuhin Anzen Iinkai, "Shokuhin ni hukumareru hōshasei bussitsu ni kakaru shokuhin kenkō eikyō hyōka ni kansuru shingi kekka (an) ni tsuite no goiken, jōhō no boshū kekka ni tsuite" [On the Results of Public Solicitation of Opinions and Information Regarding (the Draft Report on) the Review on the Food Safety Evaluation of Health Effects Due to Radioactive Substances in Food], n.d., available at www.fsc.go.jp/iken-bosyu/iken-kekka/kekka-risk_radio_230729.pdf.

54. Kōseirōdōshō, "Komiyama daijin kakugi go kisha kaiken gaiyō" [Summary of Minister Komiyama's Press Conference following the Cabinet Meeting], October 28, 2011, 8:55 to 9:20 a.m., available at www.mhlw.go.jp/stf/kaiken/daijin/2r9852000001tghx.html.

55. Yakuji Shokuhin Eisei Shin'gikai Shokuhin Eisei Bunkakai [Subcommittee on Food Safety in the Council on Drug and Food Safety], Minutes, February 24, 2012, available at www.mhlw.go.jp/stf/shingi/2r9852000002bzxb.html.

56. Subcommittee on Food Safety, Minutes.

57. Kōseirōdōshō, "Komiyama daijin kakugi go kisha kaiken gaiyō."

58. Subcommittee on Food Safety, Minutes.

59. Hōshasen Shingikai [Radiation Council], Minutes, 116th session, November 22, 2011, available at www.nsr.go.jp/archive/mext/b_menu/shingi/housha/gijiroku/1313890.htm.

60. Subcommittee on Food Safety, Minutes, December 22, 2011, available at www.mhlw.go.jp/stf/shingi/2r98520000024g9a.html.

61. Subcommittee on Food Safety, Minutes, February 24, 2012.

62. Nihon Shōhisha Renmei, "Hōshanō osen no jishu kijun o mitomenai Nōsuishō tsūchi ni kōgi" [Protesting the Directive of the Ministry of Agriculture against Voluntary Standards Regarding Radioactive Contamination], May 14, 2012, available at http://nishoren.net/food_safety/2246.

63. Radiation Council, Minutes, 123rd session, January 17, 2012, available at www.nsr.go.jp/archive/mext/b_menu/shingi/housha/gijiroku/1316177.htm.

64. Ibid.

65. Ibid.

66. Radiation Council, Minutes, 125th session, February 2, 2012, available at www.nsr.go.jp/archive/mext/b_menu/shingi/housha/gijiroku/1316571.htm.

67. Ibid.

68. Genshiryoku Anzen Iinkai, "Kongo no hinan kaijo, hukkō ni muketa hōshasen bōgo ni kansuru kihonteki na kangaekata ni tsuite" [Basic Guidelines on Radiation Protection for the Termination of Evacuation and Reconstruction], July 19, 2011, available at www.kantei.go.jp/jp/singi/genshiryoku/dai18/18_11_gensai.pdf.

69. LCC WG, Minutes, 2nd session, 10.

70. Ibid., 11.

71. Ibid.

72. LCC WG, Minutes, 4th session, 13–20.

73. LCC WG, Minutes, 7th session, 36.

74. Ibid.

75. "Teisenryō hibaku no risuku kanri ni kansuru waakingu gurūpu hōkokusho" [Report of the Working Group on Risk Management of Low-Dose Radiation Exposure], December 22, 2011, available at www.cas.go.jp/jp/genpatsujiko/info/twg/111222a.pdf.

76. Marie Cronqvist, "Survival in the Welfare Cocoon: The Culture of Civil Defense in Cold War Sweden," in *Cold War Cultures: Perspectives on Eastern and Western European Societies*, ed. Annette Vowinckel, Marcus M. Payk, and Thomas Lindenberger (New York: Berghahn Books, 2012), 191–212; Laura McEnaney, *Civil Defense Begins at Home: Militarization Meets Everyday Life in the Fifties* (Princeton: Princeton University Press, 2000); Edward Geist, "Was There a Real 'Mineshaft Gap'? Bomb Shelters in the USSR, 1945–1962," *Journal of Cold War Studies* 14, no. 2 (2012): 3–28; Kenneth D. Rose, *One Nation Underground: The Fallout Shelter in American Culture* (New York: New York University Press, 2004).

6 Encouraging Transnational Organizational Learning

Kazuto Suzuki

Organizational learning can be defined as the process of acquiring, distributing, integrating, and creating information and knowledge among organizational members.[1] In the context of promoting nuclear safety and security, organizational learning requires not only the transfer of information and knowledge between nuclear organizations within a state but also efforts to overcome cultural, social, and political differences to promote information sharing between states. It may require changes in the beliefs or worldviews of organizational members as well as of leaders of regulatory organizations.[2] Although overcoming these barriers is difficult, transnational organizational learning is important to identifying deficiencies in nuclear safety and security regulations and practices.[3]

The objective of this chapter is to discuss why Japanese nuclear authorities have not learned from past experiences, both in Japan and other countries, and to identify how organizational learning failures led to inadequate safety and security measures in advance of the severe accident at the Fukushima Daiichi power plant in 2011. Unlike many articles and books published after 2011, this article does not aim to explain organizational learning from the Fukushima accident. The purpose of this article is to analyze why Japanese safety regulation missed opportunities to improve safety and security measures before the accident.

While there were many important indications that Japan was not prepared for a crisis of the scale of the Fukushima disaster, this chapter focuses on Japan's failure to learn from external cases, including the so-called B.5.b measures (implemented by the United States after the terrorist attacks on September 11,

2001, to secure nuclear facilities), International Atomic Energy Agency (IAEA) peer review, and the role of industry in the nuclear safety community in other countries. Although the US B.5.b measures were aimed at preventing terrorist attacks on nuclear power plants, there are many implications for general nuclear safety issues as well. The issue of IAEA peer review highlights the shortfalls of international efforts to place pressure on Japan to enact more comprehensive nuclear safety and security measures. The discussion on the role of industry suggests the different mechanism through which the nuclear safety community works in Japan and other countries.

This chapter addresses the following questions: (1) Why did Japan ignore suggestions from the United States (particularly the B.5.b clause) and the international peer community, and keep industry from playing a major role in nuclear safety measures?; (2) What could have been done to facilitate enhanced transnational organizational learning? Would it have been possible for industry, nongovernmental organizations, or international organizations to change the government's mindset?; and (3) Did the Fukushima Daiichi accident change the administrative culture and policy paradigm in Japan for nuclear safety? Will Japan's new Nuclear Regulation Authority be more open to learning from other countries' experience and practices? Will it be more open to suggestions from international and nongovernmental organizations? Answers to these questions illuminate reasons why transnational organizational learning was not successful before the accident and help us assess the prospects for future organizational learning.

INTERNATIONAL TRENDS IN NUCLEAR SAFETY REGULATIONS

The Independent Investigation Commission on the Fukushima Nuclear Accident identified "Galapagos" syndrome in nuclear safety regulation as a factor contributing to the severity of the Fukushima Daiichi accident.[4] The reference to Galapagos syndrome implies that the Japanese nuclear safety regulation regime was isolated from international standards and did not reflect up-to-date global safety protocols. Although Japanese safety authorities paid attention to those global trends and practices, they did not take actions to incorporate the guidelines into their operations. Potential explanations for Japan's Galapagos syndrome in the context of nuclear safety will be discussed below, but first this chapter examines specific cases in which Japanese safety authorities did not take positive actions despite changing global practices.

B.5.b measures

After the September 11, 2001, terrorist attacks, the United States thoroughly reviewed its security procedures for nuclear facilities. In February 2002, the Nuclear Regulatory Commission (NRC) issued an order proposing the so-called B.5.b measures on station blackout (SBO) and accident mitigation:

> Each licensee shall develop and implement guidance and strategies intended to maintain or restore core cooling, containment, and spent fuel pool cooling capabilities under the circumstances associated with loss of large areas of the plant due to explosions or fire, to include strategies in the following areas: (i) fire fighting; (ii) operations to mitigate fuel damage; and (iii) actions to minimize radiological release.[5]

Although these measures are discussed in the framework of nuclear security rather than nuclear safety, they pose strong recommendations for preventing an event such as the Fukushima Daiichi disaster.[6]

However, the B.5.b measures were not seriously discussed by the Japanese nuclear safety community, nor were they adopted into Japanese nuclear safety regulations. The Nuclear and Industrial Safety Agency (NISA) admitted in January 2012 that it had been informed by the NRC in 2002 about B.5.b measures. In 2006 and 2008, NISA officials went to the United States and were briefed in detail by NRC members about measures needed to improve nuclear safety.[7] However, there is no evidence that NISA informed operators such as the Tokyo Electric Power Company (TEPCO), owner of the Fukushima Daiichi plant; the Japan Nuclear Technology Institute (JANTI), a nongovernmental organization of nuclear safety engineers; the Atomic Energy Commission (AEC); or the Nuclear Safety Commission (NSC).

The only evidence the author could find from NISA regarding the NRC's recommendations was a brief message submitted to the Nuclear Safety and Protection Committee on the Advisory Committee for Natural Resources and Energy on March 9, 2009. The message states: "NRC of the United States has been reviewing the risk of aircraft crash and issued amendment on its regulation in February 2009. The NRC will require four important safety measures (core cooling, containment, spent fuel pool cooling capabilities, and spent fuel pool rigidity) for applications for new reactor constructors. Japan shall investigate this trend for necessary policy response in the future."[8]

This statement implies that NISA considered the B.5.b measures as designed to prepare only for aircraft collision and not other incidents, including hydrogen explosion or station blackouts as a whole. The statement also suggests that NISA was prepared to investigate NRC recommendations, but not prepared to apply those measures to Japanese safety issues. Furthermore, NISA misinformed the Nuclear Safety Committee and other relevant authorities that the B.5.b measures were applied only to new reactor construction, whereas NRC required all operating reactors to meet B.5.b requirements.

In fact, there were opportunities to include B.5.b measures in accident management (AM) procedures when the Nuclear Reactor Regulation Law (NRRL) was modified in 2005. Although the Safety Regulation Working Group in the Ministry of Education, Culture, Sports, Science and Technology (MEXT) discussed counterterrorism measures to be integrated in the new NRRL, the focus of the discussion was the internal threat posed by nuclear facility personnel. Nevertheless, as Naito's chapter in this volume explains, the measures to mitigate internal threat were not also fully implemented. Thus, recommendations aimed to improve security by strengthening background checks and monitoring capabilities. These measures were necessary to improve nuclear security in Japan but did not contribute to improved AM measures or preventing the Fukushima Daiichi accident.

IAEA Peer Review

Ignoring the B.5.b measures was not the only case in which Japanese authorities failed to implement new recommended safety measures. The Galapagos syndrome in Japan's nuclear safety regulations began much earlier. The IAEA formulated its first international safety standards, the Nuclear Safety Standards (NUSS) program, in 1974. The standards subsequently evolved after the incidents at Three Mile Island and Chernobyl.[9] While IAEA standards are not legally binding, they provide benchmarks for safety regulations and procedures. In order to increase the effectiveness of these standards, the IAEA has launched various peer review systems such as the Operational Safety Review Team (OSART), Independent Safety Culture Assessment (ISCA), International Reporting System (IRS), and Peer Review of Operational Safety Performance Experience (PROSPER). Although peer reviews can create positive political and social pressure on the reviewed states, there are a variety of obstacles for implementing review recommendations. As Washington argues, IAEA peer review lacks the legal enforcement power of the international safeguard system based on the Nuclear Non-Proliferation Treaty (NPT), for example. Also, it has a weakness as an international organization that has to take into account political and diplomatic concerns.

Since safety is primarily a domestic concern, it is difficult to place international pressure on countries that are actively pursuing domestic nuclear power—which include mostly developing countries, but also Japan up until the Fukushima Daiichi accident.[10] The only tools for enforcing review recommendations are collegiality and strong pressure from social norms. If a state like Japan ignores peer review in the name of national sovereignty and therefore prevents the implementation of the recommendations, it is unlikely that reviews will improve nuclear safety.

WANO Peer Review

After the Chernobyl accident, power plant operators worldwide pursued initiatives to improve the safety of operations. They convened a meeting in Paris in 1987 and formed the World Association of Nuclear Operators (WANO). WANO began its peer review process in 1991, with TEPCO involvement, and it conducts peer reviews of plants every six years.[11] Although WANO has been successful in improving safety and reliability as a self-regulating body, there is always a tension between industrial long-term interests in maintaining stricter safety regulations and the cost of investing in those measures. As an industrial organization, WANO was able to find the balance between cost and safety, but the contribution from Japanese operators to the peer review and standard-making processes was limited.

JAPANESE RESPONSES TO INTERNATIONAL PEER REVIEWS

Although Japanese authorities and operators were involved in international peer review processes, they did not respond properly to the groups' advice and recommendations. The IAEA implemented the OSART process for the Takahama plant Unit 3 and 4 reactors in 1988; for the Fukushima Daini plant Unit 3 and 4 in 1992; for the Hamaoka plant Unit 3 and 4 in 1995; and for the Kashiwazaki-Kariwa plant in 2004. The OSART process produced numerous recommendations for improving operational safety, but TEPCO claimed that these recommendations were already implemented and that no further action was required.[12] In 2005, TEPCO also issued a statement after receiving an OSART report on Kashiwazaki-Kariwa, citing the report's evaluation of the managers and staff at Kashiwazaki-Kariwa as "very enthusiastic in their commitment to improve the operational safety of the plant"; therefore, the statement said, TEPCO would continue to promote this behavior.[13] It is true that there was enthusiasm within TEPCO for safety improvements, but enthusiasm was eclipsed by the attitude that existing conditions were good enough to meet international standards. This attitude prevailed despite serious peer recommendations to change TEPCO's performance, including: (1) improving and integrating the monitoring of safety performance across the site; (2) review of the entire program involved in the management of safety and instituting an integrated approach; (3) enhancing preparedness for fire mitigation in the areas of fire protection organization, training, and control of combustible materials and barriers; (4) improving guidance and activities related to preventive maintenance; (5) improving the ALARA (that is, as low as reasonably achievable) radiation protection program; and (6) enhancing control of chemicals and other substances in the controlled area.[14] Although it is impossible to assess retrospectively whether OSART recommendations would have prevented the Fukushima Daiichi disaster, they would certainly have helped TEPCO to respond to the crisis.

Japan's response to the IAEA peer review—conducted by the Integrated Regulatory Review Service (IRRS)—was another lost opportunity. The IAEA carried out its review between June 25 and 30, 2007, and issued a report with recommendations for the Japanese government to review the regulatory governing system.[15] The IRRS team made the following five recommendations to improve Japanese nuclear safety governance: (1) The role of NISA, as the regulatory body, and NSC, in preparing safety guides, needed to be clarified; (2) NISA should continue to develop its efforts to address the impacts of human and organizational factors on safety in operation; (3) NISA should develop a strategic human resources management plan to face future challenges; (4) NISA should continue to foster relations with industry that are frank and open, yet formal and based on mutual understanding and respect; and (5) NISA should continue the development of its comprehensive management system.

After receiving the report and recommendations, NISA responded to the IRRS report in a press release in March 2008.[16] It stated that (1) Japan had in place a legal and administrative framework for nuclear safety. The regulatory framework had been recently modified and was evolving; (2) NISA as a regulatory agency was playing the central role for developing and coordinating elements of the regulatory framework; and (3) In order to facilitate mutual understanding and cooperation, action had been taken to improve the relationship between NISA, the nuclear industry, and other relevant authorities, and further efforts were in progress.

While the IRRS report did mention some good practices of Japanese regulatory authorities,[17] the NISA statements distorted the message from the IRRS report and repeatedly emphasized that there were no problems in Japanese nuclear safety. Furthermore, the chairman of the NSC, Atsuyuki Suzuki, issued a statement, based on the NISA's interpretation of the report, in which he thanked the IRRS team for their positive remarks. He said:

> According to the report, Japanese regulatory authorities are highly capable, in terms of international standards, and function effectively to ensure the nuclear safety. I am happy with this evaluation and its high remarks [for our program] ... The IAEA safety standards state that standards such as evaluation guidelines shall be made by the government agencies, therefore, the relationship between NSC and NISA should be clarified. It is important to explain the Japanese situation to other countries and agencies.[18]

Since the report focused on the role and capability of NISA, it is understandable that Suzuki made less specific comments on the IRRS report. However, the optimistic nature of his statement suggests that the message from the IRRS team did not reach the people responsible for nuclear safety in Japan, and the recommendations were not fully respected.

Of course, noncompliance with OSART or IRRS recommendations is not unique to Japan. For example, the OSART reports on the Philippsburg 2 and Neckarwestheim nuclear power plants in Germany mentioned instances of noncompliance.[19] However, it is important to recognize the unique elements of Japanese safety culture and the mindsets of operators and regulators that allowed them to overlook critical safety measures in the lead-up to the Fukushima Daiichi accident.

EXPLANATIONS OF THE GALAPAGOS TENDENCY IN JAPAN'S NUCLEAR SAFETY

There are various possible explanations as to why Japanese authorities ignored international trends and recommendations for nuclear safety. This section focuses on the cultural, normative, and administrative problems of Japanese nuclear issues. Although it addresses specific elements of Japanese nuclear issues, the author believes that every nuclear country's safety culture is affected in one way or another by national culture and social norms. Thus, the problems discussed here should not be considered Japan-specific.

Myth of Safety

One explanation for Japan's Galapagos syndrome is the "myth of safety":[20] the presumption that high safety standard regulations and the excellent quality of Japanese technology were enough to ensure that nuclear power plants would be 100 percent safe. The myth holds that if people assume 100 percent safety of nuclear plants, there is no need to prepare for disaster. However, the Fukushima nuclear accident revealed that this presumption was indeed a myth, and when the myth was exposed, people realized that a continued dependence on technological solutions and a lack of preparedness would make it impossible to avoid further disasters of a similar kind.

Because of the myth of safety, risk control for nuclear accidents has focused primarily on risk mitigation by improving the safety standards of the hardware. Japanese authorities investigated the safety of each piece of machinery and sought to ensure the safety of these products by a method called Probabilistic Safety Assessment (PSA).

Because the results of PSA were fairly positive for most nuclear plants, the low probability of risk was used to justify operators' lack of investment in additional safety measures. For example, Susumu Suguri, former chairman of the Reactor Safety Standard Working Group under the NSC, wrote:

> The risk of radiation exposure is as high as a road accident, so if we consider the frequency of an accident, the nuclear power plant is 10,000 times safer than driving on the road. Additionally, the Three Mile Island and Chernobyl accidents which caused complete core meltdown have different safety design from [Japanese] nuclear power plants, and therefore, these accidents cannot be used as reference to the frequency of core meltdown cases in our country.[21]

As long as the safety design was maintained and the quality of hardware remained at a high standard, the operators and regulators believed that they did not have to think about the possible scenario of a beyond-design-basis threat (BDBT) (that is, threats beyond the baseline threat that the facility is designed to withstand).

In addition to the dependence on PSA, consecutive filings of lawsuits by antinuclear movements made Japanese operators and regulators focus on the quality of hardware. A lawsuit filed in 1973 over the safety of the Ikata Nuclear Power Plant raised a number of issues that challenged the quality of the government's safety inspections. The court's judgment in 1978 confirmed that approval of nuclear reactor installations lay within the scope of government discretionary power, and the government was required during the course of the trial to produce various types of documentary evidence to prove the safety of the nuclear power plant.[22] Since then, the nuclear regulatory authorities have substantially increased the number of items to be covered during inspections, lengthened the time needed to complete inspections, and allowed the inspectors much more time and labor to produce and process the documents. Because of the 1978 ruling, the tendency to overemphasize the importance of documentation in the administration of safety regulations also grew, and the primary objective of inspections to check on compliance with safety regulations became to produce written requests to improve the safety of the hardware. The belief that nuclear accidents would not occur as long as the operators complied with rigorous paper-based inspections spread. As this kind of regulatory pattern became the widely accepted norm, the inspection of safety regulation compliance was conducted in an increasingly bureaucratic manner, and the system of securing nuclear power plant safety by improvements in microsafety became the established practice. Consequently, inspections have endlessly focused on the micromanagement of nuclear safety regulation. While this safety control system has contributed to focusing and specializing in inspecting smaller parts and subcomponents, it has at the same time spawned regulations that lack any clear means of ensuring the overall safety of nuclear plants.

Similarly, there had been a general understanding among citizens that state-of-the-art technology was safe from the beginning of the nuclear age in Japan. The view prevailed that the safety of nuclear energy could be ensured by maintaining the safety standards established in the more technologically advanced countries from which the technology was being imported.

The local municipalities in areas in which nuclear power plants were to be situated also demanded "100 percent safety." They expressed the view that "nuclear accidents themselves, let alone disasters, must never occur."[23] It was paradoxical, in light of this demand, that the government agencies, operators, and local municipalities rejected the establishment of green-belt safety zones around nuclear power plants. Local opposition to the relocation of residents within the green belt contributed to those decisions. For residents, historically inherited lands and farms were more important than efforts to reduce the risks of nuclear accidents, particularly in light of the costs that would have been associated with relocation. In other words, it was in each party's immediate interest to terminate the idea of a green belt. However, the risk of nuclear accident still existed, and in the case of an accident, those who lived near the nuclear power plants would be exposed to the most severe dangers. Thus, residents maintained the demand for 100 percent safety. In order to avoid lengthy negotiations and to speed construction of power plants, government agencies and operators asserted that nuclear power plants were completely safe, knowing that residents would accept their construction only under those terms.

Lack of Sense of Security

The second explanation for Japan's failure to faithfully adopt international nuclear safety norms is a lack of attention to nuclear security. Among the nuclear 3S's (safety, security, and safeguards), heavy attention was paid to nuclear safety and safeguards but not to security. This is partly because there was no alarming threat on nuclear material or facilities. It can be said that this mindset was due to a myth of security based on an idealistic pacifist constitution and an alliance with the United States. But more important, nuclear security was largely ignored because of the myth of safety.

For example, during a discussion about the relationship between nuclear safety and security in the Advisory Committee on Nuclear Security's technical evaluation working group in 2011 after the Fukushima Daiichi accident, one member made the following statement:

> It seems that the issue of nuclear security is, so far, considered that multilayer safety protection would be able to deal with the security situation. So, even if there was a security problem, it can be prevented by the safety measures. However, given the fact that we witnessed in Fukushima Daiichi, we have to admit that there are some issues that safety measures cannot deal with security questions.[24]

This statement is testimony that the security issue was largely neglected, or not distinguished from the safety measures. Thus, NISA did not take the B.5.b measures seriously because they might have considered the probability of a terrorist or any other kind of security threat nonexistent in Japan, and even if a security incident were to happen, safety measures would be able to deal with the situation.

Complexity of Administrative Structure and Confusion of Responsibilities

The third explanation for Japan's Galapagos syndrome is the complexity of Japan's administrative structure. First, the responsibility for nuclear safety and security was clearly separated between NISA/NSC and AEC. The AEC was responsible for nuclear safety, security, and safeguards combined when it was established in 1956. However, when the NSC was separated from the AEC in 1978, the responsibility for nuclear safety was moved to NSC, while AEC remained responsible for nuclear security and safeguards. Thus, it would be understandable that NISA and NSC did not take the B.5.b measures seriously, as they may also fall into the AEC's jurisdiction. Although NISA was mandated to improve security measures, its focus was on preventive measures for fire and other on-site accidents. It was not clear who should be in charge in the case of sabotage or large-scale explosion, as B.5.b assumes. Yet when NISA was informed about B.5.b measures by the US NRC, this complex administrative arrangement was not fully explained. Also, there was no evidence that NISA had informed AEC about these measures. Thus, the problem lay not just in the complexity of the responsibilities but also in the lack of communication between these authorities.

Second, even for nuclear safety, the share of responsibility between NISA and NSC was not clear, as the IRRS report made evident. NISA was expected to be the regulatory agency, and the NSC was responsible for double-checking NISA's work and providing safety guidelines to NISA. This type of duality of responsibility often blurs accountability. NSC would have considered that the B.5.b measures or IRRS recommendations should be interpreted and implemented by NISA, whereas NISA might have thought that they had no compliance obligation unless NSC asked them to respond.

The complication of this regulatory system was certainly not an ideal formula for governmental supervision and did not comply with international best practice. The IAEA repeatedly expressed its concerns to Japanese regulators, including through the aforementioned IRRS report. As far as major civil nuclear countries are concerned, Japanese regulatory governance was extraordinarily complicated. However, it should be noted that even in countries with simplified regulatory systems, misunderstanding over who-does-what-in-which-situation could happen.

The 1986 Chernobyl accident prompted many nuclear states to stress "constant improvement in safety" in their cultural, normative, and administrative frameworks. However, that did not happen in Japan, because of the reasons discussed above. The regulators, operators, and Japanese public shared the understanding that Chernobyl was an isolated accident that would never occur in Japan because of the differences in work ethic, technical specificities (Japan has no Chernobyl-type RBMK reactors), and technological excellence. This led Japan to be isolated from global trends of "constant improvement in safety" and to maintain the "myth of safety."

CAN POST-FUKUSHIMA REFORM CHANGE THE POLICY PARADIGM?

The Fukushima Daiichi accident changed the culture and perceptions of nuclear safety in Japan. The myth of safety has been dismantled as people realize that 100 percent safety cannot be guaranteed. The complicated administrative structure has also been reformed: NSC and NISA, together with the nuclear security and safeguard functions in MEXT, have been integrated into a newly established Nuclear Regulation Authority (NRA) under the Ministry of Environment. This change has simplified decision-making processes and clarified who is in charge in times of crisis.

The NRA was established in September 2012 following lengthy discussions about how to incorporate the lessons of the Fukushima Daiichi accident and create a more effective administrative system. It is too early to judge the extent to which the NRA has changed the old policy paradigm on nuclear safety and security, but there are several points that can be identified in the aftermath of the Fukushima Daiichi accident.

First, although the myth of safety has been heavily criticized, it still prevails in the mindsets of Japanese politicians and bureaucrats. When Prime Minister Noda decided to restart Oi nuclear plant's Units 3 and 4, he highlighted that the reactors had passed a so-called stress test based on an EU model but originally designed by NISA, and, therefore, had been proven safe. He emphasized that the health of the reactors was good enough to reopen them, so there was no reason to worry about a catastrophic disaster similar to that of Fukushima Daiichi. In other words, passing a stress test provided an excuse to bypass contingency plans and any further discussion of a possible accident or security threat.

However, the chairman of the NRA, Shunichi Tanaka, initiated a discussion about accident management (AM) measures in the case of severe accident or terrorist attack. The draft of new AM measures submitted in March 2013 takes B.5.b measures into account. Furthermore, the NRA is charged by the cabinet-level Nuclear Disaster Prevention Council to draft a nuclear accident response manual to reengineer the existing crisis response system and make it more effective. These new measures and manuals will take into account the lessons of Fukushima Daiichi as well as various recommendations from the IAEA and B.5.b measures. It took a large-scale disaster for the Japanese authorities to realize the failures and shortfalls of their nuclear safety and security regulatory system.

Although improving institutional arrangements and preparing emergency manuals are necessary for improving Japanese nuclear safety and security standards, they are not sufficient. What became clear through the Fukushima Daiichi accident was that even if manuals and institutional arrangements exist, leaders and emergency responders dealing with crises must be able to implement proper responses. The Diet-sponsored Fukushima Nuclear Accident Independent Investigation Commission stated that the accident was "made in Japan" and "a man-made disaster."[25] Understanding the mindset of officials, operators, engineers, and politicians is crucially important. Before the Fukushima Daiichi accident, the mindsets of these people were strongly influenced by the myth of safety, and there are some doubts that the myth has entirely disappeared.

As discussed above, the myth of safety was not created solely by those who wanted to promote nuclear energy but also by those who wanted to accept the nuclear power plants. The demand for 100 percent safety assurance was the driving force behind the myth. The reason PM Noda emphasized plant health before reopening Oi plant Units 3 and 4 was to meet this popular demand. It can also be said that the antinuclear movement after the Fukushima Daiichi accident was a mirror image of the myth of safety because the demonstrators' demand was to abort restarting any nuclear plants and eventually decommission all of them, based on the idea that nuclear plants should be 100 percent safe and that the Fukushima Daiichi accident proved that the government and operators could not make such a guarantee. As long as people demand 100 percent safety, the operators, regulators, and politicians have only two choices: either decommission all nuclear plants or convince the population that nuclear power plants are completely safe. This dilemma reinstates the myth of safety in nuclear safety regulation.

The current debate on the authorization process for restarting idle nuclear reactors represents the difficulty of implementing new regulations in the current political and social environment. The debate centers on who will give the final authority for restarting nuclear reactors. The NRA says that it should be the government, since the procedure requires the consent of local residents, while the government considers a green light on safety from NRA as adequate final authorization. On the one hand, the NRA understands that the nuclear safety regulation should not be limited to assessments of the health of hardware and plants, but should be extended to preparation for a severe accident. On the other, government, vis-à-vis popular demand for 100 percent safety, still wants to present an image that nuclear technology is safe, and therefore restarting plants should be based on technological assurances that reactors present no need for people to prepare for accidents.

The Fukushima Daiichi accident has changed people's consciousness about nuclear safety. Four commissions carried out extensive investigations into the incident (government-sponsored, Diet-sponsored, TEPCO-sponsored, and independent investigations), which received wide coverage by newspapers and journalists. These investigations revealed extensive deficiencies in Japan's nuclear safety regulations and the lack of attention to nuclear security. Thus, the post-Fukushima nuclear regulatory system took the findings of the investigations seriously and tried to address as many of their concerns as possible. In that context, B.5.b measures and nuclear security issues attracted attention.

However, the myth of safety has not gone away. This myth is widely shared among academics, operators, engineers, politicians, and most of all, the general public. Although people no longer subscribe to the idea that nuclear plants are safe, the mindset of demanding 100 percent safety has not changed. This mindset remains the cultural and conceptual problem for transnational organizational learning.

ORGANIZATIONAL LEARNING AT THE INDUSTRIAL LEVEL

Organizational learning can also occur at the industrial level. In the United States, the Institute of Nuclear Power Operations (INPO), which was created after the Three Mile Island accident, has been very important for promoting higher levels of safety and reliability in the operation of commercial nuclear power plants. In order to achieve its goals, INPO works to establish performance objectives, criteria, and guidelines for the nuclear power industry; conducts regular, detailed evaluations of nuclear power plants; and provides assistance to help nuclear power plants continually improve their performance. Certainly, Japanese operators were fully aware of the work of INPO through the World Association of Nuclear Operators, which was created to maximize the safety and reliability of nuclear power plants worldwide by providing a forum for operators to assess, benchmark, and improve performance through mutual support, exchange of information, and emulation of best practices. In 2005, Japanese operators established the Japan Nuclear Technology Institute (JAN-TI) as a sister organization of INPO and corresponding partner to WANO;

the newly-established organization sought to achieve high levels of safety and the world's highest level of operating performance. Some unique features of JANTI's "Action Principle" statement distinguished JANTI from other organizations such as INPO. The first principle was "JANTI shall comply with laws and regulations as a member of society, and act according to the ethics of engineers." The principle suggested that JANTI regarded the ethics of engineers as a foundation of nuclear safety, and compliance with laws and regulations a societal role, implying that the corporate operators could fulfill their duties as long as they followed laws and regulations. The second principle was "JANTI shall continue to enhance its own safety culture." This principle suggested that JANTI regarded safety culture as not universal, but unique to each country, so that it might not adopt international norms for nuclear safety. The third principle was "JANTI shall maintain a third-party standpoint that is independent of its members," which suggested that it would take an objective and neutral position. However, this principle also suggested that JANTI would not intervene with member corporations' practices and would perhaps leave them alone even if it identified deficiencies in their safety measures. Finally, the action statement said, "JANTI shall value the exchange of opinions and partnerships with related organizations." This suggested that JANTI valued exchange of ideas, but not necessarily critical peer review or other independent review processes. Compared with the principles and practices of INPO, JANTI did not put sufficient pressure, without effective peer reviews, on operators to improve their safety measures and practices, and operators did not pay attention to the activities of JANTI. Although lack of such pressure was not the direct cause of the Fukushima Daiichi accident, efforts to promote organizational learning would have helped improve TEPCO's capabilities and in turn its ability to respond to the accident.

After the Fukushima Daiichi accident, JANTI was dissolved and transformed into the Japan Nuclear Safety Institute (JANSI). Although the mission of JANSI is no different from that of JANTI—to make the Japanese nuclear power industry the world's safest—the way in which JANSI tries to achieve that goal is different. JANSI emphasizes that operators should engage in improving safety though a comprehensive approach (as opposed to the microsafety approach) and should avoid self-centered safety activities. A mechanism will be created for independent technical evaluation, the results of which will be shared with operators. In other words, before the Fukushima Daiichi accident, JANTI did not have such an independent technical evaluation mechanism.

Despite the transformation from JANTI to JANSI, Japan's nuclear operator structure has not changed since the Fukushima Daiichi accident. The system of regional monopolies on power generation and distribution is still jealously protected. Although the government's indecision on energy and nuclear policy issues has prevented operators from restarting nuclear power plants, which eventually has led to higher dependence on expensive fossil fuel power generation, operators maintain the existing systems of regional monopoly despite government efforts to introduce changes to break down this monopoly. Thus, operators in Japan are neither competitors nor collaborators in business. They coexist but independently manage their own resources and facilities. For non-TEPCO operators, the tragedy of the Fukushima Daiichi accident is "TEPCO's problem, not ours," which reflects their belief that it is unfair for them to be prevented from restarting nuclear reactors when they played no role in TEPCO's problems. Operators face the joint need to improve safety measures, but more strongly, they share an interest in maintaining the low cost of nuclear safety. Since most operators, including TEPCO, face huge financial challenges as a result of heavy reliance on imported natural gas, coal, and oil, they are not enthusiastic about investing in nuclear safety measures at any cost. As long as regional monopoly systems are protected, entities do not have to compete with other sources of energy, and other operators. This has led to suspicion that JANSI is not a completely different organization from JANTI.

CONCLUSION

Organizations are groups of people with a history of working together under certain procedures and rules with shared task objectives and meanings. Organizations have collective memories and cognitive systems even when the members and leaders change. They preserve certain ways of thinking and understanding issues, norms, and values.[26] Because each organization has its own culture, norms, and values,[27] it can be difficult to transfer know-how, experience, knowledge, and norms to other organizations even within the same cultural environment. In other words, it can be very difficult for an organization in one country to learn from a foreign organization's experience, even if the organizations share similar technical knowledge or functional expertise.[28]

Nevertheless, the time is ripe for Japan to learn from the experiences of others. Although the myth of safety still remains the dominant mindset of the politicians and general public, regulators and operators have learned that they must be prepared for any accident. The new initiative for including B.5.b and other security measures for existing reactors taken by Shunichi Tanaka, NRA chairman, opens many opportunities for incorporating the ideas and practices of other countries, such as B.5.b measures, and recommendations from IAEA peer review reports.

It is too early to tell how the culture of the NRA will develop, but given the number of activities for which the NRA is responsible, it is expected that there will be more agency-to-agency transnational learning to improve nuclear safety and security. However, cultural and normative acceptance of new initiatives by the NRA will likely be a challenge. The myth of safety may prevail, and NRA initiatives may therefore not receive enough political or public support. In fact, Tanaka's appointment took an unnecessarily long time because there were objections from the public and opposition parties that he was one of the members of the "nuclear village" responsible for the Fukushima Daiichi accident.

This chapter predicts that organizational learning will occur because the newly created NRA is hungry to learn from the lessons of the accident and the recommendations from other countries, the IAEA, and industry. However, under the current political circumstances, in which the government cannot decide when to restart idle nuclear reactors nor who will make the decision, it is hard to accurately predict the future of Japanese nuclear policy and the NRA's role in it. Perhaps, for a young organization like the NRA, this is an ideal time for learning and to incorporate international norms on nuclear safety. If the NRA is successful in creating a new culture and norms for nuclear safety, it has the potential to change the mindset of politicians and the general public. If that occurs, Japan will become a new model of nuclear safety best practices and will be able to lead other countries in Asia, where an increasing number of countries show interest in using nuclear power.

NOTES

1. Nancy M. Dixon, *Organizational Learning Cycle: How Can We Learn Collectively*, 2nd ed. (Aldershot: Gower Publishing, 1999).

2. Jack S. Levy, "Learning and Foreign Policy: Sweeping a Conceptual Minefield," *International Organization* 48 (1994): 279–312.

3. Chris Argyris, *On Organizational Learning*, 2nd ed. (Oxford: Blackwell, 1994).

4. Independent Investigation Commission on Fukushima Nuclear Accident, "Report of Investigation and Verification, March 2012," esp. ch. 11.

5. US Nuclear Regulatory Commission Regulation, Title 10, Code of Federal Regulations (10 CFR), Sec. 50.54, Conditions of Licenses, para. (hh)(2), available at www.nrc.gov/reading-rm/doc-collections/cfr/part050/part050-0054.html.

6. This understanding has been unanimous among all accident investigation commissions.

7. "NISA Knew US Accident Measures: Did Not Tell TEPCO," *Asahi Shimbun*, January 27, 2012, available at www.asahi.com/special/10005/TKY201201260723.html.

8. Minutes of 29th meeting of the Nuclear Safety and Protection Committee, the Advisory Committee for Natural Resources and Energy, March 9, 2009, available at www.meti.go.jp/committee/summary/0002400/gijiroku29.html.

9. "An Overview of the Nuclear Safety Standards (NUSS) Programme," *IAEA Bulletin* 21, nos. 2/3 (1979).

10. Monica J. Washington, "The Practice of Peer Review in the International Nuclear Safety Regime," *New York University Law Review* 430 (May 1997): 430–69.

11. "Peer Reviews," World Association of Nuclear Operators, available at www.wano.info/programmes/peer-reviews/. The author did not have access to individual peer review reports.

12. "TEPCO Says It Has Cooperated with IAEA on OSART Findings," *Nucleonics Week*, October 10, 2002.

13. "The Result of IAEA's OSART Evaluation," Tokyo Electric Power Company, available at www.tepco.co.jp/kk-np/nuclear/pdf/17060901.pdf.

14. International Atomic Energy Agency (IAEA), "Report of the Operational Safety Review Team (OSART) Mission to the Kashiwazaki Kariwa Nuclear Power Plant, Japan, 1–17 November 2004," IAEA-NSNI/OSART/04/127.

15. IAEA, "Integrated Regulatory Review Service (IRRS): Report to the Government of Japan, 25–30 June 2007, December 2007," available at www.nsr.go.jp/archive/nisa/genshiryoku/files/report.pdf.

16. "About IRRS Report," NISA/METI news release, March 14, 2008, available at www.nsr.go.jp/archive/nsc/anzen/shidai/genan2008/genan018/siryo18-2.pdf.

17. Three points were mentioned in the report: (1) NISA's relationship management program is well structured and comprehensive; (2) The regulations and standards to be applied for licensing and approval applications have been clearly stated; (3) The operating experience for major events has been thoroughly investigated and appropriate countermeasures have been enforced on the licensees.

18. Atsuyuki Suzuki, "Comment by the Chairman on IAEA/IRRS Evaluation Report," March 17, 2008, available at www.nsr.go.jp/archive/nsc/anzen/soki/soki2008/genan_so18.pdf.

19. IAEA, "Report of the Operational Safety Review Team (OSART) Mission to the Philippsburg-2 Nuclear Power Plant Germany, 9–28 October 2004," IAEA-NSNI/OSART/04/126; IAEA, "Report of the Operational Safety Review Team (OSART) Mission to the Neckarwestheim Nuclear Power Plant Germany, 8–24 October 2007 and Follow-up Visit 11–14 May 2009," IAEA-NSNI/OSART/07/142F.

20. T. N. Srinivasan and T. S. Gopi Rethinaraj, "Fukushima and Thereafter: Reas-

sessment of Risks of Nuclear Power," *Energy Policy* 52 (January 2013): 726–36; Norimitsu Onishi, "'Safety Myth' Left Japan Ripe for Nuclear Crisis," *New York Times*, June 24, 2011; Jonathan Soble, "Beware the Safety Myth Returning to Japan's Nuclear Debate," *Financial Times*, July 13, 2014; Johannis Nöggerath, Robert J. Geller, and Viacheslav K. Gusiakov, "Fukushima: The Myth of Safety, the Reality of Geoscience," *Bulletin of Atomic Scientists*, May 30, 2013; The Independent Investigation Commission on the Fukushima Nuclear Accident, *The Fukushima Daiichi Nuclear Power Station Disaster: Investigating the Myth and Reality* (London: Routledge, 2014).

21. Susumu Suguri, "How Safe Is Nuclear Power Generation?" *Nuclear System News* 15, no. 4 (March 2005), available at www.enup2.jp/newpage38.html.

22. Legal Defense Counsel, *Atomic Energy and Social Dispute on Safety: Criticism of Ikata Nuclear Plant Court Decision*, Report, Nuclear Energy Technology Research (Tokyo: Technology and Humanity, 1979, in Japanese).

23. Naoya Sekiya, "Sociopsychological Analysis relating to 'Views on Nuclear Safety': The Formation and Collapse of the Nuclear Safety Myth," JNES Survey Research on Japanese View of Safety, JNES, 2004.

24. Minutes of the Technical Evaluation Working Group of Advisory Committee on Nuclear Security, August 23, 2011.

25. See Message from the Chairman, in "Official Report of the Fukushima Nuclear Accident Independent Investigative Commission," National Diet of Japan, Tokyo, 2012, available at http://warp.da.ndl.go.jp/info:ndljp/pid/3856371/naiic.go.jp/en/.

26. Bo Hedberg, "How Organizations Learn and Unlearn," in *Handbook of Organizational Design*, vol. 1, ed. Paul C. Nystrom and William H. Starbuck (Oxford: Oxford University Press, 1981).

27. Scott D. N. Cook and Dvora Yanow, "Culture and Organizational Learning," *Journal of Management Inquiry* 2, no. 4 (December 1993): 368.

28. Barbara Levitt and James G. March, "Organizational Learning," *Annual Review of Sociology* 14 (1988): 319–40.

PART III: Lessons Learned about Lessons Learned

7 Were Japan's Nuclear Plants Uniquely Vulnerable?

Phillip Y. Lipscy, Kenji E. Kushida, and Trevor Incerti

INTRODUCTION

Most existing studies of the Fukushima disaster have singled out failures specific to Japan. These include inadequacies in Japan's nuclear regulatory structures,[1] insufficient disaster preparedness,[2] and even culture.[3] However, these conclusions are based primarily on the outcome at a single plant, Fukushima Daiichi. Without domestic and international comparisons, it cannot be established that problems specific to Japan were responsible for the disaster.

The question, put bluntly, is whether Japan was uniquely unprepared, or whether it had the bad luck of being the first country to have a nuclear power plant (NPP) overwhelmed by an earthquake and tsunami. The nature of the Fukushima disaster lends itself to a comparative, quantitative approach that was not possible for prior disasters such as Chernobyl and Three Mile Island, which were triggered by human and technical failures. The Tohoku earthquake and tsunami affected several nuclear plants simultaneously, offering a natural experiment of disaster preparedness. In addition, although disaster response in Japan had many failings, we will show that three variables were crucial at the initial stage of the crisis: plant elevation, seawall elevation, and location and status of backup generators. If the Fukushima Daiichi plant had maintained higher elevations for any of these three variables, or if the backup generators had been watertight, the disaster would likely have been much less serious. This observation allows us to perform a much broader comparative study based on the status of these three variables—assessed against plausible tsunami risk— not only for all nuclear plants in Japan but also for all seaside nuclear power plants in the world.

The ultimate goal of this research project is to determine what we can learn about nuclear politics and regulation by looking across cases within Japan and across countries. As a first step, we use data from all nuclear power plants within and outside Japan that lie next to the ocean, putting the Fukushima disaster in international context through a comparative approach.

The March 11, 2011, earthquake and tsunami affected four plants: Fukushima Daiichi (INES 7), Fukushima Daini (INES 3), Onagawa (INES 1), and Tōkai Daini.[4] The plants and reactors in which either off-site power or on-site backup electricity generation capacity survived avoided core meltdowns. Those that lost both—Fukushima Daiichi Reactors 1–3—suffered meltdowns.

This paper unfolds in two parts. Part I is a within-country comparison of the four nuclear power plants along the northeastern Japanese seaboard affected by the March 11, 2011, earthquake and tsunami. Comparing the damage among them, it is clear that securing external electric power and on-site backup electric power sources were critical. External power sources were compromised as a result of the earthquake, while backup power sources were damaged by the tsunami. The reactors losing both external and backup power incurred meltdowns. The findings in Part I allow us to identify several key variables with which we conduct a broader, cross-national analysis.

Part II presents analysis on a dataset of nuclear power plants around the world. The data include information on eighty-nine nuclear power plants in twenty countries, collected from publicly available sources as well as directly from plant operators. Using this data, we provide a cross-national comparison of NPP design features at the time of the Tohoku earthquake, particularly focusing on plant elevation, seawall height, and generator status and elevation. We then compare these features against recorded historical wave heights. Our results indicate that Japan was relatively unprepared for a tsunami disaster in international comparison, but there was considerable variation within Japan, and Japan was not the only vulnerable country.

Our data also produce several novel findings about nuclear power plants in Japan. Within Japan, plants constructed earlier, irrespective of subsequent improvements, tended to be underprotected against tsunami. In addition, plants owned by the largest utility companies exhibited particularly inadequate disaster preparations, while those owned by smaller utility companies were in line with the international average.

PART I. JAPANESE PLANTS AFFECTED BY THE DISASTER: IDENTIFYING KEY VARIABLES

The tsunami that hit northeastern Japan offers a natural experiment in disaster preparedness. Four plants were simultaneously hit by the earthquake and tsunami. The four plants were Fukushima Daiichi, Fukushima Daini, Onagawa, and Tōkai Daini. While it is well known that Fukushima Daiichi was declared an INES Level 7 event, Fukushima Daini was declared Level 3, and Onagawa a Level 1 event. As we will illustrate, Fukushima Daiichi and Onagawa encountered almost identical seismic and tsunami hazards with a wide disparity in outcomes, while the hazards for Fukushima Daini and Tōkai were somewhat less serious.

Comparing Damage across Japanese Plants

A comparison across the four reactors hit by the tsunami reveals the critical importance of procuring electricity, either from external or backup sources. The plants required pumps to cool the reactors, and these pumps required electricity. (In some cases, backup electricity generators required cooling pumps as well.)

In the simplest comparison, the plants and reactors in which either external or backup sources of power were operational survived without core meltdowns. Those that lost both—Fukushima Daiichi Reactors 1–3—suffered meltdowns. External power sources comprised the power lines from the plant to the external electricity grid, along with the transformer facilities. Backup power sources included emergency diesel generators (EDGs), batteries, generator trucks, and the transmission/transformer facilities. Table 7.1 shows the external and backup power situation after the earthquake and tsunami hit, along with the INES disaster level.

TABLE 7.1: Damage and INES Level of Four Japanese NPPs Hit by Earthquake and Tsunami

	Tsunami Height	Seawall Height	Plant Height	EDG Height	Distance from Epicenter	Maximum Gal	Surviving Off-site Power Lines	Surviving EDGs	INES Level
Fukushima Daiichi	13m	10m	10m	10m	180km	550 Gal	0/6	1/13	7
Fukushima Daini	9m	9m	12m	12m	190km	305 Gal	1/4	3/12	3
Onagawa	13m	14m	13.8m	13.8m	70km	607 Gal	1/5	6/8	1
Tōkai	4.6m	6.1m	8m	8m	280km	214 Gal	0/3	2/3	0

External power loss was primarily caused by the earthquake, which knocked down power lines and destroyed conversion facilities. In fact, while Fukushima Daiichi and Tōkai lost all external power sources, those of Fukushima Daini and Onagawa barely survived. Fukushima Daini and Onagawa lost three out of four, and four out of five power lines, respectively; only one line remained at each plant. In Fukushima Daini in particular, external power was critical for operating the limited number of backup power sources available.[5]

While the earthquake severed off-site power lines, the tsunami was the crucial factor that led to disaster. The tsunami not only directly damaged some of the backup power sources, such as diesel generators and batteries through flooding and debris, but also knocked out many of the seawater pumps required to cool the diesel generators, rendering them inoperable. Only a few diesel generators were air-cooled, and in some cases, such as at Fukushima Daiichi Reactor 6, these were the only types that survived.

Fukushima Daiichi lost twelve of thirteen EDGs.[6] As a result, Reactors 1, 2, 3, and 4 could not be cooled, leading to the meltdowns in Reactors 1–3. The plant's one functional generator cooled Reactors 5 and 6, undergoing maintenance at the time.

At Fukushima Daini three of twelve EDGs survived the tsunami, enabling Reactors 3 and 4 to be cooled until the surviving off-site power lines were rerouted. At Onagawa, six of eight EDGs remained intact. Tōkai Daini lost all off-site power for two days, but the survival of two of three EDGs enabled the reactor to be cooled until off-site power was restored.[7]

Off-site power can be severed by a variety of events, such as terrorism, tornadoes, and earthquakes. During such events, maintaining the integrity of on-site backup power is crucial. The Tōkai Daini NPP illustrates this point—the plant experienced a complete loss of off-site power but achieved cold shutdown because most EDGs survived the tsunami.

In the Japanese NPPs, off-site power was compromised as a result of the earthquake, while on-site backup power sources were damaged by the tsunami.[8] Comparing the plants affected by the tsunami shows a clear variation in plant height and seawall height relative to the tsunami (see Table 7.1). The Onagawa power plant's 14-meter seawall height was adequate for a 13-meter tsunami, the same height as the tsunami that overwhelmed the 10-meter seawall at Fukushima Daiichi.

Although the height of the tsunami was below plant elevation at Fukushima Daini, the plant was partially flooded as water reached as high as 14.5 meters in one area as a result of local geography.[9] Tōkai Daini was partially flooded by a 4.6-meter tsunami, as its 6.1-meter seawall was being retrofitted at the time and was not watertight.[10]

Securing external power sources in the face of potential disasters is clearly a critical issue. Yet, given the potential for tornados, terrorism, or major natural disasters such as the March 11 earthquake to sever external power lines, the security of backup power sources is of paramount importance. The Tōkai Daini reactor is the clearest example of this point, having incurred a complete loss of external power but safely completing a cold shutdown by utilizing its surviving backup power sources. The Higashi Dōri nuclear power plant in Aomori prefecture also lost all external power in the magnitude 7.1 aftershock on April 7, 2011. The backup diesel generators were operational, however, and the incident did not become serious.

A simple comparison of the plants affected by the tsunami shows a notable divergence in plant height and seawall height. Table 7.1 compares the recorded tsunami height at each plant to the seawall height and plant height. It is clear that the Onagawa power plant was adequately prepared for the events that unfolded, with a seawall height of 14 meters in place against a 13-meter tsunami. The 13-meter tsunami in Fukushima Daiichi overwhelmed the 10-meter-high seawall, and the 9-meter tsunami flooded part of the Fukushima Daini plant. The experience of Tōkai Daini revealed that quality was important as well, since retrofitting construction led to the seawall's not being completely watertight, resulting in flooding and the loss of one backup generator, despite the 4.6-meter tsunami being lower than the 6.1-meter seawall.

From this comparison of within-Japan variation of power plants affected by the March 11, 2011, earthquake and tsunami, it is clear that three variables were critical in contributing to the initial stages of the nuclear catastrophe at Fukushima: (1) plant height, (2) seawall height, and/or (3) EDG height, or adequate waterproofing of EDGs. Higher plant elevation would have prevented the tsunami from damaging the plant's critical systems, including the EDGs, which were located at an elevation equivalent to plant height. The tsunami would likewise not have reached the EDGs if the seawall protecting the plant had been taller, or the generators had been placed at higher elevations.[11] With the seawater pumps required for cooling destroyed by the tsunami, the availability of backup power to start the emergency cooling system became critical.[12] Because of low plant height, seawall height, and EDG height, both the primary and secondary cooling systems were compromised, leading to disaster.

PART II. DATA AND ANALYSIS: PLANT CHARACTERISTICS AND TSUNAMI RISK

Based on these observations about Fukushima Daiichi and other Japanese plants affected by the tsunami, we conducted a comparative analysis of tsunami preparedness at global coastal NPPs. We collected data for the following variables: base plant elevation, seawall height, emergency power system elevation, waterproofing of backup power systems, commission date, reactor type, maximum water height, and Soloviev-Imamura (S-I) tsunami intensity. Since our goal is to compare disaster preparedness at the time of the Tohoku earthquake, all data refer to NPP infrastructure as it existed prior to March 11, 2011.

Variables and Methodology

Base plant elevation is a measure of the height of critical components of the NPP above mean sea level. As seen in the previous section, elevation above sea level is a primary determinant of an NPP's risk of tsunami inundation. We typically measure elevation at the base of the reactor building. However, where components deemed critical for reactor operation or safe shutdown are located at elevations lower than the reactor building, the lower elevation is recorded. Primary sources for elevation data include national nuclear regulatory agencies, the International Atomic Energy Agency (IAEA), European stress tests conducted in response to the Fukushima disaster, and primary source information from nuclear plant operators.

Seawall height is similarly recorded as the maximum height of a seawall, flood barrier, levy, or natural barrier (such as sand dunes or barrier islands) above mean sea level. In the event that a plant does not posses a seawall or other barrier, or the barrier in question is not designed for protection against tsunami or storm surge, the height is recorded as zero. Sources are identical to those used in determining base plant elevation.

Emergency power system elevation is a measure of the elevation of critical backup power supply systems above mean sea level. These systems include emergency diesel generators, gas turbine-driven generators, and battery systems. Data sources for emergency power system location include national nuclear regulatory agencies, the IAEA, European "stress tests," and primary source information from plant operators. However, in some cases, we found that this information is not publicly available on national security grounds.

Because emergency power system preparedness is determined by flood protection in addition to elevation, waterproofing of emergency power supplies is also noted. Specifically, this is an assessment of whether emergency power systems are located behind flood-proof doors or in watertight bunkers. This is recorded as a dichotomous variable (1 for yes, 0 for no). Sources are identical to base plant elevation and seawall height, with greater relative reliance on information collected directly from power operators and regulators.

Construction and commission dates refer to the dates construction was initiated and the reactor became commercially operational. Where reactors have been decommissioned or are currently undergoing decommissioning, the decommissioning date is also noted.

Reactor type refers to classification of the NPP's reactor(s) by type of nuclear reaction, moderator material, coolant, and use. Construction, decommissioning, and reactor type information is provided by the IAEA.

Maximum water height is a measurement of the maximum historically reported water or wave height recorded within a 150-kilometer radius of an NPP. We use the 150-kilometer radius as recommended by the IAEA.[13] It is common for probabilistic risk assessments (PRAs) conducted by plant operators to focus on a narrower radius in the immediate vicinity of the plant. However, this approach can lead to underestimation of risk, as historical events producing extremely large waves are rare events, and waves actually observed in a very specific location may reflect idiosyncrasies specific to those events—for example, the precise location of the epicenter of an earthquake or the landfall location of a hurricane. This problem is illustrated by PRAs conducted by Japanese plant operators prior to the Tohoku earthquake that underestimated risks based on the use of narrow radii. One example is the risk assessment performed by Tohoku Electric for the Onagawa plant. The highest waves recorded in the immediate vicinity of the plant site, based on a study of the four largest historical earthquakes, were found to be 6–8 meters. However, much higher waves (10–25 meters) were recorded about 100 kilometers to the north in Iwate prefecture; these waves were discounted as being irrelevant for the plant's location. The implicit assumption was that local conditions at the plant site made the location less susceptible to high waves than the region slightly to the north. However, the March 11, 2011 wave height reached about 13 meters at the plant site, considerably higher than estimates based on a narrow radius but consistent with records from the 150-kilometer radius we use for this study.

The primary sources of historical tsunami data are the National Geophysical Data Center (NGDC), Global Historical Tsunami Database and the Russian Academy of Sciences (RAS) Novosibirsk Tsunami Laboratory Historical Tsunami Database. Where possible, independent regionally focused government and academic reports were also consulted for confirmation.[14] We use all historical data available on past events.

Several caveats about these data should be recognized: historical data are more readily available for certain geographical regions. Importantly, historical wave height data for North and South America are not available prior to European settlement. The measure therefore likely understates risk for the Americas compared with other regions of the world. Additionally, maximum water height is not always associated with earthquakes. Landslides are also a common source of large waves. In the eastern United States, waves generated by hurricane-induced storm surges typically reach heights greater than those caused by seismic events.

The Soloviev-Imamura tsunami intensity scale is another measure used to assess the relative strength of historical nearby tsunamis. This is calculated according to the formula, $I = \frac{1}{2} + \log_2 H_{av}$, where H_{av} is the average wave height along the nearest coast. As the S-I intensity is calculated from average wave height, rather than maximum, it is less likely to be influenced by extreme outliers induced by local geographic conditions. We record the highest S-I intensity associated with a 150-kilometer radius around the NPP. All S-I intensity data were collected from the NGDC and RAS tsunami databases.

International Comparisons

In this section, we use our dataset to draw comparisons across all seaside nuclear plants currently in operation in the world. We begin by considering absolute measures of tsunami preparedness and move to measures that adjust for tsunami hazard risk.

Figure 7.1 plots base plant elevation, seawall height, emergency power system elevation, and waterproofing of backup power systems for nuclear plants according to country. Particularly low-lying plants are in Finland and Sweden, presumably because tsunami risk is considered negligible. According to this measure, Japan does not look particularly underprepared in international comparison. On average, Japanese plants are located about 10.1 meters above sea level, protected by seawalls averaging 4.6 meters in height. International averages are 8.8 meters for plant height and 3.5 meters for seawall height. Waterproofing of EDGs was not common before March 11, 2011; this measure was implemented in France and the United States after events—notably, flooding at the Blayais nuclear power plant and the September 11, 2001, attacks—highlighted potential vulnerabilities in those countries.

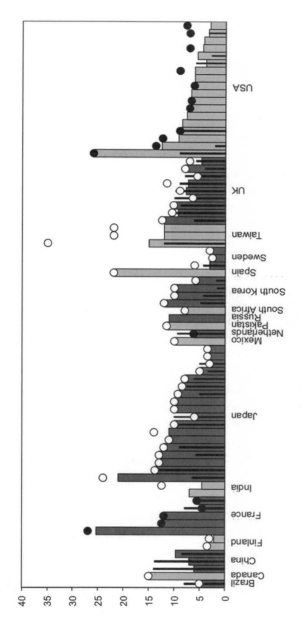

FIG. 7.1: Plant, Seawall, and Backup Power Height (m), International Comparison. Note: Dark circles indicate waterproofing of EDG; open circles indicate no evidence of waterproofing. No circle indicates plant operator declined to release information on EDGs. No vertical bar indicates no seawall.

■ Plant Height | Seawall Height ○ OEDG Height

Although these measures do not account for tsunami risk, they should not be dismissed outright for several reasons. It is not uncommon for tsunamis or major ocean surges to occur in regions of the world with limited seismic activity, for reasons such as hurricanes, landslides, and meteorite impacts. In addition, existing data on tsunami risk rely on written records to identify historical episodes, and such records are often spotty or imprecise. For example, National Oceanographic and Atmospheric Administration (NOAA) data on historical tsunamis date back to the year 123 for China and 684 for Japan, but only to 1668 for the east coast of the United States. For this reason, tsunami risk is likely to be understated for regions of the world where written records are limited, most notably North and South America. Based on these factors, the data raise questions about the adequacy of tsunami preparedness in Finland, Sweden, and the United States, countries with relatively low lying nuclear plants and seawalls.

We now move to an analysis of preparedness accounting for tsunami risk. We consider two principal measures of tsunami risk: the highest recorded wave run-up and highest recorded average run-up within a 150-kilometer radius of a NPP.[15] Our data include run-ups caused by seismic activity as well as other sources, such as hurricanes and landslides. These are blunt measures of tsunami risk, but they have several advantages over existing assessments, such as PRAs conducted by plant operators. First, the measures correctly identify Fukushima Daiichi as an at-risk plant based on data prior to the March 11 earthquake, while PRAs conducted by Tokyo Electric Power Company (TEPCO) prior to the disaster concluded that the plant was safe from inundation.[16] In combination with our data on physical features of NPPs, these measures also produce rankings that roughly correspond to outcomes during the March 11 earthquake and tsunami—Fukushima Daiichi is classified as facing the greatest risk of inundation, followed by Fukushima Daini. Onagawa and Tōkai are classified as less risky.

The first measure we examine is the highest recorded wave run-up within a 150-kilometer radius of an NPP (Figure 7.S1). We find that a large number of Japanese plants are built at elevations lower than the highest recorded run-ups. Japan has recorded particularly high tsunamis in the past; of the seven plants in our data set that lie in regions where tsunami height has exceeded 20 meters, six are in Japan (the sole exception is Taiwan's Maanshan). However, many Japanese plants are built above maximum historical water levels, and many plants outside of Japan are not. The following countries also have NPPs lying below the highest recorded wave run-up: Pakistan, Taiwan, the United Kingdom, and the United States.

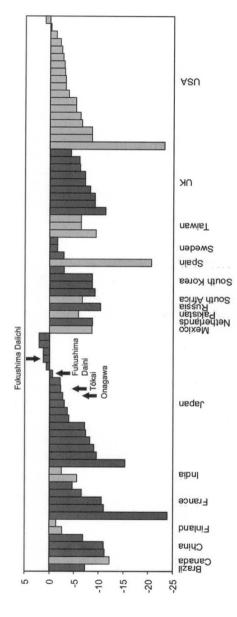

FIG. 7.2: Difference of H_{av} and Maximum of Plant and Seawall Height (m).

This finding is particularly problematic for the United States, for which historical data are likely to understate tsunami risk, as discussed above. Tsunami data for South Asia, East Asia, and northern Europe are available for a much longer period, about two thousand years, compared with only about four hundred years for the United States. The highest tsunami readings for several plants in Japan are quite old—1026 for the Shimane plant and 1341 for the Higashi Dōri plant. Any tsunamis occurring during this earlier time period remain unknown and cannot be reflected in the calculations for the United States.

The same analysis can be applied to the elevation of on-site emergency power systems (Figure 7.S2). Here Japan's disaster preparedness appears to stand out as relatively inadequate in international comparison. Aside from Pakistan's Karachi plant, all emergency power systems lying below maximum historical water levels in the data are associated with Japanese plants. However, these data are incomplete, as some plant operators, particularly in the United States and the United Kingdom, declined to release information on emergency power systems, citing security concerns.

A second measure of tsunami risk we consider is average run-up height, H_{av}. Where comprehensive data on the distribution of run-up heights are unavailable, we calculate H_{av} from the S-I tsunami intensity scale. Figure 7.2 plots the difference between H_{av} and the maximum of plant and seawall height for seaside NPPs. As this measure is based on average rather than maximum wave height, numbers above or close to zero are indicative of potential vulnerability to inundation.[17] As the figure shows, the plant and seawall height at Fukushima Daiichi was exceeded by the average height of a historical tsunami (the 1896 Meiji-Sanriku earthquake). Several other plants are located above or close to zero.

We also consider the H_{av} Ratio, calculated as H_{av}/maximum of plant and seawall height. A number above one indicates that, for a given plant, implied average wave height exceeds the maximum of plant and seawall height. Within Japan, there is a clear downward trend in the H_{av} Ratio over time (Figure 7.3 and 7.S3). NPPs constructed earlier in Japan tended toward inadequate preparation (lower plant height and seawalls) and construction in more hazardous areas (Figures 7.S4 and 7.S5). This trend may reflect improvements in regulation over time, but it is also consistent with the possibility that plant operators faced fewer incentives to enhance protection for older plants, which were closer to decommissioning. Internationally, all plants with an H_{av} Ratio exceeding or close to one were constructed prior to the early 1980s. Although there is no clear trend in H_{av} Ratios over time—old and new plants both have low ratios—

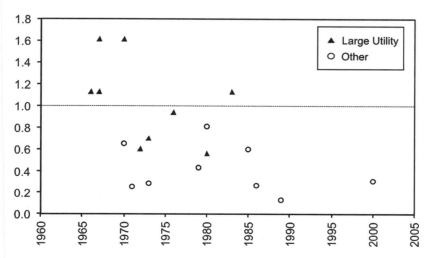

FIG. 7.3: H_{av} Ratio by Construction Date and Utility Size, Japan. Note: High numbers imply inadequate disaster preparation (i.e. high tsunami risk and low elevation of plant and seawall). A number above one means the plant and seawall both lie below the average wave height of a historical incident.

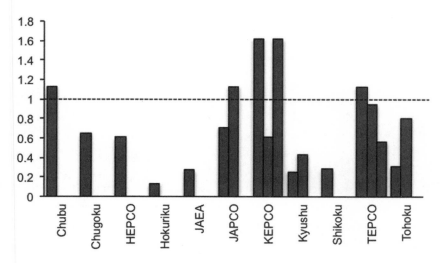

FIG. 7.4: H_{av} Ratio by Plant Operator, Japan.

excluding decommissioned plants from the data produces a downward trend similar to that of Japan (Figure 7.S6).

Also deserving attention is a comparison of H_{av} Ratios by plant operator in Japan (Figures 7.3 and 7.4). Plants operated by the three largest Japanese utilities—TEPCO, KEPCO, and Chubu—tend to have high H_{av} Ratios. Along with JAPCO—a utility 60 percent controlled by TEPCO, KEPCO, and Chubu—these companies own all nuclear plants in Japan with H_{av} Ratios above one. These companies also were the earliest builders of nuclear plants. A simple linear regression suggests that early construction date and ownership by a large utility are both associated with high risk as indicated by the H_{av} Ratio. Large utilities are also associated with low-lying emergency generators in comparison to tsunami risk.

Our measures indicate that inadequate preparedness in Japan is concentrated among the largest utilities. An international comparison underscores this point. For nuclear plants operated by small utilities in Japan (that is, excluding TEPCO, KEPCO, Chubu, and JAPCO), the average H_{av} Ratio is 0.43, indistinguishable from the international average of 0.41. In comparison, the H_{av} Ratio for plants operated by large utilities average 1.05, more than twice the international average.

We also consider operator size as a factor for all international NPPs. The results show that, within countries, larger utility companies tend to have more vulnerable plants than smaller utility companies. This result holds when Japanese plants are excluded from the analysis, suggesting that the tendency for large operators to be less adequately prepared for potential inundation is not limited to Japan.

The largest utility companies in Japan were generally the most politically influential, offering lucrative retirement positions for former bureaucrats, political contributions, and organized votes.[18] It therefore may be possible that large firms were able to push back against regulators to a degree not possible for smaller firms and secure more lax safety requirements. We also examined the number of accidents associated with each Japanese nuclear plant operator.[19] Large utility operators in Japan have experienced twice as many accidents as small operators, and the frequency of accidents is about 42 percent higher when measured on the basis of accidents per plant years in operation.

However, it is important to note that large firms may receive less regulatory scrutiny for reasons aside from regulatory capture. Research on pharmaceuticals regulation has shown that regulators may rationally place greater trust in large, well-established firms even if no political influence is exercised.[20] This effect reflects the fact that regulators care about their own reputations, and they may have a better sense of the reliability and quality of information from well-known firms than new entrants. In the context of nuclear regulation, large firms tended to be the earliest builders and operators of nuclear plants and therefore may have been considered known quantities and subject to less stringent supervision than smaller operators. Regardless of whether or not regulatory capture was responsible for the observed disparity, our results indicate that additional regulatory scrutiny ought to be exercised with respect to large utility companies.

Individual At-risk Plants

Our measures identified a number of plants with potentially high risk of inundation. According to the H_{av} Difference measure—the difference between the average height of a historical wave and the height of the plant—we identify ten NPPs at highest risk, from greatest to least, as follows (Table 7.2): Mihama (Japan), Takahama (Japan), Hamaoka (Japan), Fukushima Daiichi (Japan), Salem/Hope Creek (USA), Tsuruga (Japan), Millstone (USA), Fukushima Daini (Japan), Cook (USA), and Loviisa (Finland). Our second measure, the H_{av} Ratio, produces a similar but not identical set of NPPs. As we discuss below, the difference is most relevant for a number of low-lying plants in Europe, for which historical storm surge data are not available.

Mihama: The Mihama nuclear power plant, one of many along Japan's western coast, is built at a height of 3.5 meters above sea level and possesses no seawall. In 1927, a tsunami of maximum height 11.3 meters and implied average of approximately 5 meters struck Wakasa Bay, in which the Mihama Nuclear plant

TABLE 7.2: H_{av} Difference and H_{av} Ratio by Plant, 10 at Most Risk

Plant	Country	H_{av} Difference	H_{av} Ratio
Mihama	Japan	2.16	1.62
Takahama	Japan	2.16	1.62
Hamaoka	Japan	1.31	1.13
Fukushima Daiichi	Japan	1.31	1.13
Salem/Hope Creek	USA	1	1.33
Tsuruga	Japan	0.66	1.13
Millstone	USA	−0.2	0.95
Fukushima Daini	Japan	−0.69	0.61
Cook	USA	−1.30	0.61
Loviisa	Finland	−1.39	0.34

Source: Authors' calculations

is located. It should be noted that Mihama lies within a cove, which may mitigate extreme wave heights. However, the plant's low height, lack of a seawall, and the existence of major historical tsunamis affecting the area are cause for concern. Mihama is also under investigation for the possibility of an active fault running beneath the plant.

Takahama: We identified KEPCO's Takahama nuclear plant as equally at risk with Mihama. Takahama and Mihama both have 3.5-meter plant heights, no seawall, and are located within Wakasa Bay. Our measures therefore identified the same historical wave within 150 kilometers of both plants and arrived at the same risk assessment for Mihama and Takahama. The placement of these two plants at the top of our list indicates that greater attention needs to be paid to the risk of tsunami on Japan's western seaboard.

Hamaoka: Chubu Electric's Hamaoka nuclear plant, located on the east coast of central Japan, is situated near the site of a historical tsunami of implied average height of approximately 11 meters and maximum height of 21 meters. The wave resulted from a magnitude 8.3 earthquake off the coast of Nankai in 1498 that produced nearly thirty thousand casualties. Hamaoka sits at a height of 10 meters but possesses no seawall other than a series of sand dunes up to 10 meters that run in front of the plant. These dunes were factored into our analysis as if they were a 10-meter seawall, but the plant still made it onto our list. After the Fukushima nuclear accident, Chubu Electric Power Company acknowledged that a large earthquake could produce waves of up to 15 meters in the area, and it began construction of an 18-meter seawall. In response, the Nuclear Regulation Authority (NRA) determined that 18 meters was inadequate and instructed Hamaoka to construct a 21-meter seawall.

Fukushima Daiichi: While Fukushima Daiichi's susceptibility to inundation requires no further elaboration, it is notable that it was not the plant identified as the most vulnerable using data on the eve of the March 11, 2011 disaster. The largest known historical wave to have struck within 150 kilometers of Fukushima Daiichi resulted from the 1896 Sanriku earthquake, which produced a wave of implied average 11 meters and maximum height of 38.5 meters. The Jogan tsunami of 896 was also devastating, reaching farther inland. However, based on available data, it did not produce waves as high as the 1896 or 2011 events.

Salem/Hope Creek: The Salem/Hope Creek plant of New Jersey lies 3 meters above river level and possesses no seawall. Waves produced by the 1938 New England hurricane reached average implied heights of 4 meters and maximum heights of approximately 9 meters in the area, heights that would easily flood the plant. Plants in the United States, however, house critical components such as emergency diesel generators in watertight buildings, and the Salem/Hope Creek plant is designed to withstand a river level increase of up to 10.5 meters. Moreover, a plant such as Salem is much more likely to experience flooding as a result of a hurricane, predictable days in advance, than from a sudden tsunami. We might therefore conclude that US plants are much less likely to experience a Fukushima-type disaster, even in the event of beyond-design-basis inundation. Nevertheless, flood proofing is not infallible,[21] and the plant's low height relative to historical storm surges remains cause for concern. Salem in particular has a history of inadequate maintenance, such as 160 backlogged maintenance orders for its diesel generators.[22] Furthermore, as we indicated earlier, our measures are likely to understate risk to US NPPs resulting from the fact that historical wave height data is not available for a comparable time period.

Tsuruga: Tsuruga is the final plant located in Wakasa Bay on Japan's western seaboard identified as at risk as a result of the 11.3-meter maximum height tsunami of 1927. The plant's better relative risk assessment compared with its neighbors results from its higher height above sea level. At 5 meters, it stands 1.5 meters higher than Mihama and Takahama.

Millstone: The 1938 New England Hurricane also affected the current site of Millstone nuclear power plant in southern Connecticut. The plant sits at an elevation of 4.2 meters above sea level and has no seawalls. Estimates within our area of consideration place hurricane induced maximum wave heights at greater than 7 meters, and implied average of approximately 4 meters. Like Salem/Hope Creek, Millstone's EDGs are located behind flood-proof doors in watertight buildings, decreasing the danger of a Fukushima-type disaster.

Fukushima Daini: TEPCO's Fukushima Daini, just over 100 kilometers to the south of Daiichi, was struck by the same tsunami as Fukushima Daiichi on March 11, 2011. However, the wave reached a slightly lower maximum height, and as a result Fukushima Daini's 12-meter plant height was sufficient to allow three of the plant's twelve EDGs to survive the tsunami. As a result, the plant narrowly avoided a disaster. Fukushima Daini scored slightly better than Daiichi according to our measures because of the plant height being 2 meters higher than Daiichi's maximum height. The largest historical waves we examined at the Daini site were the same as those that struck Daiichi (that is, the 1896 Meiji-Sanriku tsunami).

Low-lying European plants: Many European plants, particularly those in Scandinavian nations, appear high on our list when measured according to the

H_{av} Difference measure. This can be attributed to low absolute plant and sea-wall heights. Sweden's Forsmark and Ringhals plants each sit at 3 meters above sea level, and Finland's Loviisa and Olkiluoto lie at 2.1 meters and 3.3 meters above sea level, respectively. However, these plants are located in areas where the likelihood of high waves caused by earthquakes and hurricanes is comparatively low.

Importantly, the ability of Swedish plants to withstand inundation may be overstated according to our measure, which is based on plant height. For Forsmark, the Swedish Radiation Safety Authority notes that "if the pumps in the secondary cooling system are started when the sea water level has passed +2.5 m, the emergency diesel generators cooling can be jeopardized."[23] EDG failures are precisely what led to the Fukushima disaster, and a 2.5-meter rise in water level leaves little margin for error. Similarly, Forsmark's cooling water flow would be severed by an increase in water levels of 2 meters, and emergency core cooling would be fully jeopardized at a water level of greater than 3 meters. At Ringhals, water levels of 3.3 meters would cause large amounts of water to enter the plant, and levels above 4 meters would break down doors and cause serious fuel damage.[24]

At Finland's Loviisa, 2.1 meters of flooding would exceed the plant's design basis, and flooding of 3 meters would jeopardize the EDGs.[25] At Olkiluoto, heights greater than 3.5 meters would cause water to enter doors, which are not watertight, and both off-site power and EDGs would likely be lost, according to the Finnish Radiation and Nuclear Safety Authority.[26]

The most plausible natural hazard likely to affect these low-lying European plants is high waves caused storm surges. However, historical data on storm surge heights is unfortunately unavailable in existing datasets except in cases where they were caused by well-defined events such as hurricanes. It should be noted that flood preparedness was considered adequate at the Blayais nuclear power plant in France until a 1999 storm generated waves that breached the seawall, knocked out off-site power to the plant, and flooded a number of internal systems. It is crucial to incorporate a margin of safety beyond what our analysis suggests in cases like this, where the historical data are likely to understate the natural hazards to the NPP sites.

CONCLUSION

These results present a mixed picture for Japan's record on disaster preparedness. According to our cross-national comparisons, it appears clear that Japan was inadequately prepared relative to the tsunami risk it confronts. This can be attributed primarily to the fact that Japan faces a higher tsunami risk than other countries because of frequent seismic activity. Japan particularly stands out with respect to the placement and lack of waterproofing of backup generators, which were a crucial element in the meltdown of the Fukushima Daiichi plant.

However, several caveats are in order. First, not all Japanese plants were inadequately prepared for a tsunami. The most vulnerable plants tended to be operated by the largest utility companies and were constructed early on. Second, Japan's lack of preparedness was not unique; we identified several power plants outside the country that were also characterized by inadequate preparation relative to tsunami risk. Finally, in an absolute sense, plants outside Japan are on average less prepared for tsunamis than those inside Japan. It is worth emphasizing again that tsunami risk is likely understated in areas of the world where historical records are limited, particularly North and South America. In this respect, the safety of NPPs in the United States should not be taken for granted. The same applies to low-lying NPPs located in Scandinavia, for which historical wave heights are likely understated because of lack of data on storm surges.

This study opens several avenues for future inquiry. First, given that Japan's highest risk plants were older plants, even after improvements such as heightening seawalls in the early 2000s, and that the largest operators were responsible for the highest risk plants regardless of the timing of construction, this study raises the question of regulatory capture. Existing reports generally contend that regulatory capture was a Japan-wide phenomenon. However, our results indicate that smaller operators have built plants with consistently less vulnerability to tsunami inundation. This observation has potential implications for policy debates within Japan over restructuring the industry, in which the possibility of breaking apart the regional electric power companies has been raised. Our results suggest that older plants and plants operated by the largest utility companies deserve further scrutiny. Additional research is required to determine if Japan's lack of preparedness is the result of capture. Second, these data suggest that nuclear power plants outside Japan should also be subject to closer scrutiny, particularly low-lying plants in Scandinavia and the eastern coast of the United States.

APPENDIX: SUPPLEMENTARY FIGURES

Supplementaray Figures 7.S1–7.S6 appear on the following three pages.

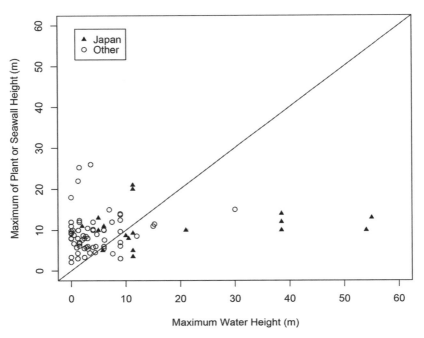

FIG. 7.S1: Maximum of Plant or Seawall Height vs. Maximum Water Height.

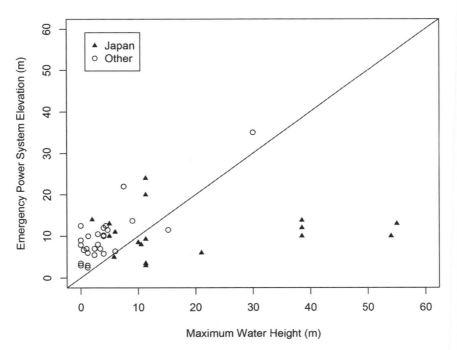

FIG. 7.S2: Emergency Power System Elevation vs. Maximum Water Height.

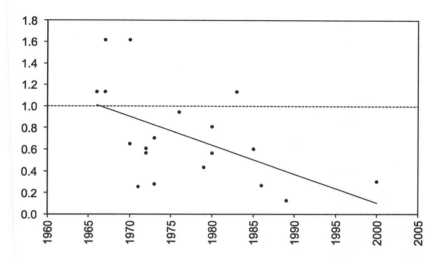

FIG. 7.S3: H_{av} Ratio over Time, Japanese Plants by Date of Construction.

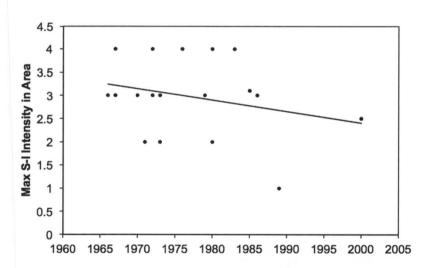

FIG. 7.S4: S-I Intensity, Japanese Plants by Date of Construction.

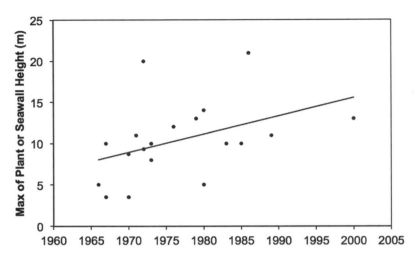

FIG. 7.S5: Maximum of Plant and Seawall Height, Japanese Plants by Date of Construction.

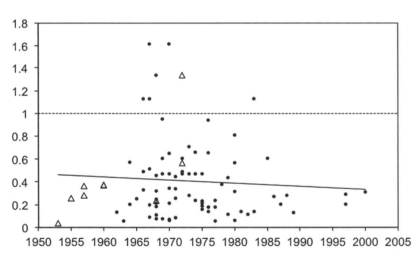

FIG. 7.S6: H_{av} Ratio over Time, All Plants by Date of Construction. Note: Dark circles indicate plants in operation; open triangles represent decommissioned plants.

NOTES

This paper is reprinted and partially modified with permission from Lipscy et al., "The Fukushima Disaster and Japan's Nuclear Plant Vulnerability in Comparative Perspective," *Environmental Science and Technology* 47, no. 12 (2013): 6082–88. Copyright 2013 American Chemical Society.

This work benefited from the support of the Japan Foundation Center for Global Partnership and the Center for International Conflict and Cooperation and Shorenstein Asia Pacific Research Center at Stanford University. We appreciate feedback received from Toshihiro Higuchi and Jacques Hymans. Full regression results are available upon request.

1. J. M. Acton and M. Hibbs, *Why Fukushima Was Preventable* (Washington, DC: Carnegie Endowment for International Peace, 2012); Masahiko Aoki and Gregory Rothwell, "A Comparative Industrial Organization Analysis of the Fukushima Nuclear Disaster: Lessons and Policy Implications," *Energy Policy* 53 (February 2013): 240–47; "Final Report of the Investigation Committee on the Accident at Fukushima Nuclear Power Stations of Tokyo Electric Power Company," Secretariat of the Investigation Committee on the Accidents at the Fukushima Nuclear Power Station, Tokyo, 2012, available at www.cas.go.jp/jp/seisaku/icanps/eng/final-report.html; "Official Report of the Fukushima Nuclear Accident Independent Investigative Commission," National Diet of Japan, Tokyo, 2012, available at http://warp.da.ndl.go.jp/info:ndljp/pid/3856371/naiic.go.jp/en/; Kenji E. Kushida, "Japan's Fukushima Nuclear Disaster: Narrative, Analysis, and Recommendations," *Shorenstein APARC Working Paper Series* (Stanford: Walter H. Shorenstein Asia-Pacific Research Center, 2012), available at http://iis-db.stanford.edu/pubs/23762/2012Jun26_FukushimaReport_draft.pdf; "Mission Report of the IAEA International Fact Finding Expert Mission of the Fukushima Daiichi NPP Accident following the Great East Japan Earthquake and Tsunami," IAEA, 2011, available at www-pub.iaea.org/MTCD/meetings/PDFplus/2011/cn200/documentation/cn200_Final-Fukushima-Mission_Report.pdf; Charles Miller et al., "Recommendations for Enhancing Reactor Safety in the 21st Century: The Near-Term Task Force Review of Insights from the Fukushima Dai-Ichi Accident," US Nuclear Regulatory Commission, July 12, 2011, available at http://pbadupws.nrc.gov/docs/ML1118/ML111861807.pdf.

2. Acton and Hibbs, *Why Fukushima Was Preventable*; Aoki and Rothwell, "A Comparative Industrial Organization Analysis of the Fukushima Nuclear Disaster"; "Official Report of the Fukushima Nuclear Accident Independent Investigative Commission"; Kushida, "Japan's Fukushima Nuclear Disaster"; "Mission Report of the IAEA International Fact Finding Expert Mission"; Miller et al., "Recommendations for Enhancing Reactor Safety in the 21st Century"; "Report on Technical Details of the TEPCO Fukushima Daiichi Nuclear Accident," Ministry of Economy, Trade, and Industry, Tokyo, February 2012.

3. "Official Report of the Fukushima Nuclear Accident Independent Investigative Commission."

4. "Report of Japanese Government to the IAEA Ministerial Conference on Nuclear Safety: Accident at TEPCO's Fukushima Nuclear Power Stations," Japan Cabinet Office, Tokyo, June 2011, available at https://www.iaea.org/newscenter/focus/fukushima/japan-report. .

5. Ibid.

6. Ibid.

7. Ibid.

8. Acton and Hibbs, *Why Fukushima Was Preventable*; "Final Report of the Investigation Committee"; "Official Report of the Fukushima Nuclear Accident Independent Investigative Commission"; Kushida, "Japan's Fukushima Nuclear Disaster"; "Mission Report of the IAEA International Fact Finding Expert Mission"; "Report on Technical Details of the TEPCO Fukushima Daiichi Nuclear Accident"; "Report of Japanese Government to the IAEA Ministerial Conference."

9. K. Ōmae, *The Final Conditions of Reactor Restart: The Last Report of the Fukushima Daiichi Accident Investigation Project* (Tokyo: Shōgakukan, 2012).

10. "Seawall Completed Two Days before Earthquake Saved the Tokai Nuclear Plant," *Yomiuri Shimbun,* February 14, 2012.

11. "Report on Technical Details of the TEPCO Fukushima Daiichi Nuclear Accident."

12. M. Saito, *The Economics of the Nuclear Crisis* (Tokyo: Nihon Hyoron Sha, 2011).

13. This standard is consistent with the radial extent of regional hazard evaluations recommended by the IAEA in 2002. In 2010, this radius was expanded to 300 kilometers. IAEA, "Seismic Hazards in Site Evaluation for Nuclear Installations," Specific Safety Guide SSG-9, IAEA, Vienna, 2010, available at www-pub.iaea.org/MTCD/publications/PDF/Pub1448_web.pdf.

14. Edward Bryant, *Tsunami: The Underrated Hazard*, 2nd. ed. (Chichester: Springer, 2008); E. Bryant and K. Haslett, "Catastrophic Wave Erosion, Bristol Channel, United Kingdom: Impact of Tsunami?" *Journal of Geology* 115, no. 3 (2007): 253–69; A. G. Dawson, D. Long, and D. E. Smith, "The Storegga Slides: Evidence from Eastern Scotland for a Possible Tsunami," *Marine Geology* 82, no. 3 (1988): 271–76; P. Dunbar and C. Weaver, *US States and Territories National Tsunami Hazard Assessment: Historical Record and Sources for Waves* (Washington, DC: US Department of Commerce, National Oceanic and Atmospheric Administration, 2008), available at http://nthmp.tsunami.gov/documents/Tsunami_Assessment_Final.pdf; A. Lau et al., "Written Records of Historical Tsunamis in the Northeastern South China Sea: Challenges Associated with Developing a New Integrated Database," *Natural Hazards and Earth System Sciences* 10 (2010): 1793–1806; C. Lim et al., "Propagation Characteristics of Historical Tsunamis That Attacked

the East Coast of Korea," *Natural Hazards* 47, no. 1 (2008): 95–118; Y. Liu et al., "Tsunami Hazards along Chinese Coast from Potential Earthquakes in South China Sea," *Physics of the Earth and Planetary Interiors* 163, no. 1 (2007): 233–44; P. Lockridge, L. Whiteside, and J. Lander, "Tsunamis and Tsunami-like Waves of the Eastern United States," *Science of Tsunami Hazards* 20, no. 3 (2002): 120–57; K. Minoura et al., "The 869 Jogan Tsunami Deposit and Recurrence Interval of Large-Scale Tsunami on the Pacific Coast of Northeast Japan," *Journal of Natural Disaster Science* 23, no. 2 (2001): 83–88; G. Papadopoulos and A. Fokaefs, "Strong Tsunamis in the Mediterranean Sea: A Re-Evaluation," *ISET Journal of Earthquake Technology* 42, no. 4 (2005): 159–70; J. Roger and Y. Gunnell, "Vulnerability of the Dover Strait to Coseismic Tsunami Hazards: Insights from Numerical Modeling," *Geophysical Journal International* 188, no. 2 (2012): 680–86; S. Shahid, "Tsunami Disaster in South Asia," *Pakistan Journal of Meteorology* 2, no. 3 (2005); D. E. Smith et al., "The Holocene Storegga Slide Tsunami in the United Kingdom," *Quaternary Science Reviews* 23, no. 23 (2004): 2291–2321; K. Zygmunt et al., "Numerical Modeling of the Global Tsunami: Indonesian Tsunami of 26 December 2004," *Science of Tsunami Hazards* 23, no. 1 (2005): 40–56; M. Takao, *Tsunami Assessment for Nuclear Power Plants in Japan* (Tokyo: Tokyo Electric Power Company, 2010).

15. IAEA, "Seismic Hazards in Site Evaluation for Nuclear Installations."

16. Takao, *Tsunami Assessment for Nuclear Power Plants in Japan.*

17. Comprehensive data on distribution of wave heights is available for only a subset of historical events. See, in particular, B. H. Choi, B. I. Min, E. Pelinovsky, Y. Tsuji, and K. O. Kim, "Comparable Analysis of the Distribution Functions of Runup Heights of the 1896, 1933 and 2011 Japanese Tsunamis in the Sanriku Area," *Natural Hazards and Earth System Sciences* 12 (2012): 1463–67.

18. B. Sovacool, "The Costs of Failure: A Preliminary Assessment of Major Energy Accidents, 1907–2007," *Energy Policy* 36 (2008): 1802–20; B. Sovacool, "A Critical Evaluation of Nuclear Power and Renewable Electricity in Asia," *Journal of Contemporary Asia* 40 (2010): 369–400.

19. Sovacool, "The Costs of Failure"; Sovacool, "A Critical Evaluation of Nuclear Power and Renewable Electricity in Asia."

20. D. Carpenter, *Reputation and Power: Organizational Image and Pharmaceutical Regulation at the FDA* (Princeton: Princeton University Press, 2010); D. Carpenter, "Protection without Capture: Product Approval by a Politically Responsive, Learning Regulator," *American Political Science Review* 98 (2004): 613–31.

21. In 2011, the NRC issued a Notice of Violation to Vogtle Nuclear plant for inadequate testing of the plant's "waterproof membrane."

22. J. Sullivan, "Problems Cited at Nuclear Plant in South Jersey," *New York Times*, October 11, 2004.

23. "European Stress Tests for Nuclear Power Plants: The Swedish National Report,"

Swedish Radiation Safety Authority 2011, available at www.ensreg.eu/sites/default/files/ Swedish%20national%20report%20EU%20stress%20tests%2020111230.pdf.

24. Ibid..

25. *European Stress Tests for Nuclear Power Plants: National Report Finland* (Finnish Radiation and Nuclear Safety Authority, 2011).

26. Ibid.

8 Beyond Fukushima: Enhancing Nuclear Safety and Security in the Twenty-first Century

Edward D. Blandford and Michael M. May

The knowledge of how to improve nuclear safety and security comes from experience and analysis—and sometimes that means the experience and analysis of accidents, close calls, and routine problems. The process of learning can be viewed as a continuous investment in both the political and financial future of the nuclear industry and of the electrical industry in general, which depends on safe, affordable, and environmentally acceptable sources of power. It has to be considered as part of the cost of power, reaching every part of the process of providing nuclear power, from qualification of materials such as concrete and steel to operations. Fortunately, most of our knowledge has come from research and day-to-day learning, not from major accidents. The process of learning, however, must be ongoing, not only for nuclear power but also for all complex engineered systems that have the potential to cause major disasters.[1]

In previous chapters in this volume, authors have discussed key lessons from the 2011 Fukushima nuclear disaster that could lead to improved nuclear safety *and* security operations. It is also important to consider these lessons alongside previous lessons learned—or not learned—from serious events since the inception of civilian nuclear operations. Many of the key lessons we learned from Fukushima are in fact not new and have emerged in previous accidents, incidents, or near misses.[2] In addition, there are critical lessons from nuclear safety that are equally applicable to nuclear security and vice versa that have not been learned. This inadequate learning between the nuclear safety and nuclear security communities is becoming increasingly concerning, as evolving threats to civilian nuclear power such as cyber security concerns could potentially play a greater role over the next several decades.

In this concluding chapter, we review the lessons learned from the Fukushima nuclear accident with respect to safety and security discussed in this edited volume and look ahead to potential policy measures that could improve nuclear safety and security. There have already been several reform measures across the global industry, with some countries opting to discontinue their nuclear programs entirely. It is fair to say that all nuclear operators were impacted by the events that started on March 11, 2011. In Japan, however, the extent to which lessons were learned from the accident remains to be seen.

We differentiate between reform measures associated with the human stakeholders responsible for the design, operation, and regulation of the technology and the response to accidents on one hand, and the "machine" or technology on the other. There are important lessons we have learned from Fukushima with respect to the individuals and organizations responsible for ensuring safe and secure nuclear operations. These include, but are not limited to, lessons and future challenges involving key ethical, risk, and safety culture considerations with respect to these individuals and organizations. There are also lessons focused on the commercial nuclear technology itself and what we have learned with respect to the design and operation of nuclear power plants following the Fukushima accident. This distinction is important as we project learning into the twenty-first century with a nuclear industry that is expecting a wide growth in nuclear newcomer states and rapidly industrializing countries with modest infrastructure. The nuclear technologies selected and the humans that will operate and regulate them are often decoupled and pose different risks.[3]

REFLECTING ON FUKUSHIMA: KEY EMERGENT THEMES

What lessons can be taken away from this retrospective survey of key pathologies associated with the Fukushima nuclear accident? Were these lessons avoidable based on previous experiences, and has the nuclear industry taken appropriate action since the accident? In this section we identify nine key themes that emerge from this edited volume and expand upon them.

1. There are important synergies between nuclear safety and security. The lack of awareness about these synergies has led to lost learning opportunities across the global nuclear industry.

A major security incident could have radiological and other consequences as serious as those of the Fukushima accident. Conversely, a major nuclear safety accident yields important insights about how plant personnel cope with accident mitigation and emergency response common to security incidents. The International Atomic Energy Agency (IAEA) has done a good job of promoting the importance of treating nuclear safety and security within a common framework through the Global Nuclear Safety and Security Framework (GNSSF) initiative. A key element of this initiative is the Global Nuclear Safety and Security Network (GNSSN), which is a mechanism for sharing knowledge among the global expert community and allows for interactions between international operators on work related to nuclear safety and security matters.

While these are critical steps in recognizing the important overlap between safety and security, there are insufficient measures to ensure that lessons from security are *also* being learned in safety, and vice versa. As pointed out in the chapters by Naito, Suzuki, and Akiyama, the B.5.b measures that the United States put in place following the 9/11 terrorist attack in 2001 to address how a licensee would respond to an accident if a plant lost large areas because of explosions or fires were not adopted in Japan. The Japanese were aware that these measures were put in place but chose not to implement them domestically on a presumed different security risk profile. While the B.5.b. measures were put in place to respond to potential vulnerabilities revealed by the 9/11 attacks, the US Nuclear Regulatory Commission (USNRC) clearly also saw the benefits to enhancing nuclear safety early on. Likewise, the events at Fukushima have taught us a good deal about nuclear security and how personnel perform key mitigation and emergency response activities.

There are signs that these cross-learning opportunities are being identified and appropriately prioritized. The 2012 report by the Japanese Advisory Committee on Nuclear Security (ACRS) discussed in Naito's chapter noted that "though initiated by a natural disaster, the accident revealed the possibility that a similar incident with serious impacts to society could result from an act of terrorism against nuclear facilities. It is Japan's duty to extract lessons learned from the accident from the viewpoints of not only safety but also security and share them with the international community in order to duly reflect them in the international efforts to strengthen nuclear security."[4] Naito drew out several important specific security implications from the Fukushima accident. Until now, regulating safety and security were handled by separate organizations in Japan, and preparation for a security incident lagged behind best practices in effect in other countries. With the reforms, both safety and security are the responsibility of the Nuclear Regulation Authority (NRA). New areas of emphasis include measures for early detection of intrusion, delay of terrorist action, enhancing the robustness of protected facilities and equipment, establishment of an adequate security regime, preparation of mitigation measures exercises, and evaluations and measures again insider threats. However, there is much work remaining in Japan. For example, key personnel reliability program elements such as employee background checks are still not required. While many nuclear operators across the world have implemented measures based on the safety lessons learned from Fukushima, it is unclear how much plant security has improved as a result of this accident.

2. A design basis (DB) is a necessary requirement for the design and construction of a nuclear power plant. However, its use as a risk acceptance mechanism has significant challenges.

Nuclear power plants are designed to maintain their integrity and performance of safety or security functions for an envelope of normal operational events as well as abnormal events that are expected to occur or might occur during the lifetime of the installation. In addition, they are designed to maintain performance of these functions for a set of design basis accidents and threats that involve failures that are possible but unlikely to occur during the facility's lifetime. As discussed by Wyss, the establishment of a design basis is usually done through three different but related mechanisms. The first mechanism is a policy-driven approach that establishes design basis requirements based on a policy solution to a perceived concern. A policy-driven design basis typically involves negotiation between multiple concerned stakeholders and relies less on a specific technical evaluation. The second mechanism is to establish design bases based on perceived physical limits where the intent is for the design basis to represent a deterministic physical bound that is very unlikely to be exceeded. Finally, the third mechanism is the establishment of a design basis based on frequency arguments. In the nuclear industry this is typically known as a risk-informed approach and is much more prevalent in establishing the design basis for safety than in security, where frequency arguments are considerably more challenging to assign to security threats.[5]

It is important to recognize that the design basis is in effect a pact among impacted stakeholders to accept some risk in return for electricity, not a guarantee of perfect safety and security. Designing to the design basis does not by itself guarantee an effective response to the worst possible conditions. A key fallacy relating to the establishment of design basis is the notion that designing a facility to withstand the maximum credible event will automatically protect against lesser events. As a result, conditions both less severe and more severe than the design basis should be evaluated and, where practicable, cost-effective modifications to the design to mitigate consequences should be considered. Most important, plans should be practiced and continually reevaluated in the light of new information.

The Fukushima accident involved conditions that vastly exceeded the design basis, as evidenced by the drastically undersized seawall that surrounded the plant (the sizing of seawalls that surround Japanese nuclear power plants in relation to perceived tsunami risk is expanded upon by Lipscy et al. and discussed later). As discussed by Wyss, competent authorities must ensure that operators evaluate plant outcomes that might occur if an event outside of the design basis occurs and evaluate cost-effective modifications to the plant that can reduce potential consequences. The decision to store critical backup equipment and locate vital electrical components in areas of the plant that were susceptible to flooding was based on the notion that a beyond-DB tsunami wave compromising the seawall was "inconceivable."

3. Responding effectively to major nuclear accidents and security events requires swift leadership, a strong incident command chain, well-trained personnel, and adequate resources. Failure of leadership, insufficient emergency response manuals, and poor training all increased the consequences of the Fukushima accident.

Any plan to deal with emergencies must include an incident command structure with clear lines of communication and well-defined areas of responsibility, including the ability to provide timely information to the actors involved and to the public at large. This plan must include all relevant participants, from top political leadership to the regulators and management structure of the licensee, and on to the local operators and first responders at the scene of the event.

The Fukushima accident revealed that both the Japanese government and Tokyo Electric Power Company (TEPCO) lacked sufficient human resource capacity for emergency response. Emergency response failures during the crisis—including the breakdown of command and control structures and lack of awareness of pre-established response procedures—are discussed at length in the Akiyama chapter. As Akiyama noted, early response failures led top-level officials to bypass the command chain and make decisions based on incomplete information. The existence of substantial distrust between Japan's political leadership and key organizations responding to the accident also encouraged political leaders to take control of the emergency response. This distrust had been building for several years in Japan with several cover-ups and small accidents eroding confidence among the government, nuclear industry, and the public. It is very important to note that courageous decision-making by the plant manager and key on-site staff was able to ensure that even worse outcomes were avoided. The importance of the control room shift supervisor having autonomous decision-making authority cannot be overstated, and this *lack* of authority in Japan is clearly a lesson to take away from Fukushima.

Akiyama attributed the breakdown in emergency response to several factors. First, the myth of absolute safety that prevailed among Japanese nuclear power stakeholders prevented the adoption of strong accident mitigation and emergency response measures. Second, because of this mindset, there was insufficient training among the different actors in the command chain to prepare for an emergency of this magnitude. In addition, the myth of absolute safety led to poor assumptions in crisis management manuals resulting in prescriptive guidances that were not useful, or impossible to implement. Finally, a technically weak nuclear regulator resulted in insufficient regulations and requirements for accident mitigation and emergency response.

4. The destructive accidents at Fukushima and previous nuclear accidents have had a significant impact on nearby local communities as a result of radioactive contamination of land, groundwater, and the ocean. Rigidity and uncertainty in radiation protection regulations through the use of strict numerical standards have only worsened these impacts.

Long-term evacuations that prevent people from returning to their homes, farms, and businesses have a lasting impact on public well-being. Managing the risks of these evacuations will always cause significant controversy in the public eye because of the uncertainty about the health effects of low levels of ionizing radiation, the inherent variability in nearby biosphere contamination, and implementation of radiation protection guidance with competing societal tradeoffs.

As Higuchi pointed out in a previous chapter, one of the key failures following Fukushima was the over-reliance on "making the magic number," which ultimately led to stifling the voices of the nearby communities and minimizing their opportunity to make informed choices. Controversies surrounding adequate radiation protection have historically surrounded reference levels established by the International Commission on Radiological Protection, which date back to 1928. Higuchi observed that confusion surrounding radiological protection management can be understood through a concept developed by Donald MacKenzie called the "certainty trough."[6] There are substantial differences in how knowledge surrounding the health risks of ionizing radiation are understood between the scientific producers of the knowledge, the public administrators charged with managing this knowledge in the form of regulations and standards, and the affected public, oftentimes with very little access to, or interest in gaining, this knowledge.

Numerical standards of radiation protection, while themselves quite conservative, were implemented quite rigidly without adequate regard for local factors, such as hot spots, land utilization, and location of habitations. As discussed by Higuchi, government officials in Tokyo used these numerical guides as an administrative cutoff to stifle local initiative and restrict their ability to make informed decisions. As a result, much of the concerned population lost faith in these standards. The government in turn resorted to lower, though still rigid, numerical standards, causing unnecessary economic and social damage. While numerical standards are necessary, they should be implemented discriminately, with regard to local conditions and in consultation with local authorities. Indeed, local populations should be considered as partners in dealing with the dangers. One key lesson from the post-Fukushima response is that radiation protection by numbers alone is a policy doomed to fail.

5. There are existing models of organizations that have had proven success in improving nuclear safety. For example, the US Institute of Nuclear Power Operations (INPO), created in the wake of Three Mile Island (TMI), has helped reduce operator-related incidents and unplanned shutdowns.

Funded and supported by the US nuclear power industry, INPO provides a forum for the ongoing process of learning lessons in the operations area. Although design features at TMI prevented any significant release of radiation, financial losses following the accident were so significant that the industry and its financial backers were moved to cooperate with regulators in establishing and maintaining much improved operator training, operations standards, and operations staffing.

Operator ratings under the system that was created following TMI are kept confidential within the industry so that criticism can be uninhibited and action can be taken in a timely manner without fear of misinterpretation. On the other hand, actual performance results, including all incidents, are made public. Expert management in the owner-operator sector has been essential to establishing and maintaining quality of operations. In addition, dealing with reactors during abnormal conditions requires well-thought-out procedures, clearly established lines of authority, and on-site personnel who are competent and authorized to make tough decisions. Operator ratings at the various plants remain private, but results with regard to operating procedures and consequences are public. However, there are industry watchdogs and concerned stakeholders who are critical of the relationship INPO has with industry. Some say the information INPO gathers through its peer-review inspections keeps critical safety information away from the public and regulatory body. Industry's response to this criticism is that INPO's inspections are deeply thorough and the release of all information could negatively affect the candor of the resultant reports. This balance is a hard one to establish and maintain.

Because of differing laws, policies, and priorities, however, it has been shown to be difficult to extend the INPO concept to the international nuclear power industry despite the fact that what happens in one country usually affects the future of the industry in other countries. As a result of Fukushima, Japan formed the Japan Nuclear Safety Institute (JANSI) in November 2012, based on the INPO model. JANSI built upon and absorbed the Japan Nuclear Technology Institute (JANTI), which had been founded on the INPO model in March 2005. Suzuki's chapter discussed some of the features of JANTI's "Action Principle" statement that distinguishes JANTI from other organizations such as INPO, and made the following observations about JANTI. First, JANTI appears to regard the ethics of engineers as a foundation of nuclear safety and compliance with laws and regulations as a societal role. This dualism implies that utilities can be seen as fulfilling their duties so long as they follow existing laws and regulations. The second observation was that JANTI viewed safety culture as specific to each country. In many ways, this is understandable, as implanting one country's safety culture into a different country with unique societal norms may not be effective.[7] However, international norms for nuclear safety culture need to be reviewed and their applicability evaluated. A strong universal safety culture encourages everyone to report problems and concerns, and to have effective corrective action programs to address these problems and concerns. Third, Suzuki noted that JANTI stated it would take an objective and neutral position with regard to member corporations' practices, and would therefore not likely have the same influence as the INPO on its members' safety practices.

Moving forward, JANSI has committed to an extensive peer review system among the Japanese nuclear licensees; the implementation of such a system might prove challenging to the Japanese, however. As Lipscy et al. have asserted earlier, there is a considerable range of size among the nuclear plant owner-utilities in Japan, with the largest utility companies typically having the most political influence. In order for JANSI to truly succeed, the peer review process must be entirely democratic, and responsibility must be demanded at all levels of operation regardless of plant size.

6. The nuclear industry has historically had difficulties with transnational learning. Many of the mechanisms that cause licensees to share information within a country have not worked across international borders.

All three of the major nuclear power accidents (that is, TMI, Chernobyl, and Fukushima), as well as several of the lesser-known close calls, had precursors in previous incidents, although often not in the same country. The lessons-learned reviews that followed most of these events produced several specific, useful recommendations. Some of those recommendations were implemented—the lessons were learned—but often they were not. Not surprisingly, implementation steps that translated into more efficient operations—such as better, more standardized operating procedures— were carried out more often than steps that required immediate expenditures to avoid uncertain disaster, such as better defenses against possible flooding. For example, the 1999 massive flood in Southwestern France resulted in a complete loss of off-site power and compromised several important safety-related systems at the Blayais nuclear power plant. Clearly preventive measures and accident mitigation lessons learned from this accident were not adopted by TEPCO prior to Fukushima. The same is true on the nuclear security side. In an earlier chapter, Naito discussed how information on B.5.b security measures was shared within certain levels of the Nuclear and Industrial Safety Agency (NISA) but was not shared across the agency or with Japanese operators.

The Independent Investigation Commission's comments on the "Galapagos" syndrome in reference to Japan's nuclear safety regulation regime's being isolated are very telling. Organizations such as the World Association of Nuclear Operators (WANO) and the IAEA offer opportunities for countries to learn from each other. Suzuki's chapter reviewed several international opportunities for enhanced learning that the Japanese did not utilize to implement improved safety measures. Although relevant stakeholders from the Japanese nuclear industry were involved in international peer review processes, there was insufficient response to resultant advice and recommendations. It is important to note that it was not just important safety measures that Japan could have adopted based upon international experience but also international practices that improve plant economics with minor or no safety consequence. The Japanese had very rigorous and expensive requirements in these areas leading to capacity factors far below the international average. Many of those requirements did not contribute to actual safety and may have further increased the complacency.

While nuclear energy offers both global promises and global dangers, transnational learning in Japan has been inadequate, where it has taken place at all. Overconfidence in technology (usually not shared by the technologists at the working level themselves), the myth of absolute safety (shared tacitly by all stakeholders including antinuclear groups), and a weak regulator all contributed to this situation. Mechanisms for sharing information and peer evaluation should be strengthened, but here again cultural changes will need to take place. The lack of transnational learning adversely affects both safety and security preparations.

7. The regulation of nuclear safety and security requires a strong and independent regulator. Many of the failures at Fukushima were the result of an operator that was weakly regulated. In some cases, regulatory capture was a clear problem. In others, overreliance on prescriptive requirements for plant operations relative to international norms created a false sense of confidence and thus a culture of complacency.

A regulating agency with appropriate power and strong technical competence—one that is well staffed, well funded, and independent of its licensees—is a necessary, though not sufficient, requirement for safety and, in particular, for the formulation and implementation of lessons learned. For different reasons and with different effectiveness, many countries have nuclear regulatory agencies that combine the promotion of the technology and the regulation of the operators. These two types of functions were originally combined in the United States and other countries because of heavy government involvement in the commercial introduction of the technology. In 1974, the United States divided the Atomic Energy Commission into the USNRC and the Energy Research and Development Administration (ERDA), primarily for public confidence reasons. Since Fukushima, the Japanese have established an independent regulator called the Nuclear Regulation Authority (NRA), which follows a model similar to that of the USNRC.

Regulatory capture by licensees through either political or administrative processes has been a problem in several countries. Many of the previous chapters discussed problems potentially resulting from regulatory capture in Japan, ranging from inconsistent seawall requirements to lax regulations surrounding critical accident mitigation and emergency response measures. However, the performance of the Japanese fleet prior to the accident does not necessarily point to an industry with a captured regulator in a traditional sense. The national capacity factor of the entire fleet in Japan was 65.7 percent, which is far below international standards.[8] One of the major reasons for this markedly low performance is the existence of highly prescriptive regulations that require plants to shut down every twelve months for refueling and time-based maintenance on critical systems, structures, and components. Several countries have moved toward condition-based maintenance, which has resulted in improved plant availability while also improving plant safety.[9] While there are many signs that regulatory capture was a problem prior to Fukushima, one of the perverse consequences of mandating much more prescriptive requirements for refueling outage frequency and online maintenance, compared with international norms, would be a false sense of confidence and thus a culture of complacency.

The decision by Japan to remove the regulating agency from the administrative structure of the operating and promoting agency is a step toward greater safety. Regulators must also encourage the identification and reporting of problems to make possible effective implementation of corrective action programs. Ensuring both safety and security at nuclear sites is not a matter of simply setting forth regulations to meet known problems. Rather, it is a continuing and dynamic set of interactions involving regulators, licensees, and other stakeholders, none of whom are independent of the others. However, it will take considerable time before this right balance can be achieved.

8. There are challenges to ensuring adequate nuclear safety and security that are unique to the country that operates the reactors. There is some validity to the comment by the chairman of the Japanese Diet's Independent Investigation Commission that Fukushima was an accident "made in Japan."

In many postmortem studies of Fukushima, people have often asked whether such an accident could happen elsewhere. Many aspects of the accident are not unique to Japan but rather the result of the technology exposed to very challenging conditions. Older vintage light water reactors, like the ones at Fukushima, were not built to withstand station blackout conditions for extended periods of time. The accident itself was caused by an extreme natural hazard and was not the result of operator action or shoddy maintenance. However, there are many aspects of the accident that are unique to Japan. The myth of absolute safety that was distinctly Japanese was a prerequisite for construction of nuclear power plants in the first place. It is a good sign that the NRA has challenged the myth by implementing a set of safety goals similar to those that were first implemented in the United States after TMI. These safety goals are both qualitative and quantitative in nature. Notably, these goals deviate from absolute safety by stating: "The possibility of health effects to the public caused by utilization of nuclear power should be limited to the level not to cause a significant increase in the public risk."[10]

Additionally, there were other nonsocietal aspects of the accident that were unique to Japan. Lipscy et al.'s quantitative study of the vulnerability of reactors against flooding worldwide showed that, while power plant sites around the world are vulnerable, the Fukushima site was especially and unnecessarily vulnerable. It also showed that, in Japan, plants owned by the largest utilities were the most vulnerable. Precautions such as improving the siting of emergency sources of electric power and water; requiring better waterproofing of pumps, valves, and other parts needed for the continued cooling of fuel elements after outside power is lost; and installing higher seawalls are needed in a number of places in and outside Japan to lessen or avoid the risk of meltdowns, which are among the largest factor in causing serious radiological accidents. But there is validity to the comment by the chairman of the Japanese Diet's Independent Investigation Commission that Fukushima was an accident "made in Japan."[11]

9. In the United States and some other countries, public fear of radioactivity and the ensuing interventions of often well-informed organizations have spurred learning from experience. But in countries in which the responsible nuclear organizations, governmental and private, were insulated from criticism, learning has been slower.

Learning from experience is never an easy process, especially when it takes place in a very public, very critical arena. Nevertheless, transparency has enhanced that process. Democracies in general have been quicker to learn from mistakes and accidents than countries with limited or no public accounting, such as the former Soviet Union and East Germany. Transparency helps learning in all three groups: the owners-operators, the government regulators, and some of the intervening organizations. Improved transparency has been associated with improved safety and security.

One key lesson from Fukushima was that lack of transparency before the accident made the political consequences of the accident more severe than they might otherwise had been. This lack of transparency stemmed ultimately from the *Zettai Anzen Shinwa* ("myth of absolute safety") that was fostered by the authorities for many decades: if safety was absolute, no risk could be admitted. As Akiyama has discussed, this mentality led to inadequate training and preparation for dealing with accidents and weak regulatory institutions. It made possible the establishment of the Japanese nuclear village, with both the social acceptance of the safety and security risks in the communities hosting nuclear power plants but also intransigent opposition from antinuclear groups. Following Fukushima, and several previous problems, most of the Japanese public lost faith in nuclear power and concluded that they could not trust either utilities or government. Based on the past fifty years of commercial operation, the risks from nuclear power to public health are lower than the risks associated with fossil fuels electricity generation.[12] However, these risks are not zero and must be communicated in a truthful and transparent manner. It is unclear whether this lesson has yet been fully learned.

Looking to the Future—Improving Nuclear Safety and Security

Lessons are learned from both success and failure. Severe reactor accidents or security events are extremely rare, and every effort should be taken to abstract key engineering or organizational successes or failures. Nuclear operators, designers, regulators, and involved stakeholders have all learned from operational experiences, both their own and that of others, and this relationship varies immensely across the globe.

Since the introduction of civilian nuclear power, there have been several reactor events—concerning both safety and security—that have served as opportunities to galvanize the industry. Many of the more significant events have been deconstructed and better understood through root-cause investigations yielding a set of lessons learned. Following the three major commercial reactor accidents—TMI, Chernobyl, and Fukushima—the lessons-learned process revealed that there were numerous human errors which contributed to the accident and in some cases greatly exacerbated the consequences. With respect to nuclear security, there have been no major security events that have resulted in successful radiological sabotage of a civilian nuclear installation. However, the sparseness of data for nuclear security events does not mean that there have not been precursor events or experiences that we should learn from now in order to reduce the possibility of future such events, as well as to improve future designs.

In examining the overarching themes from the previous chapters in this book and looking to the future of nuclear power worldwide over the twenty-first century, we come to a set of observations and policy recommendations on improving nuclear safety and security. It is important to note that there has been substantial policy reform across the global nuclear industry since Fukushima. Some of these reforms will prove to be successful and lead to enhanced nuclear safety and security, while some will be less effective. In many cases, policy changes will be well intended but in practice difficult to implement. We are reminded of the comments made by the former chairman of the USNRC, Richard Meserve: "Safety is hard work. It must be embedded in the management and cultural practices of both the operators and regulators; it is an obligation that demands constant attention."[13]

1. The Fukushima accident was initiated by a "once-in-a-thousand-years" event, as was the precursor incident at Le Blayais nuclear power plant in France. Given how many current nuclear sites are subject to infrequent major external events, and considering the lifetimes of modern reactors, there is a clear statistical basis for taking into account such events for both safety and security and spending some money to prevent or alleviate their consequences.

Reactor lifetimes today are roughly in the sixty-year range, which is 6 percent of the "thousand years" postulated for the recurrence time of the Tohoku tsunami. In addition, there are a number of sites subject to locally rare floods. Since a serious nuclear accident anywhere affects the nuclear industry everywhere, the industry should look at a much higher probability of problems than is implied in the "one-in-a-thousand-years" comment.

The current framework for managing safety and security risks based on demonstrating adequate protection against a design basis can lead to an incomplete characterization of risk, ineffective identification of cost-effective risk management options, and escalating costs. On the security side, there is substantial variation in security investment across the global nuclear fleet. In countries with substantial investment in security, some believe the existing design-basis threat (DBT) process is riddled with a number of conservatisms, principally, assuming a high-capability threat as a bounding event and acceptance criteria based on conditional probability of adversary success. These rankings and prescriptive risk management are thought to have unclear impacts on security. As Wyss observed in an earlier chapter, it is vitally important that reactor designers, licensees, and regulators better understand "rare" events that fall outside of the design basis for both safety and security and evaluate their potential outcomes to ensure that sufficient preventative and mitigation measures are put in place. However, there exist many countries with a marginal commitment to nuclear security because of a perceived lower threat. In some cases, security personnel are in fact unarmed and not subjected to stringent background checks.

If a small fraction of the total cost of Fukushima had been prudently spent on the precautions that have been identified since the accident (and that we have summarized above), some of the worst consequences of the Fukushima accident could have been mitigated.[14] While tsunamis are not the only possible external source of disaster, and while prioritization in allocating limited resources is always necessary, a new look must be taken at rare but potentially catastrophic safety and security events, as well as the precautions that could be useful and economically justifiable in dealing with such events. The United States has implemented the FLEX program, which is a major step in addressing the key safety issues faced at Fukushima. The FLEX program expands upon the earlier USNRC B.5.b requirements and provides an additional layer of backup power after an extreme event by stationing vital emergency equipment (such as backup generators and battery packs) in multiple locations. This program was a shared cost across the US nuclear industry and was regionally implemented through two hubs in different parts of the country. We recommend that other countries consider a similar approach, possibly through international partnerships whereby resources can be shared where suitable. It is encouraging that WANO is pursuing a worldwide-integrated response strategy for nuclear incidents and accidents and recognizing the importance of effective accident mitigation within this strategy.

2. The failure at Fukushima was due to the lack of a sufficient defense-in-depth approach, not a failure of the defense-in-depth philosophy in general. These lessons learned should also be applied to safety and security measures moving forward.

While there was clearly substantial failure in Japan to adequately address external natural events that *should* have been included within the design basis, it is important to recognize that there will always be events, in particular natural events or terrorist attacks, that will surprise us (for example, the 5.8 magnitude earthquake in Virginia and the Missouri River flooding, both of which took place in 2011). These types of events are why margin and defense-in-depth approaches to safety are essential to ensuring minimal public risk.

The Fukushima accident cannot be attributed solely to an inadequately high seawall. Rather, the accident followed a series of failures, including failures in plant defensive actions, mitigation efforts, and emergency response. Accounting for every potential event that falls within the tails of the respective probability distributions is an unmanageable approach. Appropriate reform should focus not solely on defensive actions but also on a robust blend of improved defensive actions, mitigation efforts, and emergency response procedures. Similarly, the lessons learned from an insufficient defense-in-depth strategy for tsunamis should be applied to security measures moving forward. A detailed review of the security implications of Fukushima has previously been given by Naito; these insights should not be ignored based on similar logic that led the Japanese to ignore the B.5.b measures.

In light of this, we recommend that there be a concerted effort through international organizations such as the IAEA or WANO to think through possible cost-effective retrofit options for entire plants, including spent fuel pools that reduce the likelihood that beyond-design-basis events will lead to catastrophic consequences.[15] Reduction in consequence potential for the existing nuclear fleet is also very helpful to reduce the potential seriousness of undiscovered or unanticipated events that fall within the design basis. Risk-informed and performance-based international standards should be established for ensuring that adequate defense-in-depth strategies have been implemented correctly for *both* safety and security. Both of the aforementioned international organizations have ongoing efforts for this. However, these activities are rarely integrated such that safety and security designers and practitioners are brought together. In parallel, there needs to be a substantial educational effort within the international industry about the synergies and conflicts between nuclear safety and security. This effort needs to span the entire complex including utilities, regulators, academia, and reactor vendors. The IAEA has taken an active role in promoting these ideas. However, they are rarely promulgated beyond a small population that participates in these activities. There is a serious problem with isolation between the nuclear safety and security communities wherein each side views these problems as separate and not of their concern.

3. Mechanisms to facilitate and incentivize mutual learning may not be adequate to make best use of lessons learned and prevent avoidable disasters.

There is a unique opportunity for the Japanese to use Fukushima as a catalyst to greatly enhance international learning across the global nuclear fleet. However, it will require a significant departure from the existing cultural norms of the absolute safety myth, and tremendous political will. The present mechanisms are unsystematic and do not have enforcement or incentive features. They include the efforts of vendors to build safer reactors, the general availability of lessons learned from particular accidents and near-accidents, and awareness of the worldwide cost of a nuclear accident anywhere. At the international institutional level, the two active organizations are the IAEA and WANO. The IAEA produces reports and submits protocols for adoption by its member states. It has major responsibilities in other areas (for example, safeguards against military use of civilian facilities), and it does not have the personnel, budget, or authority required to enforce safety standards that they have established. WANO focuses on reactor operation, an essential—but not the only—ingredient of safety. Its main activity to promote safety is information sharing. INPO, the US counterpart to WANO, is quite effective. But it is a confidential and cooperative US industry effort that seems difficult to replicate on a worldwide basis, at least without major changes.

Since the Fukushima accident, there have been considerable efforts to strengthen WANO and better coordinate activities between WANO, the IAEA, and national organizations such as INPO and JANSI. A WANO Post-Fukushima Commission was established and charged with determining what changes WANO should implement based on the lessons learned from Fukushima. This commission made five recommendations: (1) expand the scope of WANO's activities; (2) implement a "worldwide integrated response strategy" for nuclear incidents and accidents, shifting from focusing on just accident prevention to including accident mitigation; (3) increase the frequency of peer reviews; (4) improve WANO's visibility and transparency; and (5) improve WANO's internal consistency. In addition, WANO's members agreed to enhance staffing at regional WANO offices. These changes are encouraging signs that WANO and its membership will become more effective in enhancing global nuclear safety. Additionally, there has been a formal collaboration since 2012 between the World Institute for Nuclear Security (WINS) and WANO to examine the interface between nuclear safety and nuclear security. Part of this effort is to better define and identify best practices for managing this interface.[16]

In light of these reforms, we recommend that ongoing efforts to enhance WANO are strongly encouraged by operators and governments, as well as ensuring that resultant outcomes are disseminated to plant personnel accompanied with effectiveness evaluation metrics. The increase in peer review frequency is a strong step in the right direction, but it is important that these reviews result in shared learning and appropriate corrective actions. We strongly recommend that the collaboration between WINS and WANO be expanded beyond the identification of best practices with respect to nuclear security and safety. As discussed in the previous recommendation, the collaboration should involve a broader range of stakeholders in order to break down barriers between the two communities.

4. Any plan to deal with emergencies must include an incident command structure with clear lines of communication and well-defined areas of responsibility, including the responsibility to provide timely information to the actors involved and to the public. Mechanisms to improve planning should be applied to both nuclear safety and security.

This plan must include all relevant actors, from top political authorities to the regulators and management structure of the licensee, to local operators and responders at the scene of the emergency. Both Kushida and Akiyama gave detailed reviews of the organizational failures during the response to the Fukushima incident. Many of these failures were also visible during the emergency response to Chernobyl and, to a lesser extent, TMI, demonstrating that lessons were not learned from previous radiological events. Even though there has not been a major nuclear security incident involving a radiological release, there have been several other security incidents from which the nuclear industry can draw insights.

Training for serious nuclear safety and security events is challenging because of the many actors involved. With respect to managing serious nuclear accidents, nuclear plants often undergo training involving plant operators, key plant personnel, response centers, and key off-site actors. On the security side, the USNRC and other organizations mandate exercises that involve such overt use of force as attacks by armed groups or large airplanes crashing into nuclear installations. Easier to carry out but more difficult to deal with perhaps are incidents that involve a combination of insiders and outsiders.

We recommend that exercises be wide ranging, not only focusing on the direst possibilities but also providing training for incident commanders, personnel within the incident command structure, staff within communications facilities to and from the incident command center, and the political authorities involved. The failures associated with the Fukushima incident command effort were the result of a clear lack of preparation, distrust from key parties at the top of the structure, and lack of clear line of command. Two points may be particularly relevant:

• The incident command structure must be prepared to accept unexpected input from the field. Exercises therefore should not be tightly scripted in advance but should provide for opportunities to deal with such input.

• Relevant political authorities or their close advisers must be involved in the training to the point that they understand and trust it. Otherwise they may tend to take over the response without adequate preparation. Of course, if the incident command structure is not sufficiently trained, they may do so anyway.

It is also important to recognize that incident commands for serious nuclear safety or security events often involve international parties. Several nuclear power plants are located adjacent to an international border where the affected nearby population is also in a neighboring country. Many reactors are not designed and built by indigenous companies, and important expertise may lie outside the affected country. Additionally, countries may issue guidance to their citizens that may be located in the affected country, which may add additional complexities to an already challenging situation.[17]

5. Improved cooperation will rest most securely on lasting shared economic interest among vendors, owner-operators, government regulators, and the public. At the same time, the international nuclear power and nuclear fuel cycle markets will become, if anything, more competitive.

Because so much of the cost of nuclear power is incurred before the first kilowatt-hour is generated, the financial backers, including private and government insurers and guarantors, in theory have considerable leverage over the industry, as does any entity that can delay construction and operations, such as regulators and interveners.

That leverage can be obvious, as when the European Bank for Reconstruction and Development refused to put money into older Chernobyl-type reactors and insisted on safer Western-style models before it would invest in the nuclear industries of former Soviet-bloc countries. The influence of financial institutions can vary greatly, however. To be effective, financial factors must work in conjunction with an effective monitoring and regulatory organization. A key component of the IAEA's responsibility principle is the assurance that a state's nuclear law requires the licensee of the plant to carry the burden of financial liability for any damage caused by the operation of their facilities.

Another concern caused by the high upfront capital costs of civilian nuclear power is the temptation to cut corners across the nuclear supply chain and during construction. The sale of new nuclear technology is truly an international endeavor, with many vendors establishing international supply chains for critical safety-related nuclear components. Just a year after Fukushima, a whistleblower revealed that several components in existing South Korean nuclear power plants were counterfeit and had been qualified using forged safety certificates. These revelations resulted in the prosecution of numerous workers in the South Korean nuclear industry, including several top-ranking executives. Not only were several plants shut down for extensive periods, but the South Korean public's confidence in their proud domestic nuclear industry was shaken, as well as the public confidence in the United Arab Emirates, where four plants of Korean design are being constructed.

New users with no operating or regulatory experience are entering the market. Therefore, without considerable government attention and cooperation, the nuclear power industry may not become safer, even though from a purely technical point of view it has the potential to do so by adopting the more advanced Generation III and III+ passive reactor designs.

Elements of a solution might include a few factors. For one, some form of an import-export agreement—such as what the Nuclear Suppliers Group (NSG) now uses to monitor weapons-sensitive materials and components—might be effective. NSG efforts rest on voluntary agreement at the state level; the same would be true of a safety-oriented agreement. If there were such agreement among states, one could envisage that any vendor wishing to export reactors or other potentially dangerous nuclear facility would need a license certifying that the design meets modern safety standards. With only a few international reactor vendors, implementation of such an agreement seems feasible.

Reactor design is not the only safety consideration. Siting, construction practices with effective quality and control, and operations with strong safety and security culture also enter the mix in essential ways, as do accident management, regulatory review, and lessons-learned feedback. Agreement at the state level that would strengthen cooperation among regulatory authorities—perhaps even setting standards for independence of those authorities—would be a positive step. There is no clear consensus on what structure best ensures such independence—or, rather, effectiveness—in managing an inherently interdependent process that involves many stakeholders. A conversation that would take into account national precedents and institutions is needed before any attempt is made to discuss standards.

6. Modern reactors are of safer design and can be operated more safely than the ones that have caused major accidents. Many of these reactors offer improved security benefits as well. But it is not clear how many of these evolutionary designs will be built.

Most reactors being built today are of the Gen II+ design and are significantly safer than the RBMK design involved in Chernobyl and the Mark 1 BWR design involved in Fukushima. With the Gen II+ design, both the reactor vessel and the spent fuel are under two layers of containment. Even safer designs, such as the Gen III and Gen III+, feature more passive cooling systems, which can keep all fuel cool for days without electricity or high-pressure water injection, among other improvements. Many of these newer reactors also offer significant benefits with respect to improved security from radiological sabotage. Several of these designs utilize improved containment that harden the facility from larger aircraft attacks or are located below grade so as to minimize such a threat. Additional features include co-location of critical safety equipment inside primary containment so as to minimize security force requirements needed to ensure that multiple targets across the plant are adequately protected from attack.

With much of the global nuclear infrastructure between thirty and fifty years old, an important question is how long existing users will extend the lifetimes of their existing plants rather than replace them with modern designs. The recent experience in the United States (which has one of the oldest fleets) has shown that the combination of low natural gas prices and mismanaged large-scale component replacements[18] has resulted in premature loss of valuable assets. It is unclear how this dynamic will play out globally, where minimal access to cheap natural gas and existing nuclear manufacturing capabilities may force a different outcome.

Therefore, there should be a concerted effort by the global industry to promote the inclusion of enhanced safety and security considerations in new nuclear power technologies *early* in the design process. This requires safety and security experts to be involved throughout the design process and work together. As discussed by Wyss, a spiral, parallel, development approach can be used in which both disciplines explicitly consider how design decisions will affect design objectives for other disciplines. The safety and security designers can then be challenged to find possible synergies among their proposed concepts. This can result in a potentially valuable new way of designing nuclear power plants where potential conflicts among safety and security requirements are recognized early, to the benefit of each discipline and the final design. It should also be noted that such an approach could identify strong synergies between nuclear safety and security that could produce positive economic benefits. One example of this is the common use of passive decay heat removal systems in advanced Gen IV reactor concepts, which allow for more compact facilities and can improve plant economics. These systems are expected to improve plant safety because they do not require on-site or off-site power to operate, and also have a security benefit, as they require substantially less in-service inspection than their active counterparts thus reducing potential sabotage risk.

NOTES

1. For a detailed review of the challenges in "trial and error" learning for organizations managing complex engineered systems, see Scott D. Sagan, *The Limits of Safety Organizations, Accidents, and Nuclear Weapons* (Princeton: Princeton University Press, 1993).

2. Edward D. Blandford and Michael M. May, *Lessons Learned from "Lessons Learned": The Evolution of Nuclear Power Safety after Accidents and Near-Accidents* (Cambridge, MA: American Academy of Arts and Sciences, 2012).

3. One NRC spokesperson put this point a different way: "A really good careful driver can probably drive a poorly designed car with no bumpers, but a poor driver can easily wreck a well-designed car." See Joseph V. Rees, *Hostages of Each Other: The Transformation of Nuclear Safety since Three Mile Island* (Chicago: University of Chicago Press, 1994).

4. "Report of Advisory Committee on Nuclear Security, Strengthening of Japan's Nuclear Security," Japan Atomic Energy Commission, March 9, 2012, available at www.aec.go.jp/jicst/NC/senmon/bougo/kettei120309.pdf.

5. Initiating events that can lead to safety concerns are generally treated as stochastic, while security-initiating events involve a strategic interaction with reactive adversaries trying to optimize their success.

6. Donald MacKenzie, "The Certainty Trough," in *Exploring Expertise: Issues and Perspectives*, ed. Robin Williams, Wendy Faulkner, and James Fleck (Basingstoke: Macmillan, 1998), 325–29.

7. A good overview of some of the important relationships between nuclear safety culture and organizational culture can be found in William E. Kastenberg, "Ethics, Risk, and Safety Culture: Reflections on Fukushima and Beyond," *Journal of Risk Research* (2014), DOI: 10.1080/13669877.2014.896399.

8. Even if one were to remove Kashiwazaki-Kariwa Units 1–5, which remained shut down because of a massive earthquake in 2007, the Japanese national fleet capacity factor would still have been only 74.2 percent, which is well below international standards. See Yangbo Du and John E. Parsons, "Capacity Factor Risk at Nuclear Power Plants," Center for Energy and Environmental Policy Research, 10-016, Revised January 2012, available at www.mit.edu/~jparsons/pubs.html.

9. While perhaps counterintuitive, there is a strong synergy between plant availability and safety. The introduction of condition-based maintenance has had a positive impact on plant operations in several countries. As an example, performing time-based maintenance for prescriptive time periods can result in increasing the likelihood of "infant failures" over the life of the equipment. For examples, see Douglas M. Chapin et al., "Application of Condition-based Maintenance in Japanese Nuclear Power Plants," 7th International Conference on Nuclear Engineering, Tokyo, Japan, April 19–23, 1999.

10. More on the NRA safety goals can be found in a presentation to the IAEA by Hiroshi Yamagata, NRA Senior Coordinator for Severe Accident Measures Director, available at wwwpub.iaea.org/iaeameetings/cn205p/Monday/Yamagata.pdf.

11. The same could be said about the Chernobyl accident, which could be viewed as an "accident made in the USSR."

12. See the results of an ongoing joint initiative between the US Department of Energy and the European Commission called the ExternE project. See also *Hidden Costs of Energy: Unpriced Consequences of Energy Production and Use* (Washington, DC: National Research Council of National Academies, 2010).

13. Richard A. Meserve, "The Global Nuclear Safety Regime," *Daedalus* 138, no. 4 (Fall 2009): 102.

14. For example, the US industry, which has almost twice as many plants as Japan, has spent approximately $3 billion taking actions and making plant modifications to address lessons learned from Fukushima. The overall cost of Fukushima is currently estimated to be $105 billion. Additionally, if the 48.9 GWe of Japanese reactors had operated at a more reasonable 85 percent capacity factor, the fleet would have produced an additional 6.2 GWe of power with improved safety, which at $100/MWh would have been worth $5.4 billion per year. This added revenue would have been more than enough to offset plant modifications that could have greatly minimized the damage at the plant. See "US Nuclear Industry Spends Billions on Post-Fukushima Upgrades," *Platts*, July 31, 2014, available at www.platts.com/latest-news/electric-power/washington/us-nuclear-industry-spends-billions-on-post-fukushima-21004195; and "Fukushima Disaster Bill More than $105bn, Double Earlier Estimate—Study," *Japan*

Times, August 27, 2014, available at www.rt.com/news/183052-japan-fukushima-costs-study/.

15. It is important to differentiate between the older Generation II plants, where there are limits to what can reasonably be retrofitted given inherent design characteristics, and more modern reactor technologies.

16. See Vasiliy Galkin and Andrii Pidipryhora, "WANO Post-Fukushima Severe Accident Management Project," International Experts' Meeting on Severe Accident Management in the Light of the Accident at the Fukushima Daiichi Nuclear Power Plant, IAEA, March 17–20, 2014, available at www-pub.iaea.org/iaeameetings/cn233p/OpeningSession/4Gakin.pdf.

17. An example of this was the recommendation by Gregory Jaczko, then chairman of the USNRC, for US citizens within 50 miles of the Fukushima reactors to evacuate. This recommendation can be compared with the Japanese government's recommendation that those within a 12-mile radius evacuate.

18. The recent failed steam generator replacement projects at both the San Onofre Nuclear Generating Station and Crystal River Nuclear Power Plant have resulted in premature plant shutdowns.

Index

Independent Investigation
Commission, 5–6, 69, 137, 148, 191,
194
INES, *see* International Nuclear Event
Scale
Information technology: at nuclear
power plants, 66; SPEEDI, 89–90, 95,
112–14, 129
INMM, *see* Institute of Nuclear Material
Management
INPO, *see* Institute of Nuclear Power
Operators
Institute of Nuclear Material
Management (INMM), 72
Institute of Nuclear Power Operators
(INPO), US, 11, 44, 149, 189–90, 199
Integrated Regulatory Review Service
(IRRS), 141–42, 146, 153n17
Integrated Response Office (IRO), *see*
Government-TEPCO Integrated
Response Office
International Atomic Energy Agency
(IAEA): Advisory Group on
Nuclear Security, 59; evacuation
approach, 113–14; Fundamental
Safety Principles, 101; Global Nuclear
Safety and Security Framework,
185; Japanese regulators and, 146;
nuclear safety role, 198, 199; Nuclear
Safety Standards program, 139–40;
nuclear security conference (2013),
74; nuclear security responsibility,
59, 77; on nuclear security risks,
58–59; Nuclear Security Series, 59,
60–61, 73, 77; peer reviews, 137, 139–41,
142, 152, 191–92; Physical Protection
Recommendation, INFCIRC/225,
59, 60, 64, 66, 73, 75–77, 76 (table);
report on Fukushima accident, 11, 81;
responsibility principle, 202
International Commission on
Radiological Protection (ICRP), 110,
118, 119–20, 123–24, 126, 127, 128, 188–89

International Convention for the
Suppression of Acts of Nuclear
Terrorism (Nuclear Terrorism
Convention), 77, 79n21
International Nuclear Event Scale
(INES), 11, 23, 109, 159
International Risk Governance Council,
84
Iodine, 109, 119. *See also* Radioactive
material
IRO, *see* Government-TEPCO Integrated
Response Office
IRRS, *see* Integrated Regulatory Review
Service
Iwaki, 116–17

JANSI, *see* Japan Nuclear Safety Institute
JANTI, *see* Japan Nuclear Technology
Institute
Japan Atomic Power Company, *see* Tōkai
Daini nuclear power plant
Japanese culture, 5, 83. *See also* Cultural
factors
Japanese government: emergency
operations headquarters, 14;
evacuation orders, 13, 17, 18, 19;
peaceful use agreement with United
States, 75. *See also* Diet; Prime
minister's office; Tokyo Electric Power
Company, relations with government;
*and individual ministries and
regulators*
Japan Federation of Bar Associations
(JFBA), 65, 118
Japan Medical Association, 118
Japan Nuclear Energy Safety
Organization (JNES), 89, 101, 102,
108n49
Japan Nuclear Safety Institute (JANSI),
150–51, 190–91, 199
Japan Nuclear Technology Institute
(JANTI), 138, 149–50, 190
Japan Society of Civil Engineering, 98, 99

evacuation guidelines, 113–14; radiation protection, 118, 119; Reactor Safety Standard Working Group, 143; regulations, 99, 100, 107n37; replacement agency, 147; responsibilities, 70, 141, 145–46
Nuclear security: B.5.b measures (US), 68–70, 136–37, 138–39, 145, 146, 151–52, 185; best practices, 74–75, 198–200; definition, 59; design bases, 36; implications of Fukushima accident, 61–62; improvements in Japan, 60–61, 65–67, 73–74, 139; insider threats, 62, 64–65; international legal framework, 59, 60, 75–77, 79nn21–22; interplay with safety, 44–51, 67–75, 145, 184–86, 198; Japanese institutions, 60–61, 70, 72, 185–86; lessons for, 45, 48–49; lessons from Fukushima, 3–4, 51–53, 60–65, 67, 71–74, 183, 184–86; national regimes, 60; neglect in Japan, 145; peripheral security, 62–63, 65–67; physical protection of nuclear materials, 58–59, 60, 65–67, 70, 73, 74, 75–77; policy recommendations, 195–204; potential risks, 58–59; procedures, 60; scope, 59; training exercises, 64, 66, 200
Nuclear security index, 65
Nuclear Security Series (NSS), 59, 60–61, 73, 77
Nuclear Suppliers Group (NSG), 202
Nuclear Threat Initiative (NTI), 65
Nuclear village, 102, 152, 195
Nuclear weapons: designs, 38; Partial Test Ban Treaty, 109–10; protection of nuclear materials, 58–59; risk of theft, 58. See also Nuclear security

Obama, Barack, 101
Ohkoshi, Kiyoko, 116
Oi nuclear power plant, 147, 148
Onagawa nuclear power plant: backup

power sources, 160; earthquake and tsunami damage, 23–24, 158, 159 (table), 159–60; seawall height, 160, 161; tsunami risk assessment, 163, 166
Operational Safety Review Team (OSART), 139, 140–41, 142
Organizational learning: challenges, 136, 151, 152; definition, 136; in future, 152; incentivizing, 199–200; at industry level, 149–51, 183, 184; as ongoing process, 183; transnational, 136–37, 151, 190, 191–92, 197, 198–200. See also Lessons learned
OSART, see Operational Safety Review Team

Pacific Ocean, see Seawater
Pakistan, nuclear power plants, 166, 168
Partial Test Ban Treaty, 109–10
Police, 66, 81, 93
Political leadership, 82–83, 87–88, 95–96, 187–88, 201. See also Leadership; Prime minister's office
Politics: influence of power companies, 170; of nuclear power, 113–14, 148, 195; of radiation protection, 130. See also Antinuclear activists
Power companies: financial liability, 202; industry associations, 44, 140, 149–50, 189–91, 199; peer reviews of nuclear safety, 140–41, 142, 200; political influence, 170; preparedness for tsunamis, 169 (fig.), 170; regional monopolies, 151, 175; relations with regulators, 100–102, 170–71, 175; responsibilities, 101; sizes, 158, 170–71, 175, 191
PRAs, see Probabilistic risk assessments
Prefectural governments, 13, 121, 122
Prime minister's office (Kantei): communication with Yoshida, 87; Crisis Management Center, 88–90, 95–96; emergency response, 13, 82–83,

93–94; information flows, 89–90, 90
(fig.), 91 (fig.); Nuclear Emergency
Response Head Quarters, 85, 93; staff,
95, 104; TEPCO liaison, 16, 18, 87, 89.
See also Kan, Naoto
Probabilistic risk assessments (PRAs), 36,
38, 163, 166
Probabilistic safety assessments (PSAs),
99, 102, 107n42, 143

Radiation exposure: from atomic bombs,
123–24; biological effects, 127; cancer
risks, 110, 120, 123–24, 127, 128; from
Chernobyl accident, 109, 127; dose-
response models, 110, 111 (fig.); efforts
to reduce, 109–10; low-dose, 110, 128,
188; risk assessments, 123–24, 127–28;
risk of, 58–59; SPEEDI information
system, 89–90, 95, 112–14, 129
Radiation exposure from Fukushima
accident: amount of, 11, 109; food and
water contamination, 119–27, 129;
in Fukushima Daiichi plant, 13, 15,
16, 17–18; measurements, 115–18, 130;
persistence, 109; predictions, 112–13;
in region, 109, 114, 115–23, 128–29; soil
contamination, 116, 117; of staff, 17;
from venting reactor buildings, 16.
See also Evacuation
Radiation protection: decontamination
guidelines, 127; fallout shelters,
129–30; laws, 112; lessons from
Fukushima, 110, 112, 129–30, 188–89;
in power plants, 141; reference
levels, 6, 110–12, 113, 115–21, 123–29,
130, 188–89; responsibilities, 130;
situation-dependent, 110. *See also*
Nuclear safety
Radioactive material: in dirty bombs, 58,
59; protection of, 58–59, 60, 65–67, 70,
73, 74, 75–77
Reactor designs: boiling water reactors,
12–13, 23, 203; Gen II, 206n15; Gen

II+, 203; Gen III and Gen III+, 202,
203; Gen IV, 204
Rebuild Japan Initiative Foundation, 82
Regional Nuclear Emergency Response
Team, 85
Regulators: complex structure, 146, 147;
failure to implement international
best practices, 191–92; functions, 192;
information sharing, 191; lessons
from Fukushima, 192–93; policy
recommendations for, 200, 202–3;
reforms, 147, 185–86, 192–93; relations
with power companies, 100–102,
170–71, 175; weakness, 192. *See also
individual regulators*
Regulatory capture, 100–101, 102, 103–4,
170, 175, 192, 193
Residual risk, 97–98, 99, 101
Rice straw, 122
Risk: of cancer, 110, 120, 123–24, 127,
128; managing, 80, 97–98, 196–97;
probabilistic risk assessments, 36,
38, 163, 166; probabilistic safety
assessments, 99, 102, 107n42, 143;
public views, 195; residual, 97–98, 99,
101; scientific assessments, 123–24,
127–28; seismic, 107n37. *See also*
Design bases

Sabotage: potential risks, 59, 61–62;
prevention, 203. *See also* Nuclear
security
Safety, *see* Myth of absolute safety;
Nuclear safety
"Safety, Security and Safeguards by
Design" (3SBD), 50
Salem/Hope Creek nuclear power plant,
172–73
Sanriku earthquake, 98, 168, 172, 173
Sasaki, Yoshihiko, 100
Schools, 117–19, 129
SDF, *see* Self-Defense Forces
Seawall heights: definition, 162;

Island, 6, 36, 37, 143, 189; tsunami risk assessment, 166–68, 171, 172–73; upgrades after Fukushima, 205n14
UNSCEAR, *see* UN Scientific Committee on the Effects of Atomic Radiation
USNRC, *see* Nuclear Regulatory Commission, US
Utilities, *see* Power companies

Vicarious learning, *see* Organizational learning

Wakasa Bay, 171–72, 173
WANO, *see* World Association of Nuclear Operators
WASH-1400 "Reactor Safety Study," 36
Water: contaminated, 119; drinking, 119, 121, 124; floods, 191; storm surges, 164, 166, 172–73, 174; used by nuclear power reactors, 12–13. *See also* Seawater; Tsunamis
Weick, Karl E., 91, 92
Willis, Henry, 40

WINS, *see* World Institute for Nuclear Security
Workers: evacuated, 19, 20; firefighters, 81, 82, 93; injured, 17, 19, 20; insider threats, 62, 64–65; radiation exposure, 13, 15, 16, 17–18; risks taken, 15; trustworthiness checks, 64–65, 73–74; unidentified, 52, 56–57n22, 62
World Association of Nuclear Operators (WANO), 44, 140, 149, 191, 197, 198, 199–200
World Institute for Nuclear Security (WINS), 71, 74, 199, 200
World Trade Organization (WTO), 124

Yamazoe, Yasushi, 123, 124
Yoshida, Masao: commitment to stay at plant, 20, 21, 26n19; emergency response, 13, 15, 16, 17, 18, 91, 106n20; evacuation plans, 20; meeting with Kan, 17, 87

Zettai Anzen Shinwa, *see* Myth of absolute safety